"Barak constructs a grand narrative which attests to the pervasiveness of corporate crime, the state routinization of the crimes of the powerful, and the unsustainability of multinational capitalism. Traversing the globe, and incorporating financial, health, safety and environmental crimes, financialization and the commodification of the commons, this empirically and historically rich, theoretically sophisticated tour de force at the same time holds out the promise of effective challenge to unchecked corporate power."

Steve Tombs, Professor and Head of the Department of Social Policy and Criminology and Co-Director of the International Centre for Comparative Criminological Research, Open University, UK

"Gregg Barak advances a chastening indictment of contemporary capitalism. Both liberal capitalism and the growing strength of authoritarian capitalism in societies like China afflict profound domination upon citizens. Gregg Barak enriches the conversation about options for strategic regulation and strategic socialist innovation to temper if not tame their power."

John Braithwaite, Distinguished Professor, RegNet School of Regulation and Global Governance, Australian National University, Australia

"*Unchecked Corporate Power* is a thoughtful and thought-provoking examination of contemporary corporate harms, how economic, political, and media elites have made them appear to be the unavoidable collateral damage of honorable profit-seeking, and how the regulatory system tasked with controlling these harms has not only turned them into non-crimes, but has often facilitated their perpetration. More than a critique of corporate harms, *Unchecked Corporate Power* offers both a call and a model for fundamental restructuring of the political relationships between corporations, the public, and government. It is a must read for both scholars and citizens concerned with the rising power of corporations and the declining power of average citizens."

Raymond J. Michalowski, Arizona Regents Professor, Department of Criminology and Criminal Justice, Northern Arizona University, USA

"In this pathbreaking book, Barak critically examines the roles of multinational corporations and the state in both routinizing and trivializing major crimes and massive global harms. Using case studies he effectively exposes both the inherent contradictions and the need for change in current regulatory policies. The work not only offers a number of potential solutions, but is a major addition to the sociological and criminological understanding of global white-collar and corporate criminality. I highly recommend it."

Henry N. Pontell, Distinguished Professor and Chair of the Department of Sociology, John Jay College of Criminal Justice, and Professor Emeritus, Department of Criminology, Law and Society, University of California, Irvine, USA

UNCHECKED CORPORATE POWER

Why are crimes of the suite punished more leniently than crimes of the street? When police killings of citizens go unpunished, political torture is sanctioned by the state, and the financial frauds of Wall Street traders remain unprosecuted, nothing succeeds with such regularity as the active failures of national states to obstruct the crimes of the powerful.

Written from the perspective of global sustainability and as an unflinching and unforgiving exposé of the full range of the crimes of the powerful, *Unchecked Corporate Power* reveals how legalized authorities and political institutions charged with the duty of protecting citizens from law-breaking and injurious activities have increasingly become enablers and colluders with the very enterprises they are obliged to regulate. Here, Gregg Barak explains why the United States and other countries are duplicitous in their harsh reactions to street crimes in comparison to the significantly more harmful and far-reaching crimes of the powerful, and why the crimes of the powerful are treated as beyond incrimination.

What happens to nations that surrender ever-growing economic and political power to the globally super rich and the mammoth multinational corporations they control? And what can people from around the world do to resist the criminality and victimization perpetrated by multinationals, and generated by the prevailing global political economy? Barak examines an array of multinational crimes— corporate, environmental, financial, and state—and their state-legal responses, and outlines policies and strategies for revolutionizing these contradictory relations of capital reproduction, criminality, and unsustainability.

Gregg Barak is Professor of Criminology and Criminal Justice at Eastern Michigan University, USA. He is the editor of *The Routledge International Handbook of the Crimes of the Powerful*, author of *Theft of a Nation: Wall Street Looting and Federal Regulatory Colluding*, and recipient of the National White Collar Crime Center/White Collar Crime Research Consortium's Outstanding Publication Award for 2012.

CRIMES OF THE POWERFUL

Series Editor: Gregg Barak is Professor of Criminology and Criminal Justice at Eastern Michigan University and a 2016-17 Fulbright Lecturer/Research Scholar at the School of Law, Pontifical Catholic University do Rio Grande do Sul, in Porto Alegre, Brazil. For more than 40 years, Barak has researched and written widely on crime and justice. He is the author of several books, including two award-winning titles—*Gimme Shelter: A Social History of Homelessness in Contemporary America* (1991) and *Theft of a Nation: Wall Street Looting and Federal Regulatory Colluding* (2012).

Crimes of the Powerful encompasses the harmful, injurious, and victimizing behaviors perpetrated by privately or publicly operated businesses, corporations, and organizations as well as the state mediated administrative, legalistic, and political responses to these crimes.

The series draws attention to the commonalities of the theories, practices, and controls of the crimes of the powerful. It focuses on the overlapping spheres and inter-related worlds of a wide array of existing and recently developing areas of social, historical, and behavioral inquiry into the wrongdoings of multinational organizations, nation-states, stateless regimes, illegal networks, financialization, globalization, and securitization.

These examinations of the crimes of the powerful straddle a variety of related disciplines and areas of academic interest, including studies in criminology and criminal justice; law and human rights; conflict, peace, and security; economic change, environmental decay, and global sustainability.

1. Unchecked Corporate Power
Why the Crimes of Multinational Corporations Are Routinized Away and What We Can Do About It
Gregg Barak

UNCHECKED CORPORATE POWER

Why the Crimes of Multinational Corporations Are Routinized Away and What We Can Do About It

Gregg Barak

Routledge
Taylor & Francis Group

LONDON AND NEW YORK

First published 2017
by Routledge
2 Park Square, Milton Park, Abingdon, Oxon OX14 4RN

and by Routledge
711 Third Avenue, New York, NY 10017

Routledge is an imprint of the Taylor & Francis Group, an informa business

British Library Cataloguing in Publication Data
A catalogue record for this book is available from the British Library

Library of Congress Cataloging in Publication Data
A catalog record for this book has been requested

ISBN: 978-1-138-95142-6 (hbk)
ISBN: 978-1-138-95144-0 (pbk)
ISBN: 978-1-315-66824-6 (ebk)

Typeset in Bembo
by Taylor & Francis Books

This book is dedicated to moving beyond Bernie's "political revolution" and toward a sustainable world for all.

CONTENTS

ILLUSTRATIONS

Tables

Boxes

OTHER BOOKS BY GREGG BARAK

In Defense of Whom? A Critique of Criminal Justice Reform.

Crimes by the Capitalist State: An Introduction to State Criminality (editor).

Gimme Shelter: A Social History of Homelessness in Contemporary America.

Varieties of Criminology: Readings from a Dynamic Discipline (editor).

Media, Process, and the Social Construction of Crime: Studies in Newsmaking Criminology (editor).

Representing O.J.: Murder, Criminal Justice, and Mass Culture (editor).

Integrating Criminologies.

Integrative Criminology (editor).

Crime and Crime Control: A Global View (editor).

Violence and Nonviolence: Pathways to Understanding.

Violence, Conflict, and World Order: Critical Conversations on State-Sanctioned Justice (editor).

Battleground: Criminal Justice, a two-volume encyclopedia (editor).

Criminology: An Integrated Approach.

Theft of a Nation: Wall Street Looting and Federal Regulatory Colluding.

Class, Race, Gender, and Crime: The Social Realities of Justice in America, 4th edition (co-authored with Paul Leighton and Allison Cotton).

The Routledge International Handbook of the Crimes of the Powerful (editor).

PREFACE

The world of power in its many forms is barbaric but inventively adept at enlisting our consent.[1]

With our consent, if not necessarily our backing, nothing succeeds with such regularity as the active failures of national states to obstruct the crimes of the powerful. This is true whether we are discussing the contradictions of the state to not punish "unjustifiable" police killings of citizens, to sanction within and without borders "outsourced" political torture, or to "bailout" the fraudulent financial transactions of Wall Street traders. To clarify, there are similarities as well as dissimilarities between the state routinization of governmental crime, multinational corporate crime, politically corrupt crime, and syndicated crime, which depending on the object of the inquiry, needs to be considered and taken into account.

The *Routledge International Handbook of the Crimes of the Powerful* (2015) that I edited documents the systemic inability of states globally to thwart the crimes of the powerful. It was during the writing of the introduction to and overview of this volume along with the sequential editing of thirty-eight chapters in which the workings of a "state-routinizing crime and crime control" first came together, and subsequently became a viable and unifying framework for explaining the richness of, and even patterned, failures of national states to not only resist, but even worse, to not collude with those crimes of multinational corporations. A few years before completing my examination of high-risk securities frauds for *Theft of a Nation: Wall Street Looting and Federal Regulatory Colluding* (2012), the idea of "state-routinized crime" was already alive in my criminological imagination. Looking back, I now regard the financial abuses, moral hazards, high-risk speculation, banking on the Federal Reserve, and the failure of the capitalist state to criminally sanction any of Wall Street securities frauds or orchestrated lootings as prima facie evidence of state-routinized crime and crime control.

With *Unchecked Corporate Power: Why the Crimes of Multinational Corporations are Routinized Away and What We Can Do About It*, I continue to develop a transdisciplinary and reciprocal political economy of why and how people with excessive power—financial and corporate—are historically unencumbered from performing and/or are proportionately punished lightly for their widespread contribution to the devastation and victimization of human, physical, and social ecologies. From a globally sustainable perspective, this book investigates how legalized authorities and political institutions charged with the democratic duty of protecting its citizens from traditional law-breaking and injurious activities, especially from those with excessive or oligopolistic power, have increasingly become coddlers, enablers, and colluders with the very enterprises they are obliged to monitor, police, and regulate. What is more, by proceeding in routinized ways, these state actors rationalize, suppress, and normalize the habitually repetitive multinational corporate harms and injuries into anything other than the ordinary crimes that they are.

Unlike *Theft of a Nation* that focused "only" on financial crime and the pre- and post-treatment of the criminal epidemic responsible for the 2008 Wall Street implosion and the Great Recession that followed, the focus here on the unfamiliarity of multinational corporate crime and its relationship to the unsustainability of global capital, is more sweeping in the scope and content of the state routinization of the crimes of the powerful. Many of the true-life stories of crime and crime control found within the individual chapters, especially Chapters 3, 4, and 5, could easily be expanded into book length treatments. On the other hand, the numerous short, medium, and long stories found throughout this book are all part and parcel of one grand narrative on the globalization of capital, multinational corporate crime, and the integrated historical development of political power and social movements.

Finally, as social science experimentation and research has born out, not only can wealth be bad for your soul, but on average affluence yields less empathy, less respect for norms and laws, and more dishonesty compared to those occupying the less affluent positions in society. All of which begs two fundamental questions, whose answers this investigation seeks to understand: What happens to any one nation or to an alliance of nations worldwide that conveys and/or surrenders ever-growing economic and political power to mammoth multinational corporations and to the globally super rich? Of equal importance, what can people from around the world do to collectively resist, and ultimately, bring to a halt the vast economic carnage and environmental fallout caused by the prevailing relations of the global political economy?

G.B.
Ann Arbor, July 2016

Note

1 Wypijewski, JoAnn. 2015. "James Baldwin, a Guide in Dark Times." *The Nation*. February 9. www.thenation.com/article/195641/james-baldwin-guide-dark-times.

PART I

Routinizing the crimes of the powerful

INTRODUCTION

On the state routinization of unchecked corporate power

As global corporations have grown richer and more powerful than many nations, they increasingly operate without limits on their power or influence. Around the world, global corporations drive governmental policies, unchecked by strong global policies to protect public health, human rights and the environment.[1]

In 2015 Apple Inc. reported a quarterly profit of $18 billion, the largest in history. During the same year its market-capital valuation of $765 billion reached the highest ever for any U.S. corporation. Based on total revenues of $233 billion for 2014/2015 for a private, public, or state-owned company, Apple ranked twelfth in the world.[2] However, its record for design and technological innovation has been second to no other companies. The Apple brand is also the most admired brand in the world. Several factors have contributed to Apple's success, including the vision of the late Steve Jobs, the work executed by Apple engineers, the failure or refusal of Apple to pay a fraction of its fair share in taxes, and the super-exploitation of the workers who manufacture Apple products.[3] In the case of tax thieving, a 2013 U.S. Senate investigation discovered that by "creating mail-slot entities all over the world and attributing its profits to them, Apple [had] managed to pay just 2 percent in taxes on $74 billion of income overseas."[4]

More significantly, after a lengthy investigation the European Competition Commissioner Margrethe Vestager ruled on August 30, 2016 that Ireland must recover from the local Apple subsidiary up to as much as 19 billion euros ($21 billion), including interest for unpaid taxes dating back more than a decade. This ruling, a temporary bombshell at the very least, left at the tax doors of the world's leading multinational corporations, was based on a "decision that tax benefits provided to Apple's subsidiaries in Ireland through two tax rulings amounted to 'state aid' that was illegal" under the European rules of business competition.[5] The case of Apple's Irish operations is a radical illustration of tax avoidance accounting schemes enjoyed by such mega multinational companies as Facebook, Google, and General

Electric. The Apple example involves two subsidiaries: Apple Operations Europe (AOE) and Apple Sales International (ASI). The value of these legal arrangements is that "any Apple product sold outside the Americas is implicitly first bought by ASI, Ireland from different manufacturers across the globe and sold along with the intellectual property to buyers everywhere except the Americas. So all such sales are by ASI and all profits from those sales are recorded in Ireland",[6] and are subject to much lower negotiated tax rates than permitted by the EU.

In the case of worker exploitation, the state routinization of the inhumane conditions under which Apple's subcontracted employees work in China is well known thanks to the performance artist Mike Daisey's one-man show at the Public Theater in New York in 2011, a *New York Times* follow up story in January 2012, and finally the BBC documentary *Panorama* that aired in December 2014. The film reveals a series of broken promises made in 2012 by Apple to various human rights and labor rights groups to improve the working conditions inside of a number of Chinese facilities where employees of Pegatron and Foxconn busily assemble the newest iPhones. The filmmakers recorded the regular breaching of the standards established for workers hours, ID cards, dormitories, work meetings, and juvenile employees. They also documented that in Indonesia, children were working in dangerous open cast mines and that the tin from these illegal digs was being used in iPhones.

Apple's annual report for 2014 acknowledges that the compliance rate regarding its own standards was only 70 percent, down from 77 percent a year earlier. The enforcement of workers' hours was also down from the previous year. In a nutshell, these subcontracted workers are exploited in various ways despite the reality that Apple's labor costs amount to a tiny fraction of its profits, especially in the context of the generous compensation packages enjoyed by top executives. In 2011 and 2012, "the top nine members of Apple's executive team received compensation packages equal to that of fully 90,000 Chinese factory workers."[7]

Subsequently, in April 2015, Li Qiang, founder and executive director of the workers' rights organization China Labor Watch, reported that "workers from Foxconn factories in Chengdu and Shenzhen were [being] sent to the Quanta factory in Changshu to work 12-hour days making Apple watches in order to meet the company's April 24 release deadline."[8] As there was a shortage of dormitory space for the workers at the factory, they found themselves forced to sleep in buses. These workers also found themselves producing watches in freezing temperatures while wearing thin work uniforms, and where close to 100 workers became ill and had to be hospitalized.

Certainly one can argue that it's not fair to single out Apple. Its record is far from the worst of the technology companies:

> But Apple is undoubtedly the world's leader, its customers the most loyal. (Hollywood isn't making movies about the founders of Samsung, after all). The corporation could easily demand structural changes in the way its supply chains are constructed and workers are treated. But it can get away with only

pretending to do so because the vast majority of its customers—to say nothing of its fan boy media following—care only about the coolness of its latest gadgets, and not a whit about the exploitation and misery experienced by the people who actually make them.[9]

In a similar vein, Apple is not alone in avoiding taxes. According to Citizens for Tax Justice, eighteen of America's largest corporations, led by Apple, deployed the same tactics to avoid paying $92 billion in U.S. taxes in 2014. If this was not bad enough, the same Senate report found that

> Apple—which has $181.1 billion socked away in offshore accounts—is among the group of multinational corporations lobbying Congress to grant them a second repatriation tax holiday so they can bring an estimated $1.7 trillion home at the significantly reduced rate of 6.5 percent. The last tax holiday passed in 2004 led to a cut of more than 20,000 U.S. jobs and lowered R&D spending—directly contrary to the arguments made on its behalf.[10]

In September, 2014, Louisiana District Judge Carl Barbier found British Petroleum, one of the world's leading oil and gas companies with more than $400 billion in economic value in 2013 and with more than 80,000 employees working in eighty countries, liable for *gross negligence* under the Clean Water Act of 1972. Before that ruling came down, BP had already paid out about $28.3 billion in cleanup costs and fines, in compensation claims from injured businesses, and in relation to pleading guilty to criminal manslaughter charges for eleven men who died in the Gulf of Mexico from the Deepwater Horizon oil rig explosion. Under the Clean Water Act, gross negligence imposes penalties of $4,300 per barrel of oil spilled, as compared to only $1,100 per barrel for *simple negligence*. This could add up to an additional $18 billon in fines with some of that money charged to or paid by rig owner Transocean Drilling, the largest offshore drilling contractor in the world, or by Halliburton, one of the world's largest providers of products and services to the energy industry. Not surprisingly, the "gang of three" has appealed the Barbier civil ruling to a higher court.[11] BP had already spent more than $1 billion for outside lawyers' fees related to the oil spill. Meanwhile, there are estimates for the legal costs facing those state governments (e.g., Louisiana, Mississippi, Alabama, and Florida) most affected by the spill projected to reach as much as $100 million.[12]

Back in April 2010 the Deepwater Horizon rig exploded, resulting in a devastating 200-million-gallon oil spill, the biggest in U.S. history. While the well was capped in July 2010, oil and tar balls were still washing ashore in surrounding areas at least as late as 2015. For years after the spill and until recently, BP cleanup crews and government officials maintained that they did not know what happened to as much as 10 million gallons of oil. Thanks to a team of oceanographers from Florida State University, the "lost crude" was located in 2015 buried under sediment in the Gulf of Mexico. The contaminants from the oil portend not only long-term dangers for marine life, but these toxins are also finding their way into the human food chain by way of consumed fish that have consumed worms living in the sediment.[13] Examination of these high-profile environmental and other related crimes committed by these three powerful multinational corporations and the responses to them, by various governmental agencies as well as news reporting organizations, reveal the extent to which the state and corporations will collude to conventionalize otherwise criminal activities. This was the case, even when these crimes were highly visible and their perpetrators were caught "red-handed" and slapped mildly with fines that have amounted to little more than adding another line item to the costs of conducting their business-as-usual affairs.

In "Blacking Out the Gulf," a case study of the BP oil spill, Elizabeth Bradshaw provides ample evidence of the many forms or shapes that state-routinized crime may take. Her research documents the attempts of state-corporate "cover up" to suppress both the criminality and the environmental impact caused by the oil spill. Specifically, Bradshaw exposes the coordinated ways in which state and corporate actors employed several means to conceal from the consuming public the magnitude of actual damages. For example, a media blackout was implemented in the Gulf area, cleanup workers and other employees were censored, toxic chemicals were used to disperse the oil, and a deliberate manipulation of official images and information about the spill were circulated through mass media.[14]

On the other mediated hand, the detention of a BP-chartered offshore oil supply vessel in Scotland for having a group of unpaid workers on its crew, what trade union representatives have referred to as a "blatant example of modern day slavery," made some news and was covered locally by the *Wilmslow Guardian* in June, 2016. Although the offshore oil and gas industry only accounts for a small piece of a forced labor industry that involves, worldwide, an estimated 19 million persons in domestic work, agriculture, construction, manufacturing, and entertainment who are super-exploited annually by private enterprises, while these workers generate illegal profits of $150 billion. According to the International Labor Organization, a handful of vessel detentions chartered by big oil companies like BP might not only force a bit more due diligence in the future,[15] but these detentions might also help to shine some exposure beyond a global oil price crisis and a new wave of "slavery at sea" to a more fundamental examination of unsustainable dirty energy.

What has become business as usual are not the slap-on-the-wrist civil punishments that BP and other powerful corporations like them commonly receive from the state for their myriad of transgressions, but rather that these multinational corporations are increasingly negatively sanctioned, criminally penalized, or even charged and prosecuted for their criminal violations. As Laureen Snider argued in a 2000 issue of *Theoretical Criminology*, "The brand of state regulation known as corporate crime has basically disappeared."[16] Crimes of corporations she maintained had "been argued into obsolescence through neoliberal knowledge claims advanced through specific discourses by powerful elites."[17] Quite importantly, Snider further contended that "the acceptance of these knowledge claims cannot be understood without examining their relationship to the corporate counter-revolution that has, over the last two decades, legitimized virtually every acquisitive, profit-generating act of the corporate sector, transforming the developed (and developing) world" in its wake.[18]

Perhaps no better example of the use of specific discourses by powerful elites in relation to state-organized and state-routinized crime is the ongoing and selective war on drugs. This perpetual war continues to fuel the spreading violence in contemporary Latin America as it props up at the same time the interests of multinational corporations that are in pursuit of new resources and markets. "The logic of the War on Drugs, still firmly embraced in Washington and most of Europe" today, and dating at least as far back as the rise of powder cocaine as the "hip" or cosmopolitan drug of choice in the 1980s, had decades ago "created a vicious circle of murder and excess that united the arms manufacturers of America, the traffickers of South America and the coke habits of the middle classes from Berlin to Los Angeles."[19] As one observer of the 1980s and 1990s during the transition periods to democracy in both Brazil and neighboring countries alike has recalled, the discovery of powder cocaine would lead "to the first multinational corporation of Latin America and the first example of genuine economic integration: the production, the processing and the distribution of cocaine."[20] Of course, the state violence, coca-related homicides, and police corruption revolving around cocaine cartels and heightened drug wars, cannot be historically or structurally separated from the governmentally created and neglected favelas in the Brazilian cities of Rio de Janeiro and Sao Paulo. During the months prior to the run-up to the August 2016 summer Olympics in Rio, these drug-related activities of violence and repression were a thriving, yet deadly business.

Not long ago, in 2012, there was a highly visible Summit of the Americas, held in Colombia, for the purpose of discussing an end to the failed war on drugs. "While the presidents of Guatemala, Colombia, Costa Rico and El Salvador" voiced support for ending the war, "President Obama rejected their calls for drug legalization during high-level talks at the Summit."[21] At the time of the Summit, despite Obama's warning that "legalization could lead to greater problems," many U.S. proponents for ending the losing war on drugs were optimistic, including Ethan Nadelmann, founder and executive director of the Drug Policy Alliance, a not-for-profit, New York-based advocacy group for drug law reform grounded in science, compassion, health, and human rights.

During the April 16, 2012 broadcast of the Democracy Now program, an independent global news hour on PBS radio that airs daily from coast to coast in the United States, in response to questions from host Amy Goodman about Obama's stand on legalization, Nadelmann had this to say: "That's sort of the standard patter one expects from the politicians. They've been scared of their own shadows on this issue for a very long time."[22] Notwithstanding the nuance of the comments that were made by President Obama, Nadelmann went on to say the summit "is really going to go down in a sort of historic way in terms of the transformation of the regional and global dialogue around drug policy."[23] After all, despite Obama's stance and warning, this was the first time that a U.S. President and its administration had been willing to sit down and even discuss the matter. At the very least, the U.S. government was acknowledging that decriminalization or legalization of drugs is a reasonable topic for discussion. Nonetheless, some five years later the failed policies of the "war on drugs" still persist as they have more or less for some five decades.

In the case of many Latin American countries, including Colombia for several decades and Mexico for the past decade, the so-called war on drugs policies resume with their inefficacies and blatant failures to combat the consumption of illicit drugs in North America while escalating violence terribly in countries below the Rio Grande. These failing anti-narcotic policies have been integrated into what Dawn Paley has labeled "drug war capitalism." As Paley documents, the conflicts and violence in places like Colombia, Mexico, and elsewhere are fundamentally struggles over Latin American territory, land, and resources rather than over the production and distribution of drugs. In her book, she underscores the state routinization of drug violence as well as violence allegedly related to drugs:

> The notion that there is a clear division between state forces and crime groups—that corruption and collaboration are the work of a few bad apples—is a hegemonic idea promoted by nation-states and the mainstream media. Undoing this binary means learning from the people whose lives have been directly affected by armed groups whose activity is carried out with impunity. Impunity is not the result of a weak or deficient state, but rather it is actively provided to the gamut of armed groups who commit crimes and acts of terror against citizens, migrants, and the poor. The provision of impunity to armed actors who are politically aligned with capitalism is part of a modern nation state's *raison d'être*.[24]

These ill-guided drug policies, while failing to curb the flow of illegal drugs, victimize mostly vast numbers of poor and working-class people in Latin America. At the same time, north of the Rio Grande, bank accounts and prison cells—private and public—are bursting. And thanks to the war on drugs, billions of dollars are also being made annually off the related arms trade.

Referring specifically to the escalating violence and the failures of these anti-narcotic policies, there is the Mexican example. Since Felipe Calderon assumed the Presidency in Mexico on December 1, 2006, declaring a federal war on drugs and launching his military operations against transnational criminal organizations (TCOs), these efforts had claimed by 2014 more than 100,000 lives. During this eight-year period, "more than 27,000 people vanished, with many of these disappearances linked to organized crime. Thousands of citizens have become internal refugees, displaced within Mexico, or forced to move abroad."[25] At the same time, between 2007 and 2012, the Mexican military, armed by the United States and protected by their government, killed or executed about 3,000 people. Out of 4,000 complaints of torture that the Mexican attorney general's office had reviewed since 2006, only 15 had resulted in convictions.[26]

Accompanying the war on drugs and the huge increase in violence in Mexico, which has included the execution of public officials and the widespread use of car bombs, decapitations, dismemberment, mass kidnappings, grenade attacks, and blockades, there has also been the diversification from what had previously been regionalized drug-trafficking organizations into full-blown TCOs. Today, the expanded operations of these drug cartels include such lucrative new businesses as kidnapping, extortion, migrant smuggling, human trafficking, weapons smuggling, video and music piracy, and trafficking in crude oil, natural gas, and gasoline stolen from Mexico's state petroleum companies. These state-routinized criminal activities have all been enabled or facilitated by new kinds of relationships between organized crime and a new set of state and non-state actors. For example, there are "new corruption networks" that have been "built between criminal organizations, local police and law enforcement, politicians at all levels, and federal authorities" in both Colombia and Mexico.[27] "Formal businesses, including transnational companies (e.g., financial firms, U.S. oil companies, private security firms, arms-producing companies, and gambling companies) have also established new connections with TCOs."[28] In recent years, similar types of securities apparatuses have flourished in countries like Guatemala and Honduras, also driven by the expanding territorial reaches of the extractive industries.

In short, in the name of fighting an everlasting war on drug production and distribution from south of the Rio Grande, state and capitalist interests are being advanced that are more about social, economic, and territorial control and less about cocaine or marijuana control. In fact, the war on drugs, with its mix of militarization and paramilitarization, has become a primary vehicle for escalating rather than deescalating violence and for expanding rather than limiting the crimes of the powerful. Dysfunctionally, the failed war on drugs has become a means of forced evacuation, human extermination, residential displacement, and predictable migration away from those geographically strategic areas rich in minerals and other natural resources. In the process, these state-routinized crimes of removal have cleared the land of people for the extracting industries, for the direct investment of foreign money, and for the economic growth of transnational oil and gas companies.

Similarly, the political journalist, William Greider reminds us that it has been some time since "free trade" agreements were about trade and tariff reductions. Beginning with the passage of NAFTA in 1993, the concept of free trade morphed

> into dense legalistic prohibitions that blocked governments from interfering with the multinationals' exploitation of natural resources, abusive factory conditions and financial shenanigans, as well as offshoring of jobs and production. Investors even get their own supranational courts to rule on disputes—courts weighted in their favor because judges have no settled obligations to existing laws or public accountability.[29]

This "parallel legal system" not only creates new rights for multinational corporations and international financial institutions, it also gives them power to sue national states should their investments somehow be impaired by governmental attempts to regulate social and economic behavior; for example, when those interfering governments provide rules on health and safety standards or pass environmental and worker protection laws.

In the same way, when Dawn Rothe and David Friedrichs discuss the contemporary world order, they stress, "existing forms of global governance can be regarded as more often than not enabling crimes of globalization rather than preventing or punishing them."[30] They argue that there needs to be more consideration given to the complicity of both states and international financial institutions in the commission of not only transnational crimes, but also of multinational corporate crimes. Specifically, Rothe and Friedrichs take up those international contradictions of financial institutions like the World Bank and the International Monetary Fund, on the one hand, that "promote campaigns to combat corruption in global South countries," and on the other hand, turn around and subordinate these goals to loan officials and their sponsors in the realization of meeting other bottom-line objectives of international financial institutions.[31] These and other factors come together they argue "to produce a criminogenic environment where crimes of globalization can flourish."[32]

Not unlike those criminogenic environments produced by corporate deregulation or by international financial institutions, the same can be claimed about the state-routinizing processes of crime. This is primarily the case because the prevailing national and international financial institutions as well as the well-being of the capitalist state are all interdependent on the same economic proposition of an ever-expanding global accumulation, consumption, and reproduction of capital. A proposition that Marxists and non-Marxists alike would agree is shot through with internal and external contradictions not the least of which are arguably fatal ones—such as the emphasis or stress on endless compound growth, the necessity to exploit nature and the environment and labor to its limits, and the tendency toward the universal alienation of humans from themselves, their labor, the products of their labor and their species, to paraphrase Marx.[33]

Thus, I argue that by combining the state routinization of corporate crime by multinationals with the contradictory demands of both neoliberalism and global capitalism, criminologists and other observers of the production of harm and victimization can consider why and how the world's most successful corporate, financial, and state perpetrators of injury and ruin are also, reciprocally speaking, the beneficiaries of civic etiquettes of conformity and suppression, of hegemonic discourses and regimes of truth, and of a heightened politics of fear and corruption. If this is not enough to normalize or conventionalize the crimes of these powerful organizations, then these perpetrators are also the recipients of nuanced legal interpretations and savvy political maneuverings that foster the recurrence of these offenses, allowing offenders to get away with their daily abuses and exploitation of hundreds of millions, if not billions, of people worldwide.

Whether one is discussing the conventionalization of extraordinary crimes like politically rationalized mass murder or the conventionalization of ordinary crimes like economically rationalized labor exploitation, what precisely does the conventionalization of crime refer to? Generally, conventionalization refers to those processes and/or the institutionalization of societal reactions that tolerate or allow the perpetrators of such offenses to escape criminalization from those rules that were otherwise designed and put in place to protect potential victims from these very same crimes. For example, in his analysis of nineteenth-century English manufacturers, W.G. Carson identified those "processes whereby, despite a succession of criminal laws purporting to restrict the hours of labor to be performed by children and young persons in cotton and other textile mills," their "employers successfully retained a 'right' ... to substantial immunity from the penal and other adverse substantial implications of their criminal conduct."[34]

More fundamentally, Michel Foucault in *Discipline and Punish*, identified a restructuring of "the economy of illegalities" that marked the legal order of eighteenth-century Europe, which came into its own with the rise of the bourgeoisie, or merchant class. In an earlier publication he distinguished specifically between two kinds of institutional-legal systems, one for the "illegalities of properties" and one for the "illegalities of rights." In the case of the former, for example, theft, there are the ordinary criminal courts and punishments; in the case of the latter involving, for example, "fraud, tax evasion, irregular commercial operations," there are "special legal institutions applied with transactions, accommodations, reduced fines, etc."[35] As Augustine Brannigan has underscored, Foucault's use of the word economy does not refer to the economies of the marketplace, but rather to "the sense of the actor's responsiveness to incentives: rewards and punishments replaced by profits and costs."[36] Moreover, as Brannigan also connotes, attached to these banded and commonly practiced yet infrequently punished crimes are "a series of justifications or rationalizations which tend to minimize the moralizations of the offence" as well as to "minimize the spontaneous emotional rejection of crime that Durkheim associated with retributive justice."[37]

As a preview, state-routinized crime (SRC) works in real time while relying on the integration of historical recurrences. SRC also includes what political scientists reference when they discuss complex financial systems as involving *regulatory capture*, or the condition whereby regulatory agencies become enamored with or unduly influenced by those sectors of the economy that they are responsible for monitoring. Finally, moving beyond regulatory capture or regulatory failure, SRC borrows from what scientists of knowledge refer to as *cognitive capture* and the influence of free-market ideology to shape the course of regulation and public policy more generally. While SRC focuses on regulatory capture and regulatory failure as well as cognitive capture, it also recognizes cognitive social learning and moral disengagement theories that are part and parcel of human agency and the crimes of the institutionally powerful.

Regarding social learning and moral disengagement, Albert Bandura has described two types of psychological processes that humans use to extricate themselves from morality or moral control. The first are justificatory and include people investing harmful conduct with high moral purpose as a means for reducing self-censure.

They also involve engaging in destructive exploits with self-approval. Bandura identifies three kinds of justificatory disengagement: moral justification, euphemistic language, and exonerating comparison. The second type involves moral disengagement, such as displacement and diffusion of responsibility. For example, in the case of the crimes of multinational corporations, human agents often see themselves as part of larger enterprises, of group decision-making, and of injurious activities subdivided into harmless components. These relationships, in turn, allow individuals to exploit through the anonymity of collectively irresponsible social behavior. Finally, Bandura argues that weakened moral control can come about by disregarding or distorting harm, by blaming others for harm, and by dehumanizing victims of harm.[38]

Before proceeding further into analyzing state-routinized crime and the underenforcement and/or decriminalization of the crimes of multinational corporations in particular, there are a few related analytic assumptions derived from studies in the fields of social ecology about human nature, social behavior, and environmental interaction that underpin this investigation, which I would like to share.[39] First, as members of organized groups, individuals are also social beings shaped by their mutual interdependence and by their absolute dependence on the resources from their environments. Second, within the environmental contexts of local and global capitalism, individuals and social organizations compete for access to the distribution of these resources. In turn, this competition domestically and internationally results in system-wide contradictions that shape the patterns of "over" criminalizing the crimes of the powerless and "under" criminalizing the crimes of the powerful.

Lastly, in the aftermath of 9/11, the routinization of the crimes of the powerful and the ramping up of the securitization of the corporate state has been accompanied not only by unchecked corporate power, but also by the ongoing tax breaks for the wealthy and huge tax avoidances for multinational corporations, expedited and facilitated by wartime opportunists, lobbyists, lawyers, ex-members of Congress, and bagmen for big donors.[40] To improve their bottom lines or margins of profit, these multinational corporate interests have been busy seeking out deregulation on any and all commercial fronts, such as those tax concessions for giants like General Electric that make billions in profits every year and has paid in some of those years absolutely zero in taxes, or giving coal producers and oil frackers more freedom to pollute, opening the Alaskan wilderness to drilling, and empowering the President of the United States to keep trade favors for corporations a secret, while at the same time, "enabling many of those same corporations to run roughshod over local communities trying to protect the environment and their citizens health."[41]

Flash forward sixteen years. After some three decades of engineering a winner-takes-all economy where the powerful are now consolidating their exceptionalism from the common course of American life, evidenced by the $1.15 trillion spending bill that narrowly passed a Republican dominated Congress and signed *tout suite* into law by Democratic President Obama on December 18, 2015. This bill, while

far from perfect, at least according to the usual Washington pundits, allegedly sig-
naled the legislative branch of government was no longer dysfunctional. And
besides, the same "talking heads" could be heard saying that it supposedly did a lot
of good things. Of course, at the time of the celebratory bipartisan passage of this
spending bill, for whom and at what price was typically unasked and unanswered
by the mass media.

Eventually, though, the electorate would learn that the bill turned out to be a
bonanza for the special interests of the "donor class" or those powerful corporate
executives and super rich individuals whose monetary contributions drive the
contemporary electoral process in the United States. Provisions in this spending bill
included, for example, extending tax breaks for big business, forbidding the Securities
and Exchange Commission from requiring corporations to disclose their political
spending, more gratuities for the fossil fuel industry, and, thanks to a last minute
lobbying effort, the saving of a loophole worth more than $1 billion to Wall Street
investors and to the hotel, restaurant, and gambling industries.[42]

Notes

1 Quoted from the mission statement of Corporate Accountability International at www.
  stopcorporateabuse.org/about-us.
2 Wikipedia. 2016. "List of Largest Companies by Revenue." March 4. https://en.wikip
  edia.org/wiki/List_of_largest_companies_by_revenue.
3 Alterman, Eric. 2015. "Rotten at the Core." *The Nation*. November 2: p. 6–8.
4 Ibid., p. 8.
5 Chandrasekhar, C.P. and Ghosh, Jayati. 2016. "Battling Apple and the Giants." *Naked
  Capitalism*. September 28. www.nakedcapitalism.com/2016/09/battling-apple-and-the-
  giants.html?utm_source=feedburner&utm_medium=email&utm_campaign=Feed%3A+
  NakedCapitalism+%28naked+capitalism%29.
6 Ibid.
7 Ibid.
8 Quoted in ibid., p. 6
9 Ibid., p. 8
10 Ibid.
11 Bawden, Tom. 2014. "BP's Legal Bill for Gulf Oil Spill Disaster Soars to $1bn." *The
  Independent*. February 5. www.independent.co.uk/news/business/news/bps-legal-bill-
  for-the-gulf-oil-spill-disaster-soars-to-1bn-9107849.html; Banerjee, Neela and Khouri,
  Andrew. 2014. "BP, Found Grossly Negligent, May Face $18 Billion in Gulf Spill
  Fines." *The Los Angeles Times*. September 4. www.latimes.com/nation/nationnow/la-na-
  nn-bp-reckless-gulf-oil-spill-20140904-story.html. See also, "BP Statement on Deepwater
  Horizon Oil Spill." *The Ed Show*. February 23, 2015. www.msnbc.com/the-ed-show/
  bp-statement-restitution-deepwater-horizon-oil-spill.
12 Bawden, 2014; Deslatte, Melinda and Kunzelman, Michael. 2013. "APNewsBreak: La.
  AG's Oil Spill Tab Nears $24M." *Yahoo News*. January 14. These figures are merely
  suggestive of the extent by which the legal expenditures of the states are "outgunned"
  by their powerful corporate counterparts. http://news.yahoo.com/apnewsbreak-la-ags-
  oil-spill-203038154.html;_ylt=A0LEV7kBdfBU0UUAiVsnnIlQ;_ylu=X3oDM
  TEzbWtpc2h2BHNlYwNzcgRwb3MDNgRjb2xvA2JmMQR2dGlkA1lIUzAwM18x.
13 Connolly, Amy. 2015. "Study: BP Oil Spill Left Millions of Gallons Buried in Gulf
  Floor." UPI.com. January 31. www.upi.com/Science_News/2015/01/31/Study-BP-
  oil-spill-left-millions-of-gallons-buried-in-Gulf-floor/4761422720211/.

14 Bradshaw, Elizabeth. 2015. "Blacking Out the Gulf: State-Corporate Environmental Crime and the Response to the BP Oil Spill." In *The Routledge International Handbook of the Crimes of the Powerful*, edited by G. Barak. New York: Routledge, pp. 363–372.

15 Geiger, Julianne. 2016. "Slavery at Sea: The Ugly Underbelly of Oil Shipping." *Naked Capitalism*. June 21. www.nakedcapitalism.com/2016/06/slavery-at-sea-the-ugly-under belly-of-oil-shipping.html.

16 Snider, Laureen. 2000. "The Sociology of Corporate Crime: An Obituary: (Or: Whose Knowledge Claims have Legs?)." *Theoretical Criminology* May 4: 169–206.

17 Ibid.

18 Ibid.

19 Glenny, Misha. 2016. *Nemesis: One Man and the Battle for Rio*. New York: Alfred A. Knopf, p. 62.

20 Rene Schonenberg quoted in ibid., p. 62.

21 Transcript from *Democracy Now*. 2012. "Obama Refuses to Back Growing Call for Drug Legalization to Stem Spreading Violence in Latin America." April 16. www.democra cynow.org/2012/4/16/obama_refuses_to_back_growing_call.

22 Ibid.

23 Ibid.

24 Paley, Dawn. 2014. *Drug War Capitalism*. Oakland, CA: AK Press, p. 17.

25 Correa-Cabrera, Guadalupe. 2014. "Forward." In *Drug War Capitalism*, edited by P. Dawn. Oakland, CA: AK Press, p. 3.

26 Ahmed, Azam and Schmitt, Eric. 2016. "Mexican Military Runs Up Body Count in Drug War." *The New York Times*. May 26. www.nytimes.com/2016/05/27/world/americas/ mexican-militarys-high-kill-rate-raises-human-rights-fears.html?emc=edit_th_20160527& nl=todaysheadlines&nlid=34985918&_r=0.

27 Ibid.

28 Ibid., pp. 3–4.

29 Greider, William. 2015. "This Year's 'Free Trade' Scam." *The Nation*. January 26: p. 24.

30 Rothe, Dawn and Friedrichs, David. 2014. *The Crimes of Globalization*. New York: Routledge, p. 12.

31 Ibid., p. 79.

32 Ibid.

33 Harvey, David. 2014. *Seventeen Contradictions and the End of Capitalism*. New York: Oxford University Press.

34 Carson, W.G. 1979. "The Conventionalization of Early Factory Crime." *International Journal for the Sociology of Law* 7: 37.

35 Quoted in Brannigan, A. 2013. *Beyond the Banality of Evil: Criminology and Genocide*. Oxford: Oxford University Press, p. 32.

36 Brannigan, Augustine. 2013. *Beyond the Banality of Evil. Criminology and Genocide*. Oxford: Oxford University Press, p. 32.

37 Ibid.

38 Bandura, Albert. 2001. "Social Cognitive Theory of Personality." In *Handbook of Personality: Theory and Research*, edited by L. Pervin and O. John. New York: Guilford Press, 2nd edition, pp. 154–196.

39 Lanier, Mark, Henry, Stuart and Anastasia, Desire. 2015. *Essential Criminology*, 4th edition. Boulder, CO: Westview Press, pp. 190–195.

40 Moyers, Bill. 2015. "The Plutocrats Are Winning. Don't Let Them! *Naked Capitalism*. December 22. www.nakedcapitalism.com/2015/12/bill-moyers-the-plutocrats-are-win ning-dont-let-them.html?utm_source=feedburner&utm_medium=email&utm_campaign= Feed%3A+NakedCapitalism+%28naked+capitalism%29.

41 Ibid.

42 Ibid.

1

CAPITALISM, CORPORATIONS, AND CRIMINALITY

At the end of Alan Greenspan's *The Map and the Territory: Risk, Human Nature, and the Future of Forecasting* published in 2013, the longest serving Chairman of the Federal Reserve Board (1987–2006) reveals that he no longer believes in the "free market" assumptions that he once ascribed to. Unfortunately, he has nothing to replace those assumptions with, including those of Keynesian economics that once upon a time he bought into. Reflecting on the banking crisis of 2008 and the Great Recession that followed, Greenspan had this to say:

> I have come to a point of despair where, if we continue to make banks wards of the state through TBTF policies, I see no alternative to forcing banks to slim down to below a certain size threshold where, if they fail, they will no longer pose a threat to the stability of American finance.[1]

However, if one scales the size of these mega oligopolistic banking institutions down, at what point are they no longer "competitive" in the financialization of global capital? And, would that necessarily be a "bad" thing? Whatever the answers to these hypotheticals are, most everyone knows that the banking concentrations of Wall Street wealth that contributed to the financial implosion are bigger today than they were back then.

What most people, however, do not know—including U.S. legislators on both sides of the political aisle who voted in favor of deregulation and for the Financial Services Modernization Act of 1999, which provided the final "nail in the coffin" that had been gradually eliminating the heretofore separation between commercial and investment banks established by Glass-Steagall in 1932—is the same law also known as the Gramm-Leach-Bliley Act that additionally permitted these merged banking institutions to delve into any and all economic activities that are considered "complementary to a financial activity." As a consequence of this abstruse and limitless legal clause, banks like Morgan Stanley, JP Morgan Chase, and Goldman Sachs now "own oil tankers, run airports and control huge quantities of coal, natural gas, heating oil, electric power and precious metals."[2] Thus, these banks are also buying and trading in entire industries no differently than Koch Industries while the latter oil industrialists are currently engaged in financial transactions like those of Wall Street as they try to extricate themselves from climate changing fossil fuels.

In the case of the giant Wall Street financial firms, they have been

> buying oil that's still in the ground, the tankers that move it across the sea, the refineries that turn it into fuel, and the pipelines that brings it to your home. Then, just for kicks, they [have also been] betting on the timing and efficiency of these same industrial processes in the financial markets—buying and selling oil stocks on the stock exchange, oil futures on the futures markets, swaps on the swaps markets,[3]

and so on. This allows a handful of banks to control the supply of crucial physical commodities. It further allows these institutions to trade in the financial products that might be related to those markets, such as aluminum in the case of Goldman Sachs, which not only reinforces the financial services industry's dominance of the political economy and its expanded concentration of wealth, but is also an open invitation to commit mass manipulation and fraud when required.

On the other hand, as already noted, there are a handful of "industrialists" and "technologists" that are diversifying their operations and moving aggressively into the financial markets, like the brothers Charles and Davis Koch. Koch Industries has profit revenues on the order of more than $100 billion annually, making it a non-public corporation larger than IBM, Honda, or Hewlett-Packard, second in size only to the largest private company in the United States: the agribusiness colossus Cargill.[4] Since the early 1990s the Koch brothers, for example, have also been specializing in "over the counter" or OTC trades—private, unregulated contracts not disclosed on any kind of centralized exchange. Today, they are engaging in the full spectrum of trading activities once limited to Wall Street financial giants, including such exotic securities as credit fault swaps and other derivative instruments. Koch Industries presently finds itself among the beneficiaries of the Dodd-Frank Wall Street Financial Reform and Consumer Protection Act of 2010. Case in point, the Volker Rule implemented in 2013 that bans investment banks from "proprietary trading" or investing their own money on their behalf in securities and derivatives. Accordingly, as many Wall Street banks have unloaded their commodities trading units, non-bank traders like the Koch brothers who are not prohibited from proprietary trading are able to pick up clients who would have previously traded with JP Morgan, Citigroup, or Goldman Sachs.

In preparation for the forthcoming examination of state-routinized crime and crime control—why capitalist states "fail" to control the crimes of the powerful—and how the structural relations of capitalism shape the differential responses to crime and crime control, the rest of this chapter underscores that the leading ideas and practices on or about crime and crime control are based upon the prevailing economic interests and needs at each of the stages of capitalist development (e.g., agricultural, industrial, financial). By incorporating this perspective of historical materialism, this chapter frames the study of multinational corporate crime in the context of both the globalization of capital and crime, and then pursues four objectives: (1) to provide an overview of the evolution of corporate illegalities away from criminal felonies and toward civil torts; (2) to establish what constitutes economic and political power in the contemporary era of global capitalism; (3) to characterize some of the fundamental contradictions of capitalism that help to connect the inter-related and reciprocal worlds of state and corporate fraud; and (4) to explain the dynamic relationships between capitalist state control and routinized crime control.

Globalizing capital and crime

Since the breakup of the Soviet Union almost three decades ago, the introduction of the North American Free Trade Agreement (NAFTA) in 1994, and the subsequent trading agreements between East and West, "free" trade and not "fair" trade has been integral to the globalization of both capital and crime. Globalization may be thought of as a growing interdependency among people, nations, and events that are connected increasingly throughout the world by communications, production, consumption, trade, computer networks, and transportation. Without a suitable international criminal law and/or a body of transnational regulations, and within the relations of the political economy of global capitalism, goods, services, labor, and money are allowed to move around with very limited restrictions on "setting up shop." In this process of circulation and commodification, rewards and benefits are provided to relatively few while inequality of wealth and income intensify worldwide. Although following the financial implosion and the pressure brought to the 2009 Global Economic Summit by the European Union, China, and India to resist these "unregulated" geopolitical relations and to establish international regulatory agencies, both Wall Street and President Obama rejected the idea and vetoed any attempt to create an international apparatus of regulatory control.

Two years before the global economic recession kicked in, at a Global Economic Forum sponsored by Morgan Stanley, during the opening presentation the bank's chief economist remarked:

> Billed as the great equalizer between rich and poor, globalization has been anything but … only the elite at the upper end of the occupational hierarchy have been spared the pressures of an increasingly brutal wage compression. The rich are, indeed, getting richer but the rest of the workforce is not.[5]

In some countries, the globalizing political economy has led to an expansion in pain and social injustice as measured by higher rates of disease, poverty, and hunger. The United Nations reported in 2006 that the top 20 percent of those living in high-income countries accounted for 86 percent of the world's entire private consumer spending. At the same time, tens of millions of people were succumbing annually to famine and preventable diseases. For hundreds of millions of others, life has become a daily preoccupation with obtaining safe water, rudimentary health case, basic education, and sufficient nutrition.[6] Since then, these trends have continued.

One decade later, at a time when the global economy has not yet recovered from the Global Recession, nations around the world are still submitting, though with more organized resistance to neoliberal economic policies of austerity, privatization, outsourcing, reducing taxes for the wealthy, and cutting social spending, as with a few exceptions GDP growth rates are precariously low, hovering around 2.0 at most. Moreover, wars, civil conflicts, persecutions, and oppressions have further exacerbated the global refugee crises, with numbers in 2014 exceeding 15 million refugees and 65 million displaced people worldwide. In 2015, according to the UN Refugee Agency, "one in every 122 humans is now either a refugee, internally displaced, or seeking asylum."[7] Meanwhile, in the contemporary world of free trade without regulation, multinational corporations are busy seeking business opportunities with the cheapest labor costs, least number of laborers, and weakest environmental standards.

Despite the global economic slowdown, the policies of free trade, the processes of techno-globalization, and the growing class inequality all contribute to the expanding opportunities for more crime and harm from the suite to the shop to the street. For example, the "free flow" of goods makes it easier to traffic in persons, in drugs, in intellectual property, in weapons, in contraband, in exotic wildlife, and so on. The contemporary forces of globalization also encourage the fraudulent and unfair trade practices of commerce, the laundering of unauthorized drug and arms trade profits, the smuggling of undocumented immigrants into and out of countries, the dumping of toxic waste and other forms of ecological destruction, the exploitation of workers, acts of retail and wholesale terrorism, and more.[8]

For now, one illustrative case of the globalization of capital and multinational corporate harm, crime, and misbehavior will have to suffice. In the legal case of *Caal v. Hudbay Mineral, Inc.*, the plaintiffs having no other legal options filed in the Superior Court of Justice in Ontario, Canada. In this case, ten indigenous Guatemalan women (and their families) living in a tiny village in the eastern hills of Guatemala were each evicted from their one-room homes because the land was claimed to belong to the company. Failing to find legal standing elsewhere, the women eventually filed a negligence lawsuit against the Canadian owned mining subsidiary, citing their gang rapes and other abuses perpetrated by truckloads of soldiers, police officers, and mining security personnel all working on behalf of Hudbay Mineral.

The fact that this lawsuit was filed in Canada is significant because according to government statistics 50 percent of the world's publicly listed exploration and mining companies had their headquarters in Canada in 2013. The total accounted for 1,500 companies with 8,000 properties in more than 100 countries. In a 2014 report released by the Council on Hemispheric Affairs (CHA), a policy group based in Washington, D.C., Canadian companies accounted for 50 to 70 percent of the mining in Latin America, and these companies "were often associated with extensive damage to the environment, from erosion and sedimentation to groundwater and river contamination."[9] The report has also emphasized that the oil and gas industry had demonstrated a blatant disregard for registered nature reserves and protected zones.

Legalistically, the case is very important because for decades, "overseas subsidiaries have acted as a shield for extractive companies even while human rights advocates say they have chronicled a long history of misbehavior, including environmental damage, the violent submission of protesters and the forced evictions of indigenous people."[10] The CHA has also reported that local protesters were often beaten, arrested, and in some instances, killed. Before *Caal v. Hudbay* the Canadian authorities maintained that the Guatemalan women should have standing in Guatemala, which their attorneys had rejected because of the corrupt nature of the courts. They had also failed to be heard on the basis of violations of human rights or international criminal law because they were informed that Canada had no jurisdiction. A favorable Canadian ruling on behalf of the plaintiff women would minimally establish "powerful guidelines for what constitutes acceptable corporate behavior" where no such rules presently exist.[11]

Studying multinational corporate crime and the public's right to know

A 1993 article in *The American Scholar* written by Democratic Senator Daniel Moynihan introduced the concept "defining deviancy down," referring to the ways in which the United States framed particular legal violations out of existence.[12] At the time, his phrase conjured up several earlier expressions such as the "permissive society," "being soft on crime," and "moral decay," all dealing with a need to restore "law and order." So that the reader is neither surprised nor confused from the start, this study of the routinization or defining down of multinational corporate crime does so not punitively but heuristically. In order to find tangible solutions to the problem of unchecked corporate power this examination also strives to avoid moral outrage or posturing, as challenging as that might be given the circumstances of the crimes reported here. Finally, what this inquiry does not do in the struggle to transform multinational corporate victimization is to advocate for tougher law enforcement, because the solutions to multinational crime would be better served by checking corporate power.

Although an increasing body of empirical research has demonstrated a growing concern among U.S. citizens about the dangers posed by elite or powerful offenders, the first study designed to actually measure lay or public knowledge about white-collar crime revealed that the participants were fairly ignorant about corporate crime, its harms, and victimization. At the same time, more than two-thirds of the participants thought that they were well informed on the subject.[13] This study also revealed that most people were influenced by popular crime myths about the crimes of the powerful, which resulted in more of a subjective rather than an objective or informed appreciation of, for example, the real costs in dollars or of the lives lost from the crimes of the powerful.[14] Underscoring this ignorance is Colleen Eren's investigation *Bernie Madoff and the Crisis* (2017), which reveals how the crimes of Wall Street that precipitated the financial crisis and those crimes perpetrated by Madoff, though economically and legalistically dissimilar, were culturally inseparable in the ideological and public imaginations.[15] Accordingly, one of the objectives of *Unchecked Corporate Power* is to demystify the crimes of the powerful in general and the crimes of multinational corporations in particular.

Part of the conceptual problem stems from the fact that there have been a paltry number of high-quality studies of corporate crime.[16] I would argue further there have been even fewer analyses and studies of the crimes of multinational corporations. In both types of crime the limited evidence that does exist suggests that the criminal law and penal sanctions have provided no deterrent value, while regulatory policy has fared somewhat better.[17] Either way, the perceived costs or risks by those law-violating individuals working on behalf of corporations as well as the risk of formal legal punishments for the corporations are quite small compared to the incentives or rewards (profits) for noncompliance. Another part of the conceptual problem stems from the unimaginable or unknown dark figures of multinational corporate crimes.

Thus, the conceptual and methodological position adopted here "treats theory and theory building as a device for orienting consciousness to the elusive processes" in which multinational corporate crimes are submerged. "Implicit in this approach, is a dialectical appreciation of the incongruence between appearance and reality, and the important role knowledge production plays in bridging" the divide between the symbolic and the material representations of these offenses.[18]

This perspective departs with those empirically normative assumptions that typically drive most research on corporate and state crimes, which are aimed primarily at discovering the allegedly "causative patterns" of these crimes. By contrast, my objective is similar to that of Kristian Lasslett's in *State Crime on the Margins of Empire* (2014): "to understand more fully the criminogenic potentialities inherent in actually existing capitalism, by applying classical Marxist theory to illuminate in greater clarity the different mediated processes" that contribute to the routinization of multinational corporate crimes.[19]

In the world of high-powered multinational corporate crimes[20] that we do know about, these transgressions should be studied within the legal trends and social parameters of capital accumulation and global geopolitics. In an era of financialization and globalization, these examinations need to take into account both the current developments in the internationalization of criminal law and criminal justice as well as in the application of international human rights law. Concerning International Criminal Law, Elies Van Sliedregt maintains that there has been a general trend in criminal wrongdoing to normalize complicity inside of a multitude of liability models, such as "collective agency" or "co-perpetration."[21]

Unfortunately, these and other formulations of criminal wrongdoing and collective guilt are not without their own problems and contradictions. To date, the law has only narrowly and scarcely used these liability models. For example, models of collective agency have been primarily, if not exclusively, applied to social groups like those involved in drug or human trafficking rather than to social organizations like those involved in international securities frauds or other kinds of global financial harms and injuries.[22] Even more importantly, as one of the world's leading regulatory investigators of financial institutions, Stephen Platt, has demonstrated in *Criminal Capital: How the Finance Industry Facilitates Crime*, not only do the global practices of banking act as a circulation system for criminal money acquired through drug trafficking, terrorism, piracy, human trafficking, proliferation and tax evasion, but these financial institutions also participate routinely in misselling, rate rigging, and sanctions evasion.[23]

In the context of globalization, the commonwealth, and International Criminal Justice, "the godfather of international criminal law" and the editor of *Globalization and Its Impact on the Future of Human Rights and International Law* (2015), M. Cherif Bassiouni has written:

> We are living through a period of decline in the observance of and respect for human rights as they have evolved since the end of World War II. And we may well be witnessing a setback in the evolution of international criminal justice … in a curious, not to say perverse, way—our globalized world is becoming more interdependent and interconnected at the same time that it is becoming less committed to the identification and enforcement of the common good.[24]

Comparable conclusions have also been drawn from my edited volume, *The Routledge International Handbook of the Crimes of the* Powerful (2015). Although Bassiouni's arguments and mine may vary, we both agree, as Bassiouni states, that over the past couple of decades:

> Globalization has not only enhanced the power and wealth of certain states … it has also given these states a claim of exceptionalism. That claim has also extended to certain multinational corporations and Other non-state actors because of their wealth, worldwide activities, and their economic and political power and influence over national and international institutions. For all practical purposes, many of these multinational entities have grown beyond the reach of the law, whether national or international.[25]

Probably nowhere is this statement truer than during the period that led up to and precipitated the Wall Street financial crisis of 2007–2008, when the identification and enforcement of the criminal laws, national and international, were conspicuously absent from battling an epidemic of high-stakes looting and high-risk securities frauds that were operating throughout the financial services industry. People need to appreciate that this criminally produced financial crisis "wiped away $16 trillion or 24 percent of household net wealth in the United States." It also cost more than "$20 trillion of taxpayers' money to bail out the largest financial institutions."[26] Not only were more than 5.5 million homes foreclosed on, but some 10 million people lost their jobs and millions of workers in their fifties left the economy prematurely.[27]

Between then and now, not one of the top Wall Street bankers who were collectively responsible for the biggest financial crimes in United States history has ever been charged, let alone prosecuted for or convicted of violating any criminal laws against securities fraud. One could argue in effect that these "banksters" have been rewarded for their looting and extractive financial practices. On the other side of the enforcement ledger, more than a few of those financial crimes of the past were legalized through decriminalization and deregulation, such as the repeal of the 1933 Glass-Steagall Act in 1999. Other forms of high-risk gambling, such as credit default swaps have still not been outlawed as obvious conflicts of interests, and they are also party to a derivative world of shadow banking subject to little in the way of state regulation. Historically, these types of enforcement contradictions circulate the marketing of licit and illicit securities trades. At the same time, these securities fraud enforcement dilemmas cannot be detached either from their codependency on capital accumulation or from the development of an evolving capitalist state.[28]

One fundamental difference between Bassiouni and myself in our analyses of the roles of bourgeois legality in the development and implementation of the internationalization of criminal justice has to do with how we come to terms with the non-criminal intervention into human rights violations, high-risk financial frauds, and a host of other multinational economic and environmental crimes. When Bassiouni examines the present state of globalization, he talks in terms of its positive and negative paradoxical effects on human rights violations and the lack of enforcement against such crimes. By contrast, when I examine the co-existence of the contemporary outcomes of the globalization of the crimes of the powerful and their noncriminal control, I talk in terms of the historical contradictions between the enforcement of the criminal law, on the one hand, and the enforcement of capital accumulation and the influential roles played by the World Bank, the International Monetary Fund (IMF), and a number of international trade agreements, resulting in favorable accommodations to multinational corporate interests at the expense of consumers, workers, and the environment, on the other hand.

From felonies to torts: constrained and unconstrained corporations

At the time of the ratification of the U.S. Constitution in 1789, the crime of bankruptcy was still punishable by death in the Courts of England, a long penal tradition dating at least as far back as thirteenth-century Venice, Italy. The early legal systems of mercantilism defined bankruptcy as an "act of debtor fraud, de facto theft by absconding with property and avoiding judicial process and the paying of just debts."[29] While never treated as a capital offense in the United States, plaintiff creditors could accuse defendants of bankruptcy or "debtor-perpetrated crime" in a court of law as late as the mid-nineteenth century. Eventually,

> bankruptcy was transformed from a branch of law for the relief of creditors against debtor fraud intended to foster the payment of debts into a pseudo-social welfare for debtor relief. Modern bankruptcy law legalized what antecedent jurisprudence first sought to prevent, the nonpayment of debts.[30]

Similarly, the history of what corporations were allowed to do (or not) gradually moved away from those of constrained to emancipated legal subjects, beginning with the emergence of the corporations of great wealth and criminality. Those included the three biggest traders of the seventeenth century—the British East India Company (1600), the Dutch East India Company (1602), and the Hudson Bay Company (1670)—each a product of the rise of mercantilism and the establishment of what would become an uneasy alliance of corporate and state power. In facilitating the transformation to the new imperial model of acquiring great wealth by stealing it, European Kings at the time legally contracted for three types of private services. First, there were the "adventurers" or explorers like Christopher Columbus, Hernando De Soto, Francisco Pizarro, and Hernan Cortez. Second, there were the "privateers" or mercenaries like Sir John Hawkins, Sir Francis Drake, and Sir Henry Morgan. Third, there were dozens of "joint stock companies" most of whom were not as successful as those identified at the beginning of this paragraph.[31]

By the logic of empire, these efforts in state-corporate ventures or public–private partnerships of imperial conquest were quite successful as joint enterprises. After all, midway through the nineteenth century the European colonizers ruled 67 percent of the earth's land surface. Over the course of some 250 years, these legally protected and sanctioned crime syndicates plundered, slaughtered, enslaved, and colonialized indigenous people around the globe. In exchange for a share of the Crown's booty, they also killed, looted, and stole the spoils from the ships of their competitors. Backed by their home governments, these chartered corporations had their own private armies and navies. They even assumed responsibilities previously carried out by the states such as maintaining embassies, forts, and trade facilities. All in all, these state-contracted companies were able to monopolize the markets, trade in slaves, export tribute, expropriate land and other forms of wealth, and profit from other financial scams.[32]

The joint stock companies such as the British South Sea Company, which had been chartered to transport and/or sell African slaves to the Spanish colonies in America, represented the creation of a new corporate legal form that rendered mergers and monopolies of limited social responsibility. Basically, the joint stock company as part of the New Feudalism combined two ideas from the Middle Ages:

(1) the sale of shares in public markets; and (2) the protection of owners from personal liability for the corporation's obligations. These two features made it possible for chartered corporations

> to amass virtually unlimited financial capital within a single firm, assured the continuity of the firm beyond the death of its founders, and absolved owners of personal liability for the firm's losses or misdeeds beyond the amount of their holdings in the company.[33]

Across the Great Pond, during the early days of the New Republic, state legislatures issued charters to serve narrowly defined public purposes for fixed periods of time. Moreover, the common practice was for states to place specific limits on corporate borrowing, ownership of land, and profit making. There were a host of other constraints ("regulations") particularly bothersome to powerful interests, such as: (1) a corporation was not allowed to own shares in another corporation; (2) interlocking corporate directorates were prohibited; (3) large and small investors had equal voting rights; and (4) owners were held personally liable for all debts incurred during the period of their participation. If these controls or regulations were not enough, governments also kept a close watch on corporate operations. States retained the power to revoke corporate charters at will and renewals were subject to quality of performance.[34] For example, shortly before the charter of the First Bank of the United States was about to expire in 1811, Congress rejected its application for renewal because:

> The bank's charter, issued in 1790, called for a total capitalization of $10 million, of which $2 million was to come from government and $8 million from private investors. The government put in its contribution. The private shares were quickly bought, but many of the private subscribers made only small down payments and never paid the balance. It appears that the private investors who place little or none of their own capital at risk reaped significant profits as the beneficial owners of an enterprise financed almost entirely by public money and credit.[35]

After the funding of the War of 1812 proved difficult without a central bank and the nation's financial system was in a state of chaos, Congress was able to muster enough votes to establish a Second Bank of the United States in 1816, which lasted until 1836. Under essentially the same working relations as the First Bank with a larger capitalization of $35 million, this bank was able to put the central banking system in order and prospered under new management. However, state banks and frontiersmen criticized the Second Bank "on the grounds that it was too powerful and that it operated in the interests of the commercial classes of the East."[36] Local versus national banking interests became a hotly contested issue for President Jackson's fight for re-election in 1832. Interpreting his defeat of Henry Clay at the polls as an expression of popular will on the subject, Jackson instructed his

Secretary of Treasury in 1833 to begin depositing government monies into state banks. These "pet banks" as Jackson's opponents referred to them became wildly speculative with their newly found funds.

A few years later during the financial Panic of 1837, these "pet banks" collapsed. Afterward, from the mid-1840s to 1921, in one form or the other, there was an Independent Treasury System in the U.S. that retained governmental funds in the Treasury and in its subtreasuries independent of the national banking and financial systems. However, the complete separation never occurred as the financial markets were still influenced by the Treasury. The Federal Reserve was created in 1913, putting an independent treasury system to rest. Still in charge today, the Fed appears to be a public institution but is actually run by private bankers. For the last 100 years or so, the outcome of these arrangements has remained pretty much the same, namely the creation of "private wealth from public assets and credit through a more sophisticated and less transparent process" than that of the first and second chartered banks of the United States.[37]

Despite the profits that flowed to monopoly capital during the nineteenth century from the public–private funding and constructing of canals, turnpikes, railroads, and prisons, chartered corporations wanted to emancipate themselves further from their legal obligations to the commons and from their restrictions to the communal welfare. During the Civil War, deregulation of these corporation charters began in earnest because the federal government was dependent on private military contractors for its troops' provisions in the field. In turn, these contractors started using their oversized profits from military contracts as leverage to curry favor in their campaigns to reduce legal constraints on behalf of greater freedom and corporate profits.

Step by step the corporations eliminated their restrictions through both the legislatures and the courts. There was little, if any, public discussion of these legal changes even as politically contentious as they were. In one of the early victories for corporate emancipation, the Pennsylvania legislature removed the restriction limiting one corporation from owning shares in another corporation. By the beginning of the twentieth century, owners had gained exemptions from corporate liability, while protections for small shareholders had been largely eliminated, and charters were being issued automatically on demand. There were no longer any limits on the life of corporate charters. They could be passed down from one generation to the next and so on and so forth. Corporations were free to move wherever they liked and there were no longer limits on their purposes. Very quickly the largest shareholders consolidated their corporate wealth and power.

The first major corporate victory came in 1886 with the strangely ruled on decision in *Santa Clara County v. Southern Pacific Railroad*. As history has revealed, the majority of nine Justices did not decide this case. Rather, this law initially came about when the notes scribbled down by the Chief Reporter of the Court opined that the Chief Justice of the Court had declared that "a corporation is a person the same as any other individual."[38] Immediately after this "legal fiction" became the law of the land and established that corporations were people too, corporate lawyers began, and have not stopped, preparing litigation to assert and expand on those rights/fictions.

Calling this legal precedent a legal fiction refers to the fact that even though human beings cannot and corporations can "live forever, exist in several different places at the same time, change their identities at will, and even chop off parts of themselves or sprout new parts," the latter would become entitled to the same constitutional rights and protections accorded human beings.[39] One other contradiction of bourgeois legality is the illogic that corporate persons are not as liable or responsible for their actions as real individual persons are. Additionally, once corporations were legally freed to both declare bankruptcy and dissolve as companies with relatively few lasting consequences, they were able to be "reborn" again and again as newly chartered companies with fresh corporate logos and/or aliases. Overlooked in these bankruptcy proceedings are those creditors, investors, and pensioners who have often been left stranded with millions of dollars still owed to them.

Following the *Southern Pacific Railroad* case, corporate America was quick to go after its newfound legal rights; coveting the first, the fourth, and the fourteenth amendments of the U.S. Constitution. For example, corporations as a person argued for the "right of free speech" and successfully struck down laws that had in the past prevented corporations from lobbying Congress or giving money either to political candidates or to elected officials. Next, claiming the personal "right to privacy," corporations successfully struck down earlier state laws that required corporations to open all of their records and facilities to the U.S. government. Subsequently, corporations were also able to strike down surprise safety inspections of workplaces by the Occupational Health and Safety Administration. They also were able to stop the Environmental Protection Agency from inspecting some chemical factories altogether. Finally, charging discrimination and a lack of "equal protection under the law," the J.C. Penny chain store successfully sued the state of Florida, ending a law designed to help small, local businesses by charging a regional or national corporate chain a higher business license fee than locally owned stores.[40]

For most of the twentieth century, when capital was primarily national rather than global, market-oriented laws were still comparatively interventionist. That is to say, these laws were embedded in or propelled by the ideas of liberalism, Keynesianism, and regulation to offset monopoly power. However, with the rise of globalization during the last third of the century, market-oriented laws began to downplay competition and the enforcement of antitrust law. In this period the transformation in the relations of production, and the accumulation and reproduction of monopoly power nationally were remade internationally or globally. As Brett Christophers has demonstrated in his sweeping economic history of law and capitalism, the last four decades have ushered in new interpretations of what since the Great Depression had been "fixed" law, including the unencumbered deregulation of corporations and the non-enforcement of competitively oriented laws in a concerted effort "to stabilize a capitalist system whose smooth reproduction as a vehicle of class-based profit generation and accumulation was at risk."[41]

Paradoxically, capitalist law has reverted back to a new twenty-first century form of "laissez-faire" with its pre-antitrust days of

> privileging the forces of monopoly over the forces of competition because, ultimately … capitalism's stability and reproducibility had come to be threatened by a deep imbalance in its core monopoly-competition relation, only this time with the excess existing in the latter rather than the former.[42]

As a result of this paradigmatic shift in economic thinking and practice, the tenets of liberalism were supplanted by those of neoliberalism, Keynesianism by monetarism, and regulated finance by deregulated finance. Historically, these 180-degree changes in ideologies and policies reveal once again how capitalist laws will transform as necessary to come to the aid of capital accumulation and reproduction, especially during times of economic crisis.

Power, growth, and inequality in early twenty-first century capitalism

When contextualizing the contemporary state of global capitalism, most economists will agree that the complexities of forces shaping macroeconomic institutions today are a product of the fact that the rates of output growths have declined worldwide, a legacy at least in part from the Eurozone and the supranational economic crises still prevalent in most countries today. With respect to these global forces, there are to varying degrees high levels of debt—public, corporate, and household—that continue to suppress spending and growth. There are also the failed and non-performing loans as well as a more limited supply of credit for new borrowers. Moreover, the declining consumption and output growth that threatens the exponential expansion of capital reproduction of "developed" countries were occurring even before the global economic crisis made them worse by decreasing investment lending and by weakening growth productivity.

In "emerging" countries, the effects have been even more pronounced, especially where ageing populations, lower capital accumulation, and slower productivity growth are combining to foreshadow a weaker overall potential for sustainable expansion in the future. In a few words, growth or the lack of growth is uneven at best and catastrophic at worst, particularly as winners and losers are created ordinarily in relation to larger monetary movements and extraordinarily during international economic crises that precipitate global depressions. In the case of ordinary monetary relations, there are, for example, the relative prices between the exchange rates of the dollar, the euro and the yen or whether the price of oil or corn is increasing or decreasing, or in establishing the international prime borrowing and other benchmark interest rates. In response to the extraordinary debt crises brought about by the ripple effects of the Wall Street financial implosions of 2008, central banks from around the world have spent more than $10 trillion trying to stimulate the global economy.

As a result, a tidal wave of cheap money has been key to propping up or sustaining growth in many countries, to cutting unemployment, and to staving off, if not preventing, economic panic. Nevertheless, the prospects of Greece's 2015 default created a panic of sorts that reverberated in stock markets around the world as nervous investors sold off stocks, pushing down the value in several major stock markets, including a decline of more than 20 percent in China. Similar bear runs occurred in other stock markets as sellers turned to safer government bonds paying less and adding to the problem of tighter money. The point is that while Greece and Puerto Rico, too, represent extreme cases of borrowing, high borrowing by governments and corporations generally is also bogging down the globally relevant economies of Brazil, Turkey, Italy, and China. In terms of the future economic climate, the question becomes: how long can credit be extended to member nations for unpayable debts?[43]

In addition to the global economic slowdown, if not outright stagnation in some geographic locales, there is increasing competition among multinational corporations, coupled with the geopolitical and neoliberal economic policies of austerity and privatization that synergistically facilitate a social and economic, if not technological "race to the bottom" between nation-states. These are facilitated, for example, by the development of such asymmetrical international trading deals as the North American Free Trade Agreement (NAFTA) in the 1990s or the recently authorized Trans-Pacific Partnership Agreement (TPPA) of 2015. Not yet ratified, highly controversial, supported by President Obama and allegedly not supported by 2016 presidential candidates Donald Trump and Hillary Clinton, this agreement would set in motion the trading relations of some forty nations while reflecting the world's concentrating pockets of multinational corporate wealth that aspires exponentially to accumulate capital and to grow its transnational leverage—political, economic, and legal. There are, globally, however, other nations from varying geographic regions that are developing trading blocs and associations, such as the Brazil, India, China, and South Africa (BRICS) nations or the newly formed Regional Comprehensive Economic Partnership in 2015, which involves ten Southeast Asian nations, including China but excluding the United States. This partnership constitutes 50 percent of the world's population, compared to the TPPA's 40 percent.

In the meanwhile, the more common irregular trading agreements lower tariffs, depress wages, bring havoc to environments, and disenfranchise citizens as well as the sovereignty of states having the combined effects of minimizing corporate risks and of decriminalizing numerous kinds of institutionalized harms and injuries. Former U.S. Labor Secretary Robert Reich has described TPPA as NAFTA on steroids. As part of the newest generation of global trade agreements, TPPA and others such as the Trade in Services Agreement (TISA), which if universally adopted, would gut the abilities of democratic governments to protect their citizens en masse from multinational abuse. For example, investor arbitration clauses have established specialized corporate courts and a framework of international corporate law, allowing multinationals to sue governments as well as regulators for laws that interfere with the growth of their corporate bottom lines.

All of these changes are occurring as developed nations are moving toward "irregular" economies where it is forecast, for example, that by 2020 and 2025, respectively, 40 and 50 percent of the U.S. labor force will be dependent on uncertain work. That is to say, these workers will have no predictable earnings, hours or benefits. This rapidly growing group of contingent rather than permanent workers, inclusive of "software programmers, journalists, Uber drivers, stenographers, childcare workers, TaskRabbits, beauticians, plumbers, Airbnb'rs, adjunct professors, or contract nurses,"[44] will only depress consumer demand and slow down growth further. In this age of globalizing capital and shifting labor, workers are finding themselves not only increasingly on their own to survive, but they are also increasingly bearing most, if not, all of the risks associated with a changing global political economy.

With respect to the expanding global concentration of wealth and inequality, the corruptibility of representative and non-representative governments, and the prevailing corporate policies of global capitalism, economic and political power is exercised most often by keeping issues like hedge fund taxes or corporate crime, for example, off of the U.S. electoral and lobbying agendas. Likewise, most analyses of the economic and criminal rules as well as their application or enforcement typically disregard the allocation of social power within the political-economic system and in determining what those rules will be, so that those actions taken and decisions made often result in a stream of future decisions that further entrench the most powerful. Most non-critical analyses of course never bother to ask "whether a different balance of power might be preferable to the prevailing one?" Similarly, where the problem of widening inequality at home and abroad reflects "both the failure of democracy and the strategic use of political power by large corporations, Wall Street banks, and some of the richest people in the nation to alter the rules of the game in their favor,"[45] critical analyses are asking, "what can be done to change these political, economic, and social arrangements as a necessary prerequisite for 'eliminating' multinational corporate crime?"

As for the accumulation and distribution of financial wealth, the U.S. economy is "twice as large as it was four decades ago, but the median wage has barely risen, adjusted for inflation. Almost all of the gains have gone to the top."[46] In fact, corporate profits before taxes have reached their highest share of the total U.S. economy since 1942. From 2000 to 2014, "quarterly corporate after-tax profits rose from $529 billion to $1.6 trillion. Meanwhile, labor's share of the economy has dropped, representing a shift from labor to capital of about $750 billion a year."[47] This inequality in wealth also reflects an inequality in income as CEO pay in large corporations relative to the pay of average workers has gone from 20–1 in 1965 to 123–1 in 1995 to around 300–1 today.[48]

As for the political accountability of elected and/or appointed officials, this has lessened precisely because the distribution of power has become so unequal that there are so few votes over basic distribution issues as the powerful set the legislative and public agendas by not allowing, for example, a discussion of the underlying contradictions between the escalation of corporate profits versus a sustainable (livable) income for ordinary workers. Public relation specialists, lobbyists, lawyers, and so on, are constantly marketing what the public should think is important, what facts should be considered, and even what scientific truth is:

> Coca-Cola wants you to believe sugary soft drinks and unhealthy diets are not as responsible for obesity, diabetes, and heart disease as is lack of exercise. Koch Industries wants you to view climate change skeptically. Large Wall Street banks would have you believe that Dodd-Frank law and attendant regulations—far easier on banks than a resurrection of the Glass-Steagall Act would be—are harming their international competitiveness. The National Restaurant Association wants you to believe an increase in the minimum wage will throw millions out of work. Monsanto wants you to believe that genetically modified foods are perfectly safe.[49]

Moreover, in courtrooms, hearing rooms, and other regulatory proceedings where laws are interpreted and enforced, corporate power is exercised through "platoons of lawyers and economic experts—so ubiquitous and well staffed, armed with so many studies and so much data, that they're able to completely dominate proceedings."[50] Too often, weaker players and interests avoid the fray altogether as the costs of entering are too prohibitive. Sometimes, the less powerful interests refrain because they fear retaliation.[51]

As for the determination of the hegemonic rules of the financial and global economies, these have undergone considerable change on behalf of the expansion of inequality and the concentration of wealth, especially within the financial sector. Since the early 1980s, laws and regulations instituted in the wake of the Great Crash of 1929 to constrain high-risk finance and a reoccurrence of another implosion were abandoned. These included undoing the restrictions on interstate banking, on the intermingling of commercial and investment banks, and on banks becoming publicly held corporations. Not only did these rule changes precipitate the Wall Street collapse of 2008, but they also "necessitated" the policy of TBTF (too big to fail) that bailed out the big banks' executives and shareholders while ignoring the millions of homeowners who found their homes underwater (owing more money on their homes than they are worth) and/or unable to meet their monthly mortgage payments.[52] Even after the passage of the Dodd-Frank Wall Street Reform and Consumer Protection Act of 2010, securities laws have been

> relaxed to allow insider trading of confidential information, as long as investors who were tipped off don't know from whom the original tip came. CEOs are now allowed to issue stock buybacks to boost share prices when they cash in their own stock options, without shareholders knowing.[53]

Meanwhile, special tax loopholes continue to allow the partners of hedge funds and private-equity funds to treat their income as capital gains even though these traders have not invested any of their own money in the transactions.

More generally, market reorganization has not been limited to the financial sector. Over the last few decades it has occurred across the economy. For example, intellectual property rights, including patents, trademarks, and copyrights, have been enlarged and extended, creating windfalls for high tech, biotechnology, and pharmaceuticals. This market reorganization has resulted in higher prices for the consumers. At the same time, antitrust law has become more lenient, "allowing vast segments of American industry—including big cable, high tech, airlines, health insurers, hospitals, and giant retailers to consolidate and gain market power."[54] By contrast, governmental policies have shown "less tolerance toward another form of economic collusion—that of workers seeking to combine forces to gain greater bargaining leverage."[55] In other words, many states have now adopted so-called right-to-work laws where some workers who have tried to form unions have been fired for doing so by management with impunity.

In similar veins of weakening worker and consumer power as well as expanding corporate power, contract law now allows for mandatory arbitration of any kind of contractual disputes before private judges selected by the corporations. And, while bankruptcy laws have become easier for corporations, they have become increasingly more difficult for individuals. For example, bankruptcy filings used by large corporations, notably airline and automobile manufacturers as well as the city of Detroit, have permitted the abrogation of labor contracts and the threatening of closures in order to receive wage or pension concessions. By contrast, U.S. college graduates overburdened with student debts are denied all forms of bankruptcy protection.

Capitalism and the contradictory nature of capital accumulation, capitalist crisis, and corporate criminality

Capitalism is a socioeconomic system based on private ownership of the means of production and the exploitation of the labor force. Capitalism rules most parts of our world. It is based on trade, industries, investment in and ownership of the means of production, distribution, and exchange of wealth, or goods and services, which are created and maintained chiefly by individuals and corporations. Modern day capitalism also refers to political, social, and economic arrangements that are built on the idea that individuals can own private property and operate businesses for the purpose of making a profit. Other characteristics of contemporary capitalism include the contradictions of capital accumulation, wage labor, competitive and monopoly markets, and a financial system where the prices at which assets, goods, and services are exchanged have been previously arranged by some combination of those parties actually involved in market transactions and the federal or central banking institutions establishing the different rates of interest for borrowing and lending money.

As for corporations, the modern version is a nineteenth-century invention of capitalism that created a separate entity, a "legal person," which is not the same as an individual or a shareholder who owns (a part of) the company. Like a real person this corporate legal person can enter into contracts, borrow money, and sue for damages. However, a corporation, unlike a real person, has limited rather than full liability. That is, a corporation may be sued without exposing its owners or shareholders to personal liability because neither they nor any of the directors, executives, or employees is the corporation by definition. Thus, the corporation is a legal invention that allows individuals to personally profit from their legal and productive activities without having to be fully liable for their illegal and harmful activities.

In the worlds of both corporate and financial capitalism, size or magnitude has always mattered. JP Morgan Chase CFO Marianne Lake answered "no" when questioned by shareholders, at the annual investor day meeting in February 2015, if they would they be better off if the company were smaller or broken up. Smaller banks would not be better because as she stated: "Scale has always defined the winner in banking."[56] Historically, there always have been benefits that accrue to the giants of any industry, not just banking. In the case of the megabanks of Wall Street, when these financial institutions got into trouble in 2008, they simply lined up for their share of the corporate bailouts at the federal trough. Meanwhile, some 1,500 smaller banks disappeared, declaring bankruptcy or being absorbed by those larger banking institutions left standing after the Wall Street implosion. Also hurt by the contradictory financial crisis bailout processes were the ordinary consumers and taxpayers who lost their jobs, pension funds, and/or homes.[57]

These contradictions of capital expansion are also present during the "good times" for Wall Street, such as after the financial crisis period when profits were soaring and the lasting situation may have had an even more detrimental impact on several other areas of the economy. As the paper, "Why Does Financial Sector Growth Crowd Out Real Economic Growth?" published by the Bank for International Settlements in 2015 concluded: "overall productivity gains were dragged down in economies with rapidly growing financial industries" as money crowded toward the less productive sectors of the economy, such as in real estate where "bubbling" forms of collateral are acquired when loans are defaulted on.[58]

Today, capitalist economic systems, or the practices of capitalism, are mostly "free enterprise" or market-driven with varying degrees of state intervention and regulation into the affairs of capital production. Since the 1980s, most of the key areas of market activity, including oil, food, finance, pharmaceuticals, tobacco, aircraft, defense contracting, utilities, energy, insurance, hotels, and mining have become oligopolized.[59] There are also those less common "mixed economies" or planning-driven systems where private and state ownership of capital coexist.

Either way, in the words of Karl Marx, the capitalist mode of production "rests on the fact that material conditions of production are in the hands of non-workers in the form of property in capital and land, while the masses are only owners of the personal conditions of production, of labor power."[60] For the past century or so, the "social relations of production" or the degrees of competition, roles of intervention and regulation, and the scope of state versus private ownership of property, have depended on the arrangements of the differently recognized models of capitalism, including laissez-faire, welfare, crony, and state. Initially, capitalism moved around the world by way of the systems of imperialism and colonialism. Today and for the foreseeable future, the forces of globalization and oligopoly, and to a lesser degree those of neocolonialism, are shaping the contours of capital production and are propelling the spreading markets of consumer capitalism.

More than a century ago, in making sense out of imperialism in the context of the aftermath of the Industrial Revolution, Rosa Luxemburg in her posthumous work, *The Accumulation of Capital* (1913), argued that accumulation was impossible in an exclusively capitalist environment. For capital to accumulate and reproduce, it has "to expand into non-capitalist strata and nations" and that without "constant expansion into new domains of production and new countries," the survival of capitalism is not possible. Unfortunately, "the global drive to expand leads to a collision between capital and pre-capitalist forms of society," resulting in violence, war, and revolution.[61] More recently, Satyajit Das in *The Age of Stagnation: Why Perpetual Growth is Unattainable and the Global Economy is in Peril* (2016), argues that in a post-industrial, technologically advanced world, the "forever-expanding" global economy has become overridden with debt and to slow or no growth economies.

As already suggested with respect to the slow down in growth and capital accumulation worldwide before and, exacerbated by, the financial crisis of 2008, the global financial system has a multitrillion-dollar problem that seems to be having a long-term effect on weakening both developed and emerging economies. Toward the end of 2015 and the beginning of 2016, there were signs that the threat posed by the overhang of bad debt, unpaid or toxic loans, was getting worse. For example, by early 2016, some financial analysts had estimated that China's troubled credit had already exceeded $5 trillion or the equivalent of about one half of the size of the nation's annual economic output. In Europe, the debt in bad loans was exceeding more than $1 trillion. And in South America's biggest banks, toxic debt was also on the rise.[62]

Historically, the demand for profits or the accumulation and reproduction of capital and the periodic crises of capitalism following each period of economic growth or round of new technology, has depended on a combination of skill, effort, and entrepreneurship, on the one hand, by those who own and organize the means of production and, on the other hand, by the same capitalists to employ force, fraud, violence, corruption, and state power. In the latter instances, for example, before there was the compiling of stocks and the appropriation of land, the original (or "primitive") accumulation of capital resulted from the Enclosure movement or the thefts of the commons by the rich during the European decline of late feudalism and the rise of early capitalism, circa 1000 to 1500 AD. This booty, or what would become the initial stockpiles of wealth, were held by nobles and aristocrats who, with the assistance of the developing nation-states and their laws, militia, patents, and corruption, were able to use violence against peasants and workers in order to seize personal property and land.[63]

This colonization of non-capitalist sectors has always been central to the accumulation and reproduction of capital. As Hannah Arendt argued about "superfluous wealth" in *The Origins of Totalitarianism* (1951), referring to what Marx called surplus wealth, the Industrial Revolution had created enormous wealth for the capitalists with little or no domestic utility for reinvesting in profitable markets. A European crisis in capital set the stage for decades of financial and real estate fraud in the business sector that victimized artisans, tradesmen, and small merchants, accompanied by corruption in nation-states as well as by economic depressions and the massive unemployment of superfluous people. Outside of Europe, this crisis in capital reproduction and unrestrained markets set the stage for the imperialism to come. By the 1870s, these capitalists had secured the services of their states to protect by force their international investments. This re-alliance of corporate-state power enabled "the productive use of superfluous capital" and "the employment of superfluous men as soldiers and sailors" as well as "supervisors or workers in the new colonies, or in the transportation of imports and exports."[64]

More recently, one has to look no further than the economic crashes of 1929 and 2008 to appreciate the many ways that capital accumulation and the avoidance of or accommodation of financial crises have been aided not only through monopoly, oligopoly, fraud, and corruption, but also by the continuous expansion into non-capitalist sectors or to the privatization of the social commons both at home and abroad. Domestically, for example, capitalists and the Tories in the UK are intent on privatizing the National Health Service. Although the NHS operates in a market society, it is not part of the process of capital accumulation. These free-marketers "look at the way the U.S. medical/drug system works for the benefit of the rich and they want that for themselves."[65] Meanwhile, capitalists and their political allies in the United States have been struggling for nearly two decades to transform the public educational system into a cash cow for private gain. Similarly, portions of the public prison and immigration systems in both of these countries have already been turned over to the privatization and accumulation of capital.

As for the different forms of criminality in capitalist societies, whether these are the products of the powerful or the powerless, they result from the ways in which capitalist societies are organized. Hence, just as capitalism shapes social institutions, social identities, and social actions and just as capitalism creates conflicts and contradictions, capitalism also shapes both the types of crimes and types of control societies have.[66] Accordingly, crimes of the powerful that are "functional" for or promote the accumulation and reproduction of capital are subject to laws and legal processes that often conceal, enable or facilitate these "crimes of domination and repression."[67] Meanwhile, crimes of the powerless that are "dysfunctional" or threaten the accumulation and reproduction of capital are subject to laws and legal processes that reveal, inhibit or obstruct those "crimes of accommodation and oppression."[68] Finally, consistent with "constitutive criminology" and its view of criminality and crime as a reflection of the total production of the cultural and structural relations of power differentials and hierarchical relationships in capitalist societies, crimes of the powerful and crimes of the powerless are also reciprocally related to the other.[69] In short, both of these types of criminals/crimes represent two sides of the arbitrary capitalist coin.

For example, in the U.S, a death caused by manslaughter applies only to individuals, as conveniently there is no such thing as "corporate manslaughter." This arbitrary legal exemption is unlike such countries as Australia, Canada or Great Britain where various corporate manslaughter provisions apply to workplace deaths caused by the negligent conduct of supervisors and/or executive officers.[70] In a similar vein, the U.S. Supreme Court did not declare that a corporation has religious rights in the 2014 Hobby Lobby case because it was confused about whether or not a corporation could pray. Rather, the Court narrowly decided 5–4 not only to allow business owners to retain the powerful protection of limited liability, but also to expand this benefit or right by exempting corporations from one of their basic financial obligations under the Affordable Care Act.

Without the contemporary forms of capitalism, there would be no need for corporations, and without corporations or the right to incorporate, there could be no crimes by corporations. Legally, corporate crimes are those illegal acts or omissions that are committed by either a business entity (e.g., a corporation) or by individuals on behalf of a business entity. Socially, corporate harms refer to those organized activities that injure or victimize people, animals, and/or the environment. In a functional way, corporate crimes may also collude with state crimes and/or state omissions or non-regulatory enforcement to become state-corporate crime. The opportunity to "pull these crimes off" successfully with minimal liability, criminal or otherwise, depends upon the failures and/or selective practices used by the social control apparatus of the capitalist state. For example, on 14 September 2014 *The New York Times* published an extensive investigation into the record of the National Highway Traffic Safety Administration (NHTSA) that expresses the interconnected relations of state-routinized crime. The newspaper's examination went well beyond the NHTSA's publicly acknowledged failure to detect an ignition switch defect in several models of GM cars linked to some twenty-eight deaths by Thanksgiving of that year.

In addition, the investigation probed the handling of major safety defects as far back as 2004 and found that the NHTSA had "been slow to identify problems, tentative to act and reluctant to employ its full legal power against companies."[71] After analyzing agency correspondence, regulatory documents, and public databases as well as interviewing congressional and executive branch investigators, former agency employees and auto safety experts, *The New York Times* learned that in many of the major vehicle safety issues during this ten-year period that the agency had not taken "a leading role until well after the problems had reached a crisis level, safety advocates had sounded alarms, and motorists were injured or died."[72] These safety issues included the unintended acceleration in Toyotas, the fires in Jeep fuel tanks, the air bag ruptures in Hondas, and the GM ignition switch problem.

The year 2014 was, to say the least, a particularly disturbing one in terms of automobile safety. After all, there was the deadly ignition "scandal" at GM, the billion-dollar Toyota criminal settlement, and the ever-expanding number of air bag recalls. In fact, in 2014 automakers "recalled more than 48 million vehicles in the United States, surpassing the previous record of about 30 million in 2004."[73] The GM ignition recall "compensation program" managed by Kenneth Feinberg is alleged to have paid out $70 million to the families of 15 killed auto victims.[74]

Perhaps the most alarming charges during this period of automobile scandals was Volkswagen's admission in 2015 to a system-wide fraud program in which the company had intentionally sold millions of diesel powered cars, approximately 567,000 in the United States alone, fitted with deceptive software designed to cheat emissions tests. According to the Environmental Protection Agency (EPA), those VW and Audi diesel cars included in the recall "may emit up to 40 times the national standard for nitrogen oxide (NOX)," thereby impacting negatively on various healthcare and respiratory problems, such as asthma, bronchitis, and emphysema.[75]

State-routinized crime control and the capitalist apparatus

State-routinized crime control that seeks to repress the predatory and property crimes of the street and to normalize the multinational crimes of the suite is part and parcel of the capitalist apparatus of social control. When Foucault introduced the concept of *dispositif* that has been translated and mentioned by others as well as by Foucault himself as device, machinery, apparatus, construction, and deployment, they are referring to the various administrative, institutional, and physical mechanisms and knowledge structures that function to enrich and uphold power within a given social body. In one of his published interviews from the 1970s, when asked to explain what was meant by the term "apparatus," Foucault answered:

> What I'm trying to pick out with this term is, firstly, a thoroughly heterogeneous ensemble consisting of discourses, institutions, architectural forms, regulatory decisions, laws, administrative measures, scientific statements, philosophical, moral, and philanthropic propositions—in short, the said as much as the unsaid. Such are the elements of the apparatus. The apparatus itself is the system of relations that can be established between the elements.[76]

More recently, Giorgio Agamben has observed that the apparatus identifies a "set of practices, bodies of knowledge, measures, and institutions that aim to manage, govern, control, and orient—in a way that purports to be useful—the behaviors, gestures, and thoughts of human beings."[77]

Importantly, Foucault maintained that the apparatus is essentially strategic. This means

> we are speaking about a certain manipulation … of a rational and concrete intervention in the relations of forces, either so as to develop them in a particular direction, or to block them, to stabilize them, and to utilize them. The apparatus is thus always inscribed into the play of power, but it is also linked to certain limits of knowledge that arise from it and, to an equal degree, condition it.[78]

Similarly in pre-capitalist feudal apparatuses, these were subject to and conditioned by certain types of epistemological knowledge aimed at maintaining the prevailing economic and power relations of feudalism. These apparatuses in kind were also manipulated for the purpose of reproducing the legal order of feudalism.

Contemporary capitalist apparatuses are reflective of a different bourgeois legal order where the capitalist state not only possesses a vast monopoly over the use of force and violence, but also the joint sovereignty over the currency and the law, each striving jointly through bourgeois legality to reproduce the hegemony of global capital. These capitalist states, in addition, have the ultimate power of *eminent domain* over private and public property. This power is especially important as the shrinking commons locally and globally becomes increasingly deferential not only to the needs of capital accumulation and reproduction, but also to the contemporary policies and practices of structural adjustment programs, austerity, privatization, and neoliberalism. Relatedly, capitalist states possess the power not only to tax and to redistribute assets and incomes, but also to monitor and influence other non-economic institutions, such as education, healthcare, intelligence, the military, and law enforcement. Finally, by way of the collaboration of the state's central bank and its treasury department, constituting what David Harvey labels the "state-finance" nexus, capitalist states are capable of fulfilling their key supportive roles in managing both capital and monetary policies.[79]

Both indirectly and in conjunction with private justice/control through semi-autonomous agencies, individual capitalist states also include political networks of vested and competing interests that make up loosely affiliated and often ethically challenged bureaucracies whose discretionary powers are frequently executed in clusters of legally bound decisions that are normally subordinate to but not dictated by these crimes of the powerful. In other words, these capitalist-state apparatuses of social control are far too complex and numerous to be mere instruments of capital that efficiently absolve the crimes of the powerful without any resistance or push back. At the same time, while the interests of capitalist states are certainly not one and the same as capital, and may at times be at odds with the interests of capital, these states nonetheless increasingly protect the interests of multinational capital over the social and political interests of the vast majority of people worldwide who find themselves increasingly abandoned by those governments who are busy downsizing and deconstructing their social welfare states.

In their totalities, capitalist state control apparatuses not unlike those in the United States are comprised of, but not limited, to executive, judicial, and legislative branches of government, to corporate foundations and research institutes, and to the endowed philanthropy and orchestrated NGO-ization of politically constructed social problems. Furthermore, capitalist states are objects and subjects of those internationally powerful financial institutions formed by and dependent upon a Bretton Woods worldwide currency system, the World Bank, the International Monetary Fund, and the World Trade Organization, working as some kind of supranational capitalist state. Jointly, these legal institutions, both domestically and internationally, have been and are presently skewed in favor of the interests of the Global North, West and parts of Southeast Asia over the interests of the Global South.

However, these dominant "free-market" developed countries (DCs) are now being challenged by some emerging countries (ECs), by other appearing central and development banks and currencies, and by China's state-driven capitalism, which by 2012 had become the largest trading partner in the world with 124 countries compared to number two, the United States, with 76 countries. Also, in 2014, Brazil, India, China, and South Africa (BRICS) launched a $50 billion Development Bank and China created the $40 billion Silk Road Fund for Southeast and Central Asia as well as Europe. And, for comparative purposes, in 2013 the World Bank had dispersed $52.6 billion, the Brazilian Developed Bank had invested $85 billion, and the China Development Bank had extended loans valued at $240 billion.[80]

Despite the semiautonomous conditions of capitalist states and the contemporary differences in the types of crimes experienced daily in the Global North and Global South, similar kinds of powerful crimes are routinely normalized in countries as diverse as the United States and India. In part, their shared reality of state-routinized criminal experiences is a by-product of their congruently developing corporate security states. Likewise, in the context of legitimizing their corporate security states and the associated political assaults on those basic civil liberties and equal rights for all, both the U.S. and India are actively engaged in whatever it takes to cover-up, nullify, or white-wash the crimes of the powerful. For example, the cleansing or neutralizing of these crimes by both of these governments includes penalizing nonconforming journalists or whistleblowers for outing some selective criminal activities of corporations and especially of states. Similarly, each of these democratic states has exonerated state torturers or war criminals for engaging in a wide variety of patriotic misconduct.[81] Hence, both of these neoliberal capitalist states often find themselves in the dialectical bind of having to incorporate both the means and strategies that tend to demoralize, conventionalize, and *ipso facto*, decriminalize those otherwise bona fide criminal activities.

The respective state normalization or conventionalization of these crimes in both the U.S. and India occurs through highly adaptive democratic-legal systems of checks and balances as well as through mass-mediated corporate images of how things are and what is to be done about them. These mediated images are typically framed within nationalistic lenses that present favorable stories about themselves. Consistent with carefully managed or framed "selfie" images of their countries, the citizens of both nations are informed not only of what they should admire, consume, fear, or strive for, but also what they should deny, excuse, or overlook. Lastly, even though these mass-mediated images are at great variance with the political, social, and economic realities that millions upon millions of people of both countries live by, these partisan selfies nevertheless convey to their citizens not only the messages of what they should think, but also how they should feel and conduct themselves, quite often in their own collective worst interests.

Notes

1 Greenspan, Alan. 2013. *The Map and the Territory: Risk, Human Nature, and the Future of Forecasting*. New York: The Penguin Press, p. 298.
2 Taibbi, Matt. 2014. "The Vampire Squid Strikes Again." *Rolling Stone*. February 27: p. 34.
3 Ibid.
4 Dickerson, Tim. 2014. "Inside the Koch Brothers' Toxic Empire." *Rolling Stone*. www. rollingstone.com/politics/news/inside-the-koch-brothers-toxic-empire-20140924.
5 Roach, Stephen. 2006. "Globalization's New Underclass." Presented at the Morgan Stanley Global Economic Forum. March 3. http://apjjf.org/-Stephen-S.-Roach/1923/a rticle.html.
6 Barak, Gregg (ed.). 2007. *Violence, Conflict, and World Order: Critical Conversations on State-Sanctioned Justice*. Lanham, MD: Rowman & Littlefield.
7 UNHCR. 2015. "War and Persecution Increase." *UNHCR*. June 18. www.unhcr.org/ en-us/news/latest/2015/6/558193896/worldwide-displacement-hits-all-time-high-wa r-persecution-increase.html.
8 Barak, Gregg (ed.). 2000. *Crime and Crime Control: A Global View*. Westport, CN: Greenwood Press.
9 Daley, Suzanne. 2016. "Outcry Echoes Up to Canada." *The New York Times*. April 3: p. 11.
10 Ibid., pp. 1 and 11.
11 Ibid., p. 11.
12 Moynihan, Daniel. 1993. "Defining deviancy down" *The American Scholar* 62 (1): 17–30.
13 Michel, Cedric, Cochran, John, and Heide, Kathleen. 2015. "Public Knowledge about White-Collar Crime: An Exploratory Study." *Crime, Law and Social Change* 65 (1): 67–91.
14 Ibid.
15 Eren, Colleen. 2017. *Bernie Madoff and the Crisis*. Berkeley, CA: University of California Press.
16 Schell-Busey, N., Simpson, S., Rorie, M., and Alper, M. 2016. "What Works? A Systematic Review of Corporate Crime Deterrence." *Criminology and Public Policy* 15 (2): 387–416.
17 Ibid.
18 Lasslett, Kristian. 2014. *State Crime on the Margins of Empire: Rio Tinto, the War on Bougainville and Resistance to Mining*. London: Pluto Press, p. 16.
19 Ibid., p. 21.
20 Multinational corporate crime refers to those acts or omissions on behalf of the Modern corporation or "a body formed and authorized by law to act as a single person although constituted by one or more persons and legally endowed with various rights and duties including the capacity of succession," which has divisions in more than two countries (www.merriam-webster.com).
21 Van Sliedregt, Elies. 2012. *Individual Criminal Responsibility in International Law*. New York: Oxford University Press.
22 Papacharalambous, Charis. 2013. "Group-Based Imputation and the International Criminal Law Discourse: Individuals and Associations as International Criminal Wrongdoers." *Beijing Law Review* 14 (4): 129–136.
23 Platt, Stephen. 2015. *Criminal Capital: How the Finance Industry Facilitates Crime*. New York: Palgrave Macmillan.
24 Bassiouni, M. Cherif (ed.). 2015. *Globalization and Its Impact on the Future of Human Rights and International Criminal Justice*. Cambridge, UK: Intersentia, Preface.
25 Ibid.
26 Epstein, Gerald. 2016. "How Finance Costs Too Much and Fails to Deliver." *Naked Capitalism*. July 18. www.nakedcapitalism.com/2016/07/how-finance-costs-too-much-and-fails-to-deliver.html?utm_source=feedburner&utm_medium=email&utm_campaign=Feed%3A+NakedCapitalism+%28naked+capitalism%29.
27 Adler, Lynn. 2010. "U.S. 2009 foreclosures shatter record despite aid" *Reuters* www. reuters.com/article/us-usa-housing-foreclosures-idUSTRE60D0LZ20100114; Stanford

"The Impact of the Economic Crisis on Older Workers and Retirement Security" Accessed December 2016. https://web.stanford.edu/group/recessiontrends/cgi-bin/web/resources/research-project/impact-economic-crisis-older-workers-and-retirement-security.

28 Harvey, David. 2014. *Seventeen Contradictions and the End of Capitalism*. Oxford, UK: Oxford University Press.

29 Pomykl, J. quoted in Barak, Gregg. 2009. *Criminology: An Integrated Approach*. Lanham, MD: Rowman & Littlefield, p. 188.

30 Ibid.

31 Korten, David. 2006. *The Great Turning: From Empire to Earth Community*. San Francisco, CA: Kumarian Press, pp. 126–127.

32 Ibid.

33 Korten, p. 131.

34 Korten, p. 191.

35 Korten, p. 188.

36 Quoted in Barak, 2009, *Criminology: An Integrated Approach*, p. 191.

37 Hartmann, Thom. 2004. *Unequal Protection: The Rise of Corporate Dominance and the Theft of Human Rights*. New York: Rodale, p. 120.

38 Hartmann, pp. 5–6.

39 Hartmann, p. 120.

40 Hartmann, pp. 120–121.

41 Christophers, Brett. 2016. *The Great Leveler: Capitalism and Competition in the Court of Law*. Cambridge, MA: Harvard University Press, pp. 218–219.

42 Ibid., p. 218.

43 Eavis, Peter. 2015. "Loads of Debt: A Global Ailment With Cures." *The New York Times*. June 29. www.nytimes.com/2015/06/30/business/dealbook/trillions-spent-but-crises-like-greeces-persist.html?_r=1

44 Reich, Robert. 2015a. "In the New Economy, Workers Take on All the Risk." *Naked Capitalism*. August 25. www.nakedcapitalism.com/2015/08/robert-reich-in-the-new-economy-workers-take-on-all-the-risk.html

45 Reich, Robert. 2015b. "Economics Is Too Important to Be Left to Economists." *The Chronicle of Higher Education (The Chronicle Review)*. September 23. http://chronicle.com/article/Economics-is-Too-important-to/233335.

46 Ibid.

47 Ibid.

48 Ibid.

49 Ibid.

50 Ibid.

51 Hansen, Hans Krause and Uldam, Julie. 2015. "Corporate Social Responsibility, Corporate Surveillance, and Neutralizing Corporate Resistance: On the Commodification of Risk-based Policing." In *The Routledge International Handbook of the Powerful*, edited by G. Barak. London and New York: Routledge, pp. 186–196.

52 Barak, Gregg. 2012. *Theft of a Nation: Wall Street Looting and Federal Regulatory Colluding*. Lanham, MD: Roman & Littlefield.

53 Reich, 2015b.

54 Ibid.

55 Ibid.

56 Quoted in Morgenson, Gretchen. 2015. "Smothered by a Boom in Banking." *The New York Times*, Sunday Business. March 1: p. 1.

57 Barak, 2012.

58 Morgenson, 2015.

59 Weissman, Robert. 2007. "Corporate Power Since 1980." *Common Dreams*. www.commondreams.org/views/2007/06/01/corporate-power-1980.

60 Marx, Karl. 1875. *Critique of the Gotha Program*. Accessed from the Marxist Internet Archive. www.marxissts.org/archive/marx/works/1875/gotcha/ch01.htm.

61 Quoted in Walker, Ed. 2015. "Capitalism Versus the Social Commons." *Naked Capitalism.* www.nakedcapitalism.com/2016/01/capitalism-versus-social-commons.html?utm_source= feedburner&utm_medium=email&utm_campaign=Feed%3A+NakedCapitalism+%28na ked+capitalism%29.

62 Eavis, Peter. 2016. "Toxic Loans Around the World Weigh on Global Growth." *The New York Times.* February 3. www.nytimes.com/2016/02/04/business/dealbook/toxic-loans-in-china-weigh-on-global-growth.html?emc=edit_th_20160204&nl=todayshead lines&nlid=34985918&_r=0.

63 Polanyi, Karl. 1944. *The Great Transformation.* New York: Farrar & Rinehart.

64 Walker, 2015.

65 Ibid.

66 See Chambliss, William. 1988. *Exploring Criminology.* New York: MacMillan; Michalowski, Raymond. 1985. *Order, Law, and Crime.* New York: Random House; Spitzer, Steven. 1975. "Towards a Marxian Theory of Deviance." *Social Problems* 22: 638–651; Taylor, Ian, Walton, Paul, and Young, Jock. 1973. *The New Criminology: For a Social Theory of Deviance.* London and New York: Routledge.

67 Quinney, Richard. 1977. *Class, State, and Crime.* New York: David McKay.

68 Ibid.

69 Henry, Stuart and Milovanovic, Dragan. 1996. *Constitutive Criminology: Beyond Postmodernism.* London: Sage.

70 Barak, Gregg, Leighton, Paul, and Cotton, Allison. 2015. *Class, Race, Gender, and Crime: The Social Realities of Justice in America*, 4th edition. Lanham, MD: Rowman & Littlefield, p. 2.

71 Stout, Hillary. 2014. "After a G.M. Recall, a Fiery Crash and a Payout." *The New York Times.* September 25. www.nytimes.com/2014/09/26/business/after-a-gm-recall-a-fier y-crash-and-a-payout.html?_r=0. See also, Stout, Hillary, Ivory, Danielle, and Ruiz, Rebecca. 2014. "Regulator Slow to Respond to Deadly Vehicle Defects." *The New York Times.* September 14. www.nytimes.com/2014/09/15/business/regulator-slow-to-respond-to-deadly-vehicle-defects.html.

72 Stout *et al.*, 2014.

73 Ibid.

74 Stout *et al.*, 2014.

75 CarFraudSuit. 2015. "Has Volkswagen Defrauded You?" www.carfraudsuit.com/?utm_ source=Bing&utm_medium=cpc&utm_campaign=Bing.

76 Gordon, Colin (trans.). 1980. "The Confession of the Flesh." Interview in Michel Foucault's *Power/ Knowledge: Selected Interviews and Other Writings, 1972–1977.* New York: Pantheon Books, pp. 194–195.

77 Agamben, Giorgio. 2009. *What is an Apparatus? And Other Essays*, translated by D. Kishik and S. Pedatella. Stanford, CA: Stanford University Press, p. 14.

78 Ibid.

79 Harvey, David. 2014. *Seventeen Contradictions and the End of Capitalism.* New York: Oxford University Press.

80 Interview with Ian Bremmer. 2014. "America's Uneasy Path Abroad in 2015." *Time Magazine.* December 18: pp. 74–76.

81 Edwards, Beatrice. 2014. *The Rise of the American Corporate Security State: Six Reasons to Be Afraid.* San Francisco, CA: Berrett-Koehler; Roy, Arundhati. 2014. *Capitalism: A Ghost Story.* Chicago, IL: Haymarket Books.

2

WHY CAPITALIST STATES "FAIL" TO CONTROL THE CRIMES OF THE POWERFUL

Variations in powerful relations are essential for grasping the workings of state-routinized crime as these are currently reflected in the hegemonic rules of global capital and in the legal edicts and state enforcement patterns of those rules. Chapter 1, reflective of the changing interests, practices, and meanings of capitalism, corporation, and criminality, laid out an historical overview of the expanding power of corporate capital. After briefly discussing "global convergence" this chapter turns its attention to defining and situating the market-driven nature of the crimes of the powerful and of state-routinized crime (SRC). The rest of the chapter elaborates on three examples of normalization or conventionalization and how the state routinization of crime and crime control works. These include: (1) the police use and abuse of force; (2) the counterterrorist use of corporate torture; and (3) the Wall Street use of securities fraud.

Each of these criminological accounts of criminal immunity, or why neoliberal-capitalist states regularly decriminalize and fail to adequately regulate the illegal and harmful behaviors of powerful state or corporate actors, underscores the thesis that capitalist states generally do not pursue those crimes that do not threaten the profitability or well-being of the capitalist order of accumulation. At the same time, capitalist ruling classes of the past or oligarchies of capitalist power in the present usually "manage to keep their anti-social acts hidden from public scrutiny, or, failing that, have them dealt with administratively."[1] Legalistically, these non-criminal outcomes reinforce the asymmetrical hierarchies of class privilege, concentrated wealth, and political power. Routinizing multinational corporate criminality "beyond incrimination" also figures into the relevant costs of labor and technology.[2]

Structurally, the state routinization of crime does not resonate with the older theory of economic convergence where planned centralized economies like the former Soviet Union or contemporary China and those of decentralized free-market economies like post-socialist Russia or the United States are each supposed to adopt the "best practices" of each other's political economy.[3] SRC instead, resonates with present-day international policy analysts that recognize the convergence of "worst practices" scenarios, such as those developing similarities between a Russian oligarchic-reigning free market capitalism influenced by a political apparatus controlled by an autocratic presidency, on the one hand, or, a United States free market capitalist system dominated by financialization and state-sanctioned multi-national corporate monopolies, on the other hand. Accordingly, both of these nations and many others find themselves awash in a "nefarious confluence of corrupt economic practices and a privatized culture of unaccountability" that has also "combined with nationalistic fervor and religious intolerance to spawn a new global system of totalitarian politics."[4] Hence, John Feffer talks of "a new axis of illiberalism" where governments are "sinking into despotism with a corporate face and cosmetic democracy."[5] John Ralston Saul refers to this political transformation as the corporatization of world governments or to "corporate coup d'états in slow motion."[6] Similarly, the late Sheldon Wolin described this global state of affairs as "inverted totalitarianism" where corporate interests seize the levers of state, media, and government.[7]

This newer "theory of convergence in reverse" argues that "the most illiberal and undemocratic aspects of the capitalist and socialist models" are presently being adopted by nations worldwide,[8] and this thesis is reproduced here with three "case studies" of state-routinized crime control in the United States. This characterization of convergence in reverse includes the abandonment of and reversing of mean-ingful market regulation and consumer protection, the further reification of ideo-logical language to justify or moralize on behalf of the exploitation and unequal distribution of wealth, the use of political demagoguery and jingoistic propaganda to keep populations fearful and submissive to state authority, the employment of legalized political corruption and crony capitalism, and the development of hyper-capitalist systems that increasingly sacrifice individual liberties and civil rights as they serve to protect and expand corporate profits at the expense of workers, consumers, and the environment.[9] Consistent with convergence in reverse and reorganization, the developing corporate state has been able to militarize the police and privatize the military while outsourcing enhanced or harsh interrogation practices of torture used in homeland and international security operations, accompanied by the normalizing of drone warfare, the routinizing of the crimes of multinationals, and the omnipotent digital surveilling of individual privacy.

State-routinized crime

Reflexive of critical criminology and a definition of crime equating the cause of harm with something that does not necessarily have to be an act or illegal or criminal but could be all three, a general concept like state-routinized crime is especially useful for examining the etiologies of the crimes of the powerful, especially as these revolve around different forms of institutionalized corruption, extortion, and theft. While some of these practices may in fact be illegal—even criminal—many will be normalized or routinized through public policies, through civil, administrative, and judicial legal processes, through Congressional oversight committees and legislative bodies, and through the exercise of a slew of other political-legal behaviors, such as specialized task forces, campaign financing, or tax lobbying. Taken as a whole, state-routinized crime (SRC) refers to the "oil that lubricates" virtually all of the recurring crimes of the powerful, including those offenses of states as well as corporations, of globalization, and of the financial industries, allowing these symbiotic harms and injuries to co-exist with the non-criminal activities of these same groups of powerful people.

Theoretically, state-routinized crime is interactional in nature and is consistent with the logics of those social process, labelling, conflict, and structural models of human interaction. More specifically, SRC is consistent with the logics of "limited rationality," which assumes that human choices are not only situational, but they are also affected by cultural and environmental factors and by the variations in people's perceptions, motives, skills, and abilities to analyze events and to structure their power into negotiable outcomes. Except for the fundamental enforcement difference with respect to the guardian role of state neutrality or "equal protection under the law," SRC is also consistent with traditional economic models or rational choice theories of partial and qualified rationality, or of circumscribed reasoning. The best known criminological examples of these include: "routine activities theory," which assumes that criminal actions are related to the normal/rational or routine activities of potential victims and guardians in time and place;[10] "situational choice theory," which argues that criminal behaviors are structured by the skill sets of the offenders, the risks and payoffs associated with their offenses, and the context of situational constraints and opportunities;[11] and the integrated "evolutionary ecological theory," which maintains that criminal violations are about using accumulated and available alternative behavior strategies to satisfy needs by expropriating the valuables of others.[12]

Most importantly, the logics of the contradictions of capital accumulation, consumption, and reproduction are what drives the contours of the securitization of the corporate state and of the state routinization of crime. Let me reemphasize that state-routinized crime or state-approved crime is the outcome of systemic processes that satisfy the needs and interests of capital development. Furthermore, SRC assumes that the normalization of habitually powerful illegal behaviors and their lack of criminal punishment are facilitated through the socio-psychological realities of criminal accommodation and the human defense mechanisms of denial. SRC also identifies the conventionalization of the crimes of the powerful with the workings of the state apparatuses of capitalist social control. Together, the inter-related worlds of normalization (legitimizing) and conventionalization (approving) become the essential means by which the crimes of the powerful are neutralized or made relatively invisible as though they were not really grave matters with, often, dire consequences.

State-routinized crime argues explicitly that the reciprocal relations between the crimes of the powerful and the apparatuses of state social control are structural in nature, and that these are systemically interdependent with respect both to illegal opportunities and to legal constraints. These relations of state-capital control are especially germane in the cases of unchecked multinational corporate abuses. In the U.S., the diversification of state-routinized corporate crimes or the criminal non-enforcement of the law and the granting of immunity to these multinational corporations (MNCs) enables international victimization on a grand scale. Three recent examples of SRC or enabling were the 1999 repeal of the remaining features of the Glass-Steagall Act of 1933, the 2007 Halliburton legal loophole exempting fracking and other modes of oil production from the federal clean air and water acts, and the 2009 Congressional bailout-loans of those financial institutions TBTF. Three recent examples of non-enforcement/immunity were the epidemic of securities fraud on Wall Street that instigated the financial implosion of 2008 and global recession that followed, the exposure of the National Security Agency's universal violation of American citizens' right to privacy guaranteed by the fourth amendment of the U.S. Constitution, and the Central Intelligence Agency's inhumane detention and torture programs scattered around the world.

Felonies or otherwise, these state-routinized illegalities cause or are responsible for a wide assortment of injury and victimization, including those crimes and harms perpetrated by state agents as well as by other powerful corporate groups that the state enables through active collusion with and/or failing to criminally penalize obvious transgressions. These state-routinized behaviors of illegality provide ample economic and/or political gains for those participating individuals and networks of organized interests and alliances that are involved in enabling and/or covering up these activities. These state-routinized crimes also bring together politicians, lobbyists, and campaign fundraisers as well as those stakeholders from all areas of business, law, and the military to establish social policies that often proffer rather than deny opportunities, assist rather than prevent criminal events, and support rather than punish their criminal liability after it does occur. Together or alone, these institutional relations and other patterned interactions of agents of social control act as cultural and material transmission belts that both serve and forgive the various crimes of the powerful, turning them into relatively risk-free, utilitarian as well as non-utilitarian activities of shared lawlessness.

Furthermore, state-routinized crimes share commonality with some of the more expansive conceptualizations of organized crime. Traditionally, organized crime has been viewed rather narrowly as a monolithic organization of criminals, usually represented by some type of criminal enterprise or syndicate operating locally, nationally, or transnationally. More specifically, organized crime has typically referred to "illegal activities connected with the management and coordination of racketeering (organized extortion) and the vices—particularly illegal drugs, illegal gambling, usury, and prostitution."[13] This constricted definition excludes organized corruption, organized professional theft, organized burglary rings, organized identity theft, organized human sex trafficking, or any kind of unrelenting criminality organized by any other group. In contrast to the restrictive construction of organized crime, state-routinized crime includes those expressions of corruption, extortion, and professional theft that have been legitimated by precedent breaking interpretive changes in the law such as the 2010 decision in *Citizens United v. Federal Election Commission*, 558 US, which overturned a 49-year-old rule that prohibited unions and corporations from using their general treasuries to fund electioneering communications.

More widely, a model of state-routinized crime asks a fundamental question regarding the many facets of contemporary crony capitalism:

> Is corruption just a matter of legality, of financial irregularity and bribery, or is it the currency of a social transaction in an egregiously unequal society, in which power continues to be concentrated in the hands of a smaller and smaller minority?[14]

In the United States, the simplest answer might be that corporate corruption has been made legal and reconfigured into the business costs of tax-reducing corporate lobbying and political fundraising. Although

> lobbyists no longer shamelessly buy lawmakers with cash-filled suitcases, influence-peddling today can still be persuasive given the vast amounts of money spent legally particularly since Citizens United, when the court over-turned the ban on outside groups paying for political advertising supposedly independent of a candidate's own campaign.[15]

Actually, though, what's right and what's wrong is a bit more complicated. Putting it another way, what is one person's bribery and corruption may be another person's "honest graft," to paraphrase the early twentieth-century philosopher and politician, George Washington Plunkitt. For example, in 2014 a federal jury found former governor of Virginia Bob McDonnell guilty of deriving personal gain by promoting a product owned by one of his political contributors. Prosecutors had successfully argued that Mr. McDonnell had "violated the Hobbs Act by depriving Virginians of his 'honest services' as governor."[16] A federal appeals court upheld the jury verdict, and McDonnell's attorneys invoking the Citizens United holding that "ingratiation and access" do not constitute corruption, appealed to the U.S. Supreme Court. Interestingly, an amicus brief written on behalf of the defense by

> a bipartisan group of former attorney generals and other public officials cautioned that by upholding the conviction, an appeals court had "criminalized the routine practice by public officials of giving access to their constituents, including those who have supported the official in the past."[17]

Argued before the Supreme Court in April 2016, several of the justices seemed sympathetic to the arguments made by lawyers for McDonnell, questioning the scope of federal laws used by prosecutors to convict him of using his office for financial gain. On June 27, 2016, the last day of decisions for the season, the Court ruled unanimously to vacate the ex-governor's conviction, making it harder to prosecute political officials for corruption.

Borrowing from Michael Johnston's comparative analysis of corruption in both more and less developed economies, SRC specifically incorporates his idea that corruption can be brought forth legally into a political system of governing. SRC also extends his idea of legalized corruption to include legalized extortion as well as legalized theft in order to better understand how the crimes of the powerful are neutralized and why their invisibility remains relatively secure in spite of the corporate security state's recognition of and preoccupation with the growing worldwide political, social, and economic inequality as well as with the potentially catastrophic consequences of the next global financial crisis.

In his book *Syndromes of Corruption* (2005), Johnston characterized "influence market corruption" as a type of organized corruption found within those developed countries of the Global North, and he distinguishes this type from five other types of corruption—"elite," "cartel," "oligarch," "clan," and "official mogul"—which are often practiced in the less-developed countries of the world. Johnston argues that influence market corruption happens in advanced political economies because the roles of competitive politics and lobbying are more complex there than they are in those countries where the other types of corruption occur. Compared to the types of corruption found in the lesser-developed political economies, which work their means and ways around the formal systems of governing, influenced market corruption works primarily within the prevailing political, legal, and economic orders. Johnston contends that influence market corruption "revolves around access to, and advantages within, established institutions, rather than deals and connections circumventing them."[18] Johnston further explains: "Strong institutions reduce opportunities and some of the incentives, to pursue extra-system strategies, while increasing the risks. Moreover, the very power of those institutions to deliver major benefits and costs raises the value of influence within them."[19]

In a similar way, I am suggesting that just as corruption can be made formally legal, political extortion or professional theft can also be legalized. This may even occur under the guise of the First Amendment of the U.S. Constitution, as when the Supreme Court decision in the 2014 Hobby Lobby case, based upon the religious beliefs of its owners, exempted corporations from one of their fundamental financial obligations under the Affordable Care Act, namely, to pick up the costs of birth control for women. More fundamentally, these latest modes of influence or forms of corruption are much broader than the consequences of legalization. They also include the "structured unaccountability" built into the contemporary world of government and corporate organizations.[20]

More generally, in a discussion of the crimes of the powerful in their 1981 book *Organizing Crime*, Alan Block and Bill Chambliss included those "crimes of nation states, through the illegal and immoral acts of large corporations, to misuses of police and political office by local, state, and national power holders."[21] In addition to these commonly recognized crimes, state-routinized crime refers to those regularized activities that may or may not be illegal and whose influence enables or facilitates the harmful or injurious consequences of the crimes of the powerful, especially when these involve state intelligence agencies like the National Security Agency (NSA) and the Central Intelligence Agency (CIA), or even local branches of law enforcement. Additionally, if one takes the argument of Alan Wolfe in his 1973 book *The Seamy Side of Democracy*, which maintained that repression was an essential aspect of class societies that is neither irrational nor spontaneous but rather a calculated method of the state apparatus to shape the parameters within which decisions are made,[22] and combines this argument with Richard Quinney's thesis that almost all crimes are politically driven by the structural contradictions of capitalism from his 1977 book *Class, State, and Crime*,[23] then one is able to reinterpret the expressive crimes of capitalist state control as state-routinized criminal behavior.

For example, U.S. mass media and political discourse cut back and forth between two of the biggest crime news stories of 2014—the unpunished CIA crimes of torture and the unpunished police killings of unarmed citizens, typically African American males—without making any type of state-routinized criminal connections between these institutionalized behavioral reactions, treating each of these structurally related actions as isolated and unrelated phenomena. Nevertheless, a common source for both of these crimes is a global capitalist system experiencing increasing debts and recurring financial crises worldwide, expressed in escalating class conflicts and growing inequalities, and most poignantly, in acts of terrorism and state repression. Since 9/11 and in response to an intensification of the contradictions of capital accumulation and reproduction, there has been the stepped up militarization of U.S. law enforcement[24] and the expansion of surveillance technology utilized throughout the public and private domains to wage twin warfare against both domestic street crimes and international cyber or terrorist crimes.[25] There has also been the state routinization of all kinds of abusive behaviors, not the least of which have included the U.S. killings or assassinations of suspected terrorists by drone warfare in places like Yemen and Pakistan.

State-routinized crime control, regulation, and accountability

Historically, state-routinized crime control of the powerful are situated within and reify the changing and prevailing relations of social and political power. Accordingly, the contradictory absences or lack of the rule of law and the normalization of the crimes of the powerful across neoliberal democratic societies as different as the U.S. and India are indicative of the degree to which their economic leaders and political institutions are held (un)accountable to and/or are (not) dependent on the appropriate legal application of the rules and regulations. Thus, in periods associated with more rather than less regulation of securities trading, there seems to be less need for the state to routinize crime. Conversely, during periods of less regulation there seems to be more need for the state to routinize crime.

For example, following the 1929 stock market crash, by way of the passage of the Glass-Steagall Banking Act, the Securities Act, the Securities Exchange Act, and the National Housing Act in the 1930s and up through the 1970s, there was a period of sustained regulation of financial markets, and therefore, there was little need for state-routinized crime. However, after deregulation had picked up momentum, beginning with the passage of the Garn-St. Germain Depository Institutions Act in 1982 and culminating with the Gramm-Leach-Bliley Act, or the Financial Services Modernization Act of 1999, which ultimately repealed Glass-Steagall and unleashed those infamous collateralized debt obligations and high-risk derivative trading, state-routinized crime was in high demand, and it performed exquisitely on behalf of the Wall Street banksters.

Francis Fukuyama, not exactly a Marxist by any stretch of the imagination, has shown that political order and decay have fluctuated historically according to the changing modes and relations of production.[26] For example, throughout most of the laissez-faire nineteenth century, the U.S. had a weak, decentralized, corrupt, and pre-industrial corporate order with limited liability, as the order of the day was *caveat emptor*: "let the buyer beware." During this period, graft and other forms of bribery contributed not only to the buying of justice by those who could afford it but also to a national immorality crisis. At the time, rackets, pull, and protection were common antidotes for stubborn legal nuances.

Then, like now, the prevailing values of wealth and success predominated as the guiding principles of right and wrong. Early into the twentieth century before the trust-busting Progressives came along, the "ability to 'make good' and 'get away with it' offset the questionable means employed in the business as well as the professional world. Disrespect for law and order was the accompanying product of this scheme of success."[27] From the first Gilded Age during the late nineteenth century to the next Gilded Age at the turn of the twenty-first century, it's practically déjà vu all over again.

In between these two gilded ages, from the turn of the twentieth century through the 1960s, changes were brought about by the rising power of the working classes and a social revolution, expressed first in the ideas of the Progressives and later in those of the New Dealers. Driven by the modern forces of industrial and collective social capital, these political movements recognized the plights and the struggles of the laboring and marginal classes. In response to those masses of individuals who were not benefitting from, and who were perceived as posing an organized threat to, the expanding political economy, some sectors of the ruling strata set about to not only clean up the urban working environments as well as vast amounts of political corruption, but also to provide everyday people with a Square Deal during the outbreak of the First World War and a Fair Deal after the conclusion of the Second World War.

Over the span of some sixty years, a strong unionization movement of working Americans and a populist mind-set had gained the political support of some industrialists and other social and political leaders. The ushering in of a progressive or liberal agenda in the mid-twentieth century combined with the stock market crash of 1929 and the election of Franklin Delano Roosevelt in 1932 had brought about a more welfare-oriented capitalist state. Subject to Keynesian economic policy and a slew of legislated federal regulations, these new laws of social development would meet their ideological Waterloo with the election of President Ronald Reagan in 1980 and the rise of what would eventually become known as neoliberalism by the early 1990s. Before then, however, and following the assassination of President John Kennedy in 1963, the period of democratic reform and welfare liberalism would realize a zenith of sorts with the "due process" revolution of the Earl Warren Supreme Court, the passage of the civil rights and voting acts as well as the War on Poverty under the administration of President Lyndon Johnson, and the subsequent enactment of consumer and environmental protection laws in the late sixties and early seventies during the first term of the Richard Nixon administration.

In stark contrast, for the past thirty-five years, a reversal in welfare-oriented and regulated capitalism has been occurring. First initiated as part of the Reagan Revolution in the 1980s, it has continued and morphed into today's policies of austerity and privatization, favored to varying degrees by both Republican and Democratic administrations. This shift in the socio-political relations of the capitalist state were in reaction to the rising forces in competitive global capital, exemplified by the 1973 oil crisis, buttressed by a rebirthing of the older ideology of "free markets" and by the newer ideology of neoliberal economizing. By the 1990s, in a relatively short period, the delegitimizing processes of the welfare state had found a consensus between the two dominant political parties. Democratic President Bill Clinton not only signed the conservative North American Free Trade Agreement in 1994, but that was also the same year he signed the repressive Violent Crime Control and Law Enforcement Act built upon the myth of the "super-predator" that helped contribute to decades of mass incarceration. Clinton also signed the Welfare Reform Act, otherwise known as the Personal Responsibility and Work Opportunity Act of 1996, which twenty years later had essentially killed cash welfare benefits resulting in roughly 3 million American children, or 1 in 25, living in households with incomes of less than $2 per day per person for food, a global metric of extreme poverty. A few years later in 1999 Clinton signed the law that repealed Glass-Steagall. It should also be noted that in the United States by the mid-1990s the certification of class action lawsuits against law violating corporations had peaked and has been in decline ever since.

Not unrelated to these changing sensibilities of social accountability and responsibility, graduates from elite colleges and universities in the 1990s were abdicating medical and engineering schools and flocking to Wall Street to make their financial fortunes as investment brokers, arbitrage dealers, and derivative traders. In short, by the turn of the twenty-first century unenlightened self-interest, unregulated financial markets, and unfettered victimization were becoming the new economic order of the day. To paraphrase the Iron Lady, Margaret Thatcher, there were no societies, only individual men and women and their families. This sentiment was echoed in Robert D. Putman's now famous 1995 article: "Bowling Alone: America's Declining Social Capital."[28]

As Fukuyama argues, political and social, if not economic, development in the United States has clearly been moving in the wrong direction, spurred on by deregulation, privatization, growing inequality, and a decaying infrastructure. This reversal in social accountability and responsibility has also been aided by several U.S. Supreme Court decisions, exemplified by the Citizens United and Hobby Lobby cases. These two decisions in particular have served to expand the power and corporate rights of insiders over the power and common interests of outsiders. As part of these shifting relations in social and economic power, political institutions in America have become less democratic, less fair, less efficient and increasingly more dependent on the financial and corporate classes for their policy setting strategic agendas.

Police use and misuse of force, militarizing U.S. law enforcement, and privatizing the security industry

For the past several decades law enforcement agencies in the United States have come under increasing scrutiny and criticism for corruption, acts of police brutality, civil rights violations, racial profiling, selective law enforcement, and "predatory policing," or using violence as a means of preserving the status quo as well as extracting economic fees (fines) for all kinds of city ordinances and misdemeanor violations. More recently, the violent arrests of peaceful protestors during the Occupy Wall Street movement of fall 2011 and the images of police officers during the summer of 2014 in Ferguson, Missouri,

> arrayed in military formation and dressed in battle fatigues, clad in balaclavas and pointing high-caliber machine guns at American citizens protesting police killings of unarmed youth … have recast the image of police officer from peaceful community protector to fearful enforcer.[29]

At least outside of the ghettos or barrios this has been the case where the realities of police forces as "occupying armies" have a long history dating as far back in the U.S. as the nineteenth-century slave patrols.[30] Not all that ironically, present-day policing, seems to echo "a back to the future" scenario. As Wesley Kendall has argued, the modern-day police of the United States, when not protecting private property and citizens from common everyday crimes, serve "as proxy warriors for a corporate state seeking to impose order and control through either intimidation or force," having evolved from truncheon-wielding private armies

> protecting eighteenth-century corporate profiteers to the machine-gun armed paramilitary forces patrolling American streets in decommissioned combat vehicles in displays of force formerly only seen on foreign battlefields and now seen as a menacing presence during various corporate and political protests.[31]

In the United States, nobody has been keeping records of the police use of deadly force, lethal and non-lethal. Similarly, there are no numbers on the number of people killed in confrontations with officers, or whether or not the victims were armed or unarmed. There is also no data on how many officers have been prosecuted or convicted of some type of homicide or civilly sued for wrongful death.[32] Rarely does a shooting incident result in some form of sanction or punishment to an officer. With regard to Cincinnati, Ohio only one officer had been charged after killing someone in the line of duty between 2001 and 2014. Following the officer's acquittal the city experienced four days of protests and riots, the worst civil unrest since the 1960s. In a way, it is safe to report that the police have always enjoyed the relative if not absolute impunity for the killing of citizens in the U.S.

Importantly, the framing of police killings of citizens in both print and digital news coverage disproportionately reflects the activities, concerns, and views of the police, public officials, and elite groups.[33] And, while the media presents most murder victims in a sympathetic manner,[34] police killings are generally presented as "the logical consequences of victims' lawlessness or troubled behavior."[35] Seldom are news narratives of police shootings or cases of police brutality framed within the context of legal repression or racial oppression.[36]

From the beginning of 2001 until the end of 2014 the U.S. police force had killed over 5,000 civilians, without identifying whether they were armed or not, or approximately the same number of U.S. soldiers killed in the second Iraq war. Comparatively speaking, the FBI through at least 2015 had not yet recorded the annual number of unjustifiable homicides by police, only the number of justifiable homicides.[37] For 2013, the number reported was 320 police killings compared to 27 felonious killings of police officers. While the rate of police officers killed in 2013 by murder or manslaughter was 3/100,000, the rate for all U.S. inhabitants killed at large was 4.7/100,000. For perspective, the figure of close to 400 killed civilians annually dwarfs the handful of citizens killed by police forces in other Western nations such as Canada, Germany, France, or England. Moreover, during the past couple of decades the number of police officers killed on duty has steadily declined and the rates of urban violence have also plummeted in most areas of the United States. However, any type of comparable downward trend has not been the case for police killings of armed or unarmed civilians.[38]

As criminologist Hal Pepinsky blogged on December 27, 2014: "Any wrongful homicide or death on the job is a tragedy, but occupational risk scarcely accounts for patterns of police use of excessive force in communities of color."[39] Compared to whites, the police kill African American and Latino males at disproportionate rates ranging from two or three to thirty-one times greater, depending on the geographical location. It is also important to stress that police cultures with little training and supervision or those police forces guilty of criminal misconduct and excessive use of force may be normative in some locales, although they are not by any means universal policing experiences throughout most communities across the United States. Hence, police misconduct and excessive use of force against racial minorities is situational and is influenced by multiple factors in addition to race, such as police training, local budgeting for law enforcement, whether police functions are outsourced, and so on.

For example, one study in St. Louis, Missouri examined all police uses of deadly force—both fatal and nonfatal—that occurred between 2003 and 2012. The results indicated that neither the racial composition of neighborhoods nor their level of economic disadvantage directly increase the frequency of police shootings, whereas levels of violent crime do—but only to a point. Police shootings are less frequent in areas with the highest levels of criminal violence than in those with midlevels of violence.[40]

Like other studies, this one revealed that fatal deadly force incidents in St. Louis represented a small fraction (16 percent) of the use of deadly force, and that approximately one-third of shootings resulted in nonfatal wounding.

Similarly, an empirical assessment of police shootings in Chicago revealed that neither racial malevolence nor unconscious bias affords sufficient explanations for why officers disproportionately shoot blacks compared to non-blacks, and the study suggests a more complex relationship between race, policing, and violence.[41]

The study of 259 shooting cases in the city of Chicago between 2006 and 2011 indicated that these incidents were not necessarily motivated by the animus of white officers against black victims. Rather, the data showed that the race of officers involved in these shootings largely matched the general demographics of the departments themselves, and that the shooting victims were far more likely to be black and/or to live in neighborhoods that were far less diverse and affluent. In other words, police killings might have less to do with black and white than with blue on black. The findings also revealed that those officers who resorted to deadly force rarely did so to prevent and intervene in an ongoing act of violence. Typically, these shooting incidents happened when no other crimes had occurred than these persons attempting to get away from the officers. In fact, nearly half of the 259 killings reviewed occurred following a foot chase. Moreover, in more than 80 percent of these shootings, the officers reported a perceived gun threat and in 60 percent of the total incidents, a firearm attributable to the victims was found at the scene of the killing.

Perhaps even more revealing than these studies on the police use of deadly force and the universality of disproportionate minority contact at all phases of the administration of criminal justice were the findings released in December 2014 from the U.S. Department of Justice on its investigation into the abusive and unconstitutional police practices exhibited by the Cleveland Police Department between 2010 and 2014.[42] As these findings suggest, where such behaviors do exist they are, indeed, expressive of those cultural police milieus of excessive force and resistance to change.[43] The recent report was more than just déjà vu because the new findings were essentially the same as the old findings from a 2002 Department of Justice (DOJ) investigation into the behavior of the Cleveland police. Apparently nothing had changed since the earlier identification by the DOJ of the structural deficiencies of the Cleveland Police Department (CPD). Among these findings, the new report again makes it known that the police of Cleveland too often violate the U.S. Constitution by using unnecessary and unreasonable force, which their supervisors not only tolerate but have also endorsed on several occasions. Symptomatically, the DOJ report revealed that street cops in Cleveland were receiving little support, supervision, and guidance from their senior officers. These police officers were also immersed in and surrounded by a culture of excessive force. At the same time, they were on their own to figure out what was considered excessive in a department where officers were expected to demonstrate that they were both willing and tough enough to distribute force when called upon to do so.

In this policing environment, the use of excessive and maximum force became routine, as did the use of Tasers, stop and frisk harassment, and unprovoked searches. Arrest reports were often used as cover ups for excessive use of force and as leverage against civilians filing complaints against the police. Additionally, police use of incident reports on the use of force were not always properly addressed, documented, or investigated because the "top brass" often did not want to hear about these nor did they want to cooperate with the investigation conducted by the DOJ. In fact, only in the very worst-case scenarios of abuse where the evidence had demonstrated that misconduct had occurred beyond a reasonable doubt would the Cleveland Police Department write anything up. Nevertheless, most of those officers written up for using excessive force did not receive any disciplinary action. More than a decade of "runaway" policing since the DOJ first reprimanded the department testifies to the difficulty of reforming the CPD and other like-minded police organizations, especially because in those departments there is little evidence to suggest that the police themselves want to change their behavior.

One of the most interesting findings from this report is that the police viewed their beats as war zones and operated with the military mindset of an occupying army. In the United States this is not particularly surprising considering that the repressive measures of state-controlled law enforcement since 9/11 have been circulating by way of the fiscal-military and corporate-state-financial nexuses. This kind of privatization and outsourcing of law enforcement services, in turn, generate money and resources for all kinds of escalating (rather than deescalating) purposes, including the militarization and SWATification of police forces in urban and rural areas alike, especially used in waging wars on oppressed barrio and ghetto communities, or for coordinating and managing political dissent such as the organized coast-to-coast suppression of the 2011 Occupy Wall Street encampments. Moreover, even before the very lucrative and widespread outsourcing of military and intelligence functions to a private security industry had come to an end with President Obama's troop withdrawals from Iraq circa 2009–2011, excepting for a few security contracts worth upwards of $1 billion and $1.5 billion, respectively, to SOC, a Day and Zimmermann company, and Triple Canopy, Inc. for protecting U.S. Embassies in Bagdad and elsewhere,[44] some U.S. military contractors such as Xe Services (formerly Blackwater) were already turning their sights to domestic policing, paramilitary training, antiterrorism, private security, and corporate intelligence.

By 2011, dozens of law enforcement agencies had hired private military companies to train officers in military tactics deemed to be an absolute imperative by the U.S. Department of Homeland Security. With respect to militarizing the American police, federal incentives lie within the U.S. Department of Defense that operate the 1033 Program through the Defense Logistics Agency and the Law

Enforcement Support Office (LESO), whose motto has been "from warfighter to crimefighter." According to LESO, since 1990 the program has transferred $4.3 billion worth of property from the military to the police. More than 17,000 federal, state, and local law enforcement agencies have been the recipients of military equipment transferred through the program, which has increased from $1 million in 1990 to nearly $450 million in 2013.[45]

This escalation in weaponry and military force occurs during the same period when violent street crime in the United States has declined significantly, as evidenced by homicide rates that are now half of what they were twenty-five years ago. Meanwhile, the militarization of the police has resulted in U.S. citizens being eight times more likely to be killed by a police officer than by a terrorist. It has also quietly turned the nation into a garrison state, as was revealed recently near St. Louis, Missouri, where peaceful protesters over the police killing of Michael Brown were met by local cops who looked like they were headed for combat in Afghanistan.

Their military-like stance of occupation was immediately followed by the Governor's preemptive state of emergency and calling out of the National Guard in anticipation of violent protests that had not yet been realized at the time of his declaration. Such reactions cannot be separated from the Joint Terrorism Task Forces that were set up around the country post9/11, bringing local cops together with Homeland Security, the FBI, and other federal law enforcement agencies. As a consequence of this reconfiguration of law enforcement, Homeland Security policing has become the new standard in which "national security" is the overriding concern or principle trumping civil liberties and the rule of law. In this new world of securitized law enforcement, the corporate state has relegated an entire population to a collection of potential enemies of the state. Should the inequality and class conflicts between the 1 percent and the 99 percent flare up under the dominant practices of neoliberal capitalism and the ideological belief that there are no viable alternatives to "free-market" globalism, then it is safe to assume that the paramilitarization of law enforcement and the state-routinization of police use and abuse of repressive power will fluctuate upward.

U.S. counter-terrorist torture and the outsourcing of harsh interrogation techniques

I am arguing generally that state-routinized crime is the oil that lubricates the recurring patterns of all of the crimes of the powerful, including those offenses of the state as well as those of corporations and financial institutions, allowing these illegitimate activities to co-exist with their legitimate or state-sanctioned enterprising activities. State-routinized crime, or the normalization of harmful and injurious activities by the powerful, refers to the state and corporate alliances and to the working processes of the political economy that enable the reproduction of the crimes of the powerful to persist over time with only minor incriminations, as though they are, for the most part, excusing perpetrators from their criminal culpability and/or harmful wrongdoings.

In the case of U.S. counter-terrorist torture in Bagram Air Force Base in Afghanistan in addition to Abu Ghraib and Guantanamo Bay and the other CIA "Black Sites" sprinkled around the globe, many of these "enhanced interrogation techniques" programs have been outsourced—not unlike the privatization of many of the military, security, intelligence, and policing services of the early twenty-first century. In the case of Gitmo, there were two former survival school psychologists who had previously worked at Fairchild Air Force Base. They formed their own company and contracted to develop and implement a program of interrogation, which included practices such as waterboarding, rectal feeding, sleep deprivation, and freezing rooms of confinement. Although these two psychologists earned more than $80 million for their services, no actionable intelligence was ever elicited from their clients, according to the U.S. Senate report. However, the value of torture is not really about acquiring intelligence or even about revenge. The true value or

> the object of torture is the fear felt by family, relatives, neighbours, and colleagues, who will be bowed into submission by acts of brutality. Privatizing this power puts the tools of state-sanctioned violence into the calloused hand of the corporate state,

where these contractors were not held to the same standards of conduct, nor were they as constrained by the rule of law when it came to the use of excessive force as employees of the government or military would be, not unlike the privatization of prisons or of law enforcement.[46]

The processes of criminal conventionalization and normalization include a combination of three rational state-routinized pursuits: (1) the decriminalization and deregulation of the powerful's production of harmful behavior as well as the defunding of social control agencies to police these by way of political lobbying, campaign fundraising, legislative activism, and appellate decisions; (2) the non-indictment by prosecutorial agencies and the DOJ of obvious criminal offenses; and (3) the discursive rationalizations by ideologues for and defenders of the prevailing political and economic arrangements as well as those funding counter-research claims, which excuse these transgressions as well as undermine any moralizing about them. These interrelated processes do not happen in a social vacuum or without a lot of background and context.

For example, amidst the rise of the Islamic State, the beheading videos of American and European hostages, and the renewed fears of global terrorism (i.e., in Paris, Brussels, Sacramento, Jakarta, Ouagadougou, Istanbul, Bagdad, Charsadda, Orlando) during the 2015–2016 electoral season, the state routinization of U.S. counter-terrorist torture and the various drone killings have been exempted from all kinds of illegalities, criminal or otherwise. Better yet, the U.S. Congress has legalized the latter, if not the former. As Andrew Bacevich has underscored, the United States has normalized assassination as an instrument of policy: "George W. Bush's administration pioneered the practice of using missile-armed drones as a method of extrajudicial killing. Barack Obama's administration greatly *expanded and routinized* the practice" (emphasis in the original).[47]

What is more, the normalization of torture was also assisted by the big and little screening of torture as a counter-terrorist tactic in both film and television.[48] For eight seasons, Jack Bauer, a fictional character of a Counter Terrorist Unit and the lead protagonist of the television show *24* who worked in conjunction with the FBI, week in and week out saves civilization by torturing someone until they "spill the beans." According to these popular cultural scenarios, torture always works. *24* is one of the most viewed TV series of the past decade, so it is no wonder that a CBS poll released in late December of 2014, a few weeks after the release of the Senate's torture report, found that "though 69 percent of those asked consider waterboarding to be torture, 49 percent think that brutal interrogation methods are sometimes justified," and "57 percent believe that the tactics are at least sometimes effective in producing valuable intelligence to help stop terrorist attacks."[49]

Media representations of state terror and political domination have not only distorted the public's view of the efficacy of torture, but it also seems to be the case that the President, Congress, and even the Senate Intelligence Committee also drank the same medicated "Kool-Aid." These politicos are all on board with the CIA's new paramilitary (if legally questionable) mission of drone warfare, if not necessarily behind their older mission of detaining and torturing. Apparently, assassinations by drone are less messy than torture by forced rectal feeding. And, despite the "collateral damage" or killing of innocent civilians, the killings of alleged terrorists appear to be more inefficient than torture, especially when it means fewer boots on the ground and not funding still more regimes. Not only is the CIA moving further away from its original mission of intelligence and analysis, but the agency has also been empowered in other ways, such as allowing the Director of the CIA—and not the White House, as was the case initially—to make the final decisions about drone strikes in places like Pakistan and Yemen.

One of the most prominent examples of the non-criminal working nexus of the state failing to appropriately deal with crimes of the state committed by a former administration was when President Obama, the Congress, and the Department of Justice in a shared mind of accommodation and denial, decided not to pursue criminal charges against officials of the George W. Bush administration for authorizing the torture and other misconduct that were integral parts of their "secret" war on terrorism. While Mr. Obama signed executive orders in January 2009 to cancel the use of "enhanced interrogation techniques" or torture in the methods used to treat terror suspects and to place these suspects under the protection of the Geneva Conventions, and while he also instructed his attorney general to immediately review the evidence for any criminality, his position as President was always to ignore these patriotic ventures in torture so the United States could "look forward, as opposed to looking backward."

The Obama Administration was also unwilling to entertain the idea of a special prosecutor or of an independent investigation into the torture. Similarly, the

President had always rejected the idea of a creating a Truth Commission as one viable alternative to criminal prosecution. In particular, the DOJ investigation into the use of CIA torture tactics that had begun in January 2009 ended in August 2012 when the Attorney General announced, not surprisingly, that no charges would be brought against anyone for the torture that occurred in Gitmo. Evidently, the DOJ investigation could not find contrary to the public record any evidence that there were "high officials who knowingly, consciously broke existing laws, engaged in cover-ups of those crimes with knowledge forefront," the criteria spelled out by Obama during his successful campaign for the democratic presidential nomination over Hillary Clinton in 2008, which he stated should be worthy of criminally pursuing.

Even after the Senate Intelligence Committee finally released its long-awaited 500-page redacted but damning summary of the full 6,700-page "torture review" on December 9, 2014, and after renewed calls by the United Nations, human rights activists, and legal experts for the Obama Administration to prosecute those officials responsible for running the CIA's outsourced torture program, there will still be no prosecutions. It now appears that the U.S government will never, to the best of its capability, render forth those who arranged, encouraged, and conducted torture beginning in 2002 and lasting for at least four more years. In response to the renewed calls for prosecution, the Department of Justice was quick to disclose that it had no intentions of reopening its investigation into the CIA's methods because of any of the new revelations from the torture report. What is particularly interesting is the conspicuous absence of the word *torture* from a report that talks at length about waterboarding and other harsh procedures that satisfy the international standards for torture or torturous behavior. Aside from the usage of the word in the foreword to the summary written by California's Senator Dianne Feinstein, chairwoman of the Senate Intelligence Committee, the word torture does not otherwise appear.

Moreover, although the report reached some twenty conclusive findings, it does not specifically answer the question of whether or not the United States actually engaged in torture. It is also silent about whether or not those responsible for this treatment of imprisoned suspects should be prosecuted, despite the report's graphic depictions of state-carried-out barbarism. In part, this had to do with the rationale of the Select Committee's *Study of the Central Intelligence Agency's Detention and Interrogation Program*, which was conducted primarily for the purpose of the U.S. "coming clean" about those atrocious behaviors that are allegedly an affront to American values so that they would not happen again. As Feinstein stated at the time of the report's release: "It shows that the CIA's actions a decade ago are a stain on our values and on our history." She went on to say, the release of the summary "cannot remove that stain," however, the "releasing of this report is an important step to restore our values and show the world that we are in fact a just and lawful society."[50] I am not so sure that the world has been reassured or that most people are too concerned about the torturing of terrorists or alleged terrorists. But for those who are concerned, accountability for these actions by way of either criminal prosecutions or executive pardons for those who had been found guilty of authorizing the torture would have sent a much more meaningful and tangible message that the United States actually ascribes to its own domestic, if not international, rules of law.

Under the rule of law, the state apparatus should have focused its attention and held accountable those who had abetted or committed these torturous crimes. Under the UN convention against torture, there are no exceptional circumstances that can be used to justify torture of any kind. Those responsible for authorizing and/or carrying out torture or other ill treatment should still be fully investigated, if not prosecuted for these crimes. Accordingly, the European Court of Human Rights ordered Poland and Macedonia to pay damages to detainees for their complicity in the C.I.A.'s secret torture program. The U.S., however, like other superpowers, continue to buck the prevailing trends in international law and justice. While in August of 2014 President Obama finally publicly acknowledged "we tortured some folks," he had always resisted the consequences of that admission. For example, his administration even pressed federal judges to close the door on civil suits by former detainees, citing state secrets as a justification.[51] As a consequence, following the report's release and even before that, Mr. Obama was finding himself caught between the CIA and its director, John O. Brenna, who he had appointed and who many Democratic allies had accused the White House of assisting in covering up a legacy of torture by the Bush II Administration. As some legal commenters argue, President Obama did not want to set a precedent where in the future his own legacy could be in criminal jeopardy for illegally assassinating people by drone strikes.

Technically, U.S. officials and private contractors implicated by the Senate report on torture could face arrest and prosecution in other countries should they travel there. Similarly, the International Criminal Court could also investigate and prosecute these crimes. While the likelihood of the ICC pursuing this matter is probably low, the odds of an individual state are somewhat better. In sum, the U.S. state-routinization of these crimes of torture looks, sounds, and smells strikingly familiar to the modus operandi of accommodation and denial used by the Obama administration to clear the banksters of Wall Street for their epidemic of criminal violations and fraudulent wrongdoings that precipitated the financial meltdown of 2008 and the Great Recession that followed.

Wall Street and the routinization of securities fraud

More than eight years after the financial collapse, a stagnant global economic climate still persists throughout much of the world. During this period, the state of well-being of the relatively powerless middle and working classes has for the most part continued to deteriorate. Meanwhile, the super rich and the very powerful are getting even richer and increasingly more powerful. The top 100 billionaires from China, Russia, India, Mexico, Indonesia, North America, and Europe had added $240 billion to their combined coffers by 2012, enough money, Oxfam calculates, to end world poverty overnight. In 2015, the 85 richest people on the planet had the same wealth as the poorest 50 percent, or 3.5 billion people. Both Oxfam and banking giant Credit Suisse had calculated in 2015 that the richest 1 percent by the end of 2016 would own more than half of the world's wealth.[52]

Unfortunately, current economic policies are more likely to exacerbate inequality and concentrations of wealth rather than ameliorate them. Unless the power relations behind the neoliberal policies in place change or speak to these contradictory problems of capital accumulation, reproduction, and consumption, then the prospects of adjusting or abating the state-routinized financial crimes of the powerful will remain highly unlikely. As is now common knowledge, not one of the top Wall Street bankers who were collectively responsible for the biggest financial crime spree in United States history has ever been charged or prosecuted, or convicted of violating any criminal laws against securities fraud. On the other side of the enforcement ledger, more than a few of those financial crimes of the past were legalized through decriminalization and deregulation, such as the repeal of the 1933 Glass-Steagall Act in 1999, while other forms, such as credit default swaps, have not been outlawed as obvious conflicts of interests. Historically, these enforcement contradictions circulate around the marketing of licit and illicit securities trades. In other words, the prosecution dilemmas surrounding fraudulent securities trades cannot be detached from law enforcement's codependency on both capital accumulation and developing capitalist states. Thus, to criminalize or not to criminalize has security fraud hanging in the balance of the contradictory forces of "free-market" capitalism.

For example, when dominant interests and behaviors of the political economy are both highly profitable and illegal, as numerous financial transactions were in the rambling days and months that led up to the Wall Street meltdown, then the capitalist state finds itself in the awkward position of trying to both chastise and excuse these criminal violations. After the recent financial breakdown, these excuses were expressed in the issues of intent and probable cause and the very indictable evidence collected by the U.S. Senate investigative report, *Wall Street and the Financial Crisis: Anatomy of a Financial Collapse*, published in April 2011. Like the Senate's investigative report on CIA torture, the Wall Street report also failed to call a "spade a spade" except when referring to government regulatory failures as one of four causes behind the financial meltdown. The other causes were identified not as investment banking frauds but as investment banking abuses, not as high-risk mortgage frauds but as high-risk mortgage loans, and not as fraudulent credit ratings but as inflated credit ratings. At the end of the day, both the "doublespeak" of the Senate Investigative reports, one on torture and the other on securities fraud, became exercises in whitewashing the crimes of capitalist control. In the case of Wall Street, these contradictions of the accumulation of mass amounts of capital through an epidemic of high-risk securities frauds were reconciled or routinized through the selective enforcement of civil and regulatory laws rather than criminal law.[53]

The nonprosecution of securities fraud is precisely what the economic elites of Wall Street and the political appointees from both the Bush II and Obama administrations wanted all along. This also accounts for what the majorities in the

U.S. House of Representatives and the U.S. Senate wanted as well. The outcome of zero criminal prosecutions was neither by accident nor conspiracy but by a consensus of the powerful. Even before the economic implosion, a concerted effort not to prosecute financial fraudsters had begun in 2003, a reaction allegedly due to the overzealous criminal prosecutions of several high profile corporations and their senior officers at the beginning of the new millennium. In 2005–2006, the corporate backlash or movement to roll-back "white-collar" criminalization picked up momentum when the U.S. Supreme Court overturned the criminal fraud convictions of Arthur Anderson for helping to cook the accounting records of Enron, making future criminal prosecutions of control frauds less likely. Even with the passage of the quasi-ambitious Dodd-Frank law in 2010, except for the further concentration of wealth by a handful of big Wall Street banks, not much has changed with respect to derivatives and the shadow banking industry since the Wall Street collapse in 2008. Thus, the only real alternatives in the future to bailing out these TBTF financial institutions is to either break them up, turn them into public utilities, and/or nationalize them.[54]

More generally, in attempting to fix or address the contemporary crises of global capital the world finds itself caught between neoliberal, supply-side, and monetarist remedies as in Europe and the United States that emphasize austerity and privatization, on the one hand, or a centralized, demand-side and debt-financed expansion, on the other hand, as in China and India that ignore the Keynesian emphasis on the redistribution of money to ordinary people. Paradoxically, the economic and political outcomes are the same—widening and escalating social inequalities. In both cases the capitalist world is increasingly turning to central banks, led by the Federal Reserve of the United States, in order to manage the recurring financial global crises. These "solutions" to resolve the problem of capital accumulation and underconsumption depend on the contradictory relations of the dictatorship of the central bankers whose primary concerns are about protecting the global banking system, the plutocrats who manage worldwide a couple dozen banks, and the various subsystems of market capitalism that have very little regard for the well being of the masses except by way of the mystical economies of "trickle down" that never come.

In short, unless the contradictions of capital accumulation and of the bourgeois legal relations of the capitalist state are structurally altered, then it is very hard to imagine how any kind of tinkering or adjustment of the economic status quo will repair the crisis in reproductive expansionism and in the negative trends of capital unsustainability. Addressing these concerns requires a fundamental shift or modification of the prevailing political and economic arrangements locally and globally. Likewise, unless the driving forces of capital reproduction underpinning the crimes of the powerful and the victimization of the powerless are addressed, then no reduction in the volume of these crimes is likely to occur in the near or distant future.

What is needed, as an alternative to the current economic malaises of neoliberalism and to the slowdown in global capital expansionism, is a worldwide social movement on behalf of a system of international Keynesianism, of eco-welfarism, and of a Marshall-like strategic plan for sustainable growth. Consistent with this alternate vision is a realpolitik recognition that resisting the crimes of the powerful has little in common with trying to make the existing regulatory or penal arrangements of capitalist social control work better through reformist type changes of more business as usual. Rather, what are called for are fundamental changes of the political economy through social, cultural, and global activism. Without eliminating the basic conditions and structures that nurture these crimes of the powerful, new and improved social controls of "free" markets will not change the enduring relations of capitalist exploitation and reproduction as these controls will always find that they are no real challenge to state-routinized capitalist criminality.

A recapitulation of state-routinized crime and crime control

In the contemporary world of crony capitalism, legalized corruption, and structured unaccountability nothing succeeds with such regularity as the active failures of the government to obstruct the crimes of the powerful, especially those committed by the corporate state and its agents or by multinational corporations. This is true whether one is discussing the contradictions of the failures to prevent or punish the unjustifiable killings of citizens by police, the state authorized torture by the U.S. Secretary of Defense, or the criminal frauds of Wall Street financial institutions. The recurrent failures to deter those types of crimes domestically and internationally tend to routinize and reinforce the likelihood of their reproduction, especially when they prove to be economically profitable and/or valuable in some other political way. To review, state-routinized crime and crime control refers to three interrelated processes that help to neutralize, normalize and/or conventionalize the otherwise illegally harmful actions or inactions of the powerful:

1. The decriminalization and deregulation of the powerful's production of harmful behavior, as well as the defunding of social agencies to police these.
2. The non-indictment of obvious criminal offenses by prosecutorial agencies and the U.S. Department of Justice.
3. The discursive rationalizations by ideologues for and defenders of the prevailing political and economic arrangements as well as the funding of research to claims stating otherwise.

By incorporating these interrelated legal, political, and economic processes into its analysis, *Unchecked Corporate Power* investigates why people with excessive corporate power are routinely able to perform widespread social devastation and extensive victimization. This book also examines how state-legalized authorities and political institutions traditionally designed for and charged with the duty of protecting its citizens from the law-breaking and injurious activities of those with too much power have become enablers and, in many cases, colluders with the very industries they are charged with policing, rather than preventers of such mass criminality. This is especially true of multinational corporate violations of trusted securities, of health and safety, and of the community, both at home and abroad.[55] These are also the in-depth subject areas respectively of Chapters 3 through 5 in Part II of this book, "Violating the commons."

Notes

1 Pearce, Frank. 1976. *Crimes of the Powerful: Marxism, Crime and Deviance*. London: Pluto Press, p. 61.
2 Kennedy, Mark. 1970. "Beyond Incrimination: Some Neglected Facts of the Theory of Punishment." *Catalyst* 5 (Summer): 1–30.
3 Tinbergen, Jan. 1961. "Do Communist and Free Economies Show a Converging Pattern?" *Soviet Studies* 4 (April): 333–341; Galbraith, John K. 1967. *The New Industrial State*. Princeton, NJ: Princeton University Press.
4 Kendall, Wesley. 2016. *From Gulag to Guantanamo: Political, Social and Economic Evolutions of Mass Incarceration*. New York: Rowman & Littlefield, p. 156. See also, Johnston, Michael. 2005. *Syndromes of Corruption: Wealth, Power, and Democracy*. Cambridge, UK: Cambridge University Press.
5 Feffer, John. 2015. "Why the World is Becoming the Un-Sweden." *Tomdispatch*. May 26. www.johnfeffer.com/why-the-world-is-becoming-the-un-sweden/.
6 Saul, John Ralston. 1997. *The Unconscious Civilization*. New York: Free Press.
7 Wolin, Sheldon. 2008. *Democracy Incorporated: Managed Democracy and the Specter of Inverted Totalitarianism*. Princeton, NJ: Princeton University Press.
8 Kendall, 2016, p. 156.
9 Ibid., pp. 153–157.
10 Felson, Marcus. 1987. "Routine Activities, Social Controls, Rational Decisions, and Criminal Outcomes." *Criminology* 25 (4): 911–931.
11 Cornish, Derek and Clarke, Ronald (eds). 1986. *The Reasoning Criminal: Rational Choice Perspectives on Offending*. New Brunswick, NJ: Transaction Publishers.
12 Cohen, Lawrence and Machalek, Richard. 1988. "A General Theory of Expropriate Crime: An Evolutionary Ecological Approach." *American Journal of Sociology* 94: 465–501.
13 Block, Alan and Chambliss, William. 1981. *Organizing Crime*. New York: Elsevier, p. 12.
14 Khanna, Bhavya. 2014. "Arundhati Roy and Fallacies" at http://blog.mylaw.net/a rundhati-roy- and-fallacies/.
15 Roberts, Sam. 2016. "Bribery and Corruption, or 'Honest Graft'?" *The New York Times*. June 19: Sunday Review, p. 5.
16 Ibid.
17 Quoted in ibid.
18 Johnston, Michael. 2005. *Syndromes of Corruption: Wealth, Power, and Democracy*. Cambridge, UK: Cambridge University Press, p. 42.
19 Ibid.
20 Wedel, Janine. 2014. *Unaccountable: How Elite Power Brokers Corrupt our Finances, Freedom, and Security*. New York: Pegasus Books.
21 Block and Chambliss, 1981, p. 2.
22 Wolfe, Alan. 1973. *The Seamy Side of Democracy: Repression in America*. New York: McKay Company.
23 Quinney, Richard. 1977. *Class, State, and Crime: On the Theory and Practice of Criminal Justice*. New York: David McKay.
24 Kraska, Peter. 2007. "The Blurring of War and Law Enforcement." In *Violence, Conflict, and World Order: Critical Conversations on State-Sanctioned Justice*, edited by G. Barak. Lanham, MD: Rowman & Littlefield, pp. 161–187.
25 Edwards, Charles. 2014. "Partnership and Accountability Are the Key to Tackling Financial Crime." December 16. https://rusi.org/commentary/partnership-and-accounta bility-are-key-tackling-financial-crime.

26 Fukuyama, Francis. 2014. *Political Order and Political Decay: From the Industrial Revolution to the Globalization of Democracy.* New York: Farrar, Straus & Giroux.

27 Cantor, Nathaniel. 1932. *Crime: Criminals and Criminal Justice.* New York: Henry Holt, p. 145.

28 Putnam, Robert. 1995. "Bowling Alone: America's Declining Social Capital." *Journal of Democracy* 6 (1): 65–78.

29 Kendall, 2016, p. 160.

30 Barak, Gregg, Leighton, Paul, and Cotton, Allison. 2015. *Class, Race, Gender, and Crime: The Social Realities of Justice in America,* 4th edition. Lanham, MD: Rowman & Littlefield.

31 Kendall, 2016, p. 162.

32 McLaughlin, Shella. 2014. "What Happens When Officers Use Deadly Force?" *USA Today.* February 21. www.usatoday.com/story/news/nation/2014/02/21/police-dea dly-force-accountability/5697611/.

33 Fishman, Mark. 1981. "Police News: Constructing an Image of Crime." *Urban Life* 9 (4): 371–394; Ericson, Richard. 1989. "Patrolling the Facts: Secrecy and Publicity in Police Work." *British Journal of Sociology* 40 (2): 205–229; Kasinsky, Rene Goldman. 1994. "Patrolling the Facts: Media, Cops, and Crime." In *Media, Process, and the Social Construction of Crime: Studies in Newsmaking Criminology,* edited by G. Barak. New York: Garland, pp. 203–236.

34 Peelo, Moira. 2006. "Framing Homicide Narratives in Newspapers: Mediated Witness and the Construction of Virtual Victimhood." *Crime Media Culture* 29 (2): 159–175.

35 Hirschfield, Paul. J. and Simon, Daniella. 2010. "Legitimating Police Violence: Newspaper Narratives of Deadly Force." *Theoretical Criminology* 14 (2): 155–182.

36 Lawrence, Regina. G. 2000. *The Politics of Force: Media and the Construction of Police Brutality.* Berkeley, CA: University of California Press; Duran, Robert. 2013. *Gang Life in Two Cities: An Insider's Journey.* New York: Columbia University Press.

37 "The President's Task Force on Twenty-First-Century Policing." 2015. *Final Report.* Washington, DC: U.S. Department of Justice. The final report (see Action Item, 2.2.4) has called for the development of a comprehensive, national officer-involved shooting database.

38 Cited by Hal Pepinsky, Emeritus Professor of Criminal Justice, Indiana University, in his December 27, 2014 blog: "How Dangerous is Policing?" http://pepinsky.blogspot.com/2014/12/how-dangerous-is-policing.html.

39 Ibid.

40 Klinger, David, Rosenfeld, Richard, Isom, Daniel, and Deckard, Michael. 2016. "Race, Crime, and the Micro-Ecology of Deadly Force." *Criminology and Public Policy* 15 (1): 193.

41 Sekhon, Nirel. 2016. "Blue on Black: An Empirical Assessment of Police Shootings." Georgia State University College of Law, Legal Studies Research Paper. January 26. http://papers.ssrn.com/sol3/papers.cfm?abstract_id=2700724.

42 Oppel, Richard. 2014. "Cleveland Police Cited for Abuse by Justice Department." *The New York Times.* December 4. www.nytimes.com/2014/12/05/us/justice-dept-inquir y-finds-abuses-by-cleveland-police.html.

43 Smith, Brad and Holmes, Malcolm. 2014. "Police Use of Excessive Force in Minority Communities: A Test of the Minority Threat, Place, and Community Accountability Hypotheses." *Social Problems* 61 (1): 83–104.

44 Kendall, 2016.

45 ACLU. 2014. *War Comes Home: The Excessive Militarization of American Policing.* June. www.aclu.org/sites/default/files/assets/jus14-warcomeshome-report-web-rel1.pdf.

46 Kendall, 2016, pp. 171–172.

47 Bacevich, Andrew. 2016. "Six National Security Questions Hillary, Donald, Ted, Marco, etc., Don't Want to Answer and Won't Even Be Asked." *Naked Capitalism.* January 27. www.nakedcapitalism.com/2016/01/andrew-bacevich-six-national-security-questions-hillary-donald-ted-marco-etc-dont-want-to-answer-and-wont-even-be-asked.html?utm_source=feedburner&utm_medium=email&utm_campaign=Feed%3A+Naked Capitalism+%28naked+capitalism%29.

48 Flynn, Michael and Salek, Fabiola (eds.). 2012. *Screening Torture: Media Representations of State Terror and Political Domination.* New York: Colombia University Press.
49 Dutton, Sarah, De Pinto, Jennifer, Salvanto, Anthony, and Backus, Fred. 2015. "Most Americans Consider Waterboarding to Be Torture." *CBS News.* December 15. www.cbsnews.com/news/torture-and-reaction-to-the-senate-intelligence-report/.
50 670KBOI News/Talk Radio: Political News. 2014. Quoted in "Senate Report Reveals CIA's 'Brutal' Interrogation Tactics." December 10. www.670kboi.com/common/more.php?m=58&ts=1418159102&article=538D44F17FC111E4B51EFEFDA DE6840A&mode=2.
51 Hafetz, Jonathan. 2014 "Don't Execute Those We Tortured." *The New York Times.* September 24. www.nytimes.com/2014/09/25/opinion/dont-execute-those-we-tortured. html.
52 "Richest 1% to own more than rest of world, Oxfam says," *BBC News.* 2015. January 19.
53 Barak, Gregg. 2015a. "Limiting Financial Capital and Regulatory Control as Non-Penal Alternatives to Wall Street Looting and High-Risk Securities." In *The Routledge International Handbook of the Crimes of the Powerful,* edited by G. Barak. New York: Routledge, pp. 525–536.
54 Barak, Gregg. 2012. *Theft of a Nation: Wall Street Looting and Federal Regulatory Colluding.* Lanham, MD: Roman & Littlefield.
55 Barak, Gregg (ed.). 2015b. *The Routledge International Handbook of the Crimes of the Powerful.* New York: Routledge; Rothe, Dawn and Friedrichs, David. 2014. *The Crimes of Globalization.* New York: Routledge; Friman, E. Richard (ed.). 2009. *Crime and the Global Political Economy.* Boulder, CO: Lynne Rienner.

PART II
Violating the commons

3

FINANCIAL CRIMES

Violations of trusted securities

The London Interbank Offered Rate (Libor) scandal was a series of fraudulent rate submissions by those banks who submit interest rates for calculating an average interest rate used as a measure of the cost of borrowing between banks as well as a benchmark for setting interest rates worldwide. Until the Libor was taken over in January 2014 by the NYSE Euronext, a Euro-American multinational financial services corporation that operates multiple securities exchanges, the process of supervising its daily Libor rate—a collection of rates generated for ten currencies across fifteen different time periods, ranging from one day to one year—it had been overseen by the British Bankers' Association. The Libor calculating process works as follows:

> Between 7 and 18 large banks are asked what interest rate they would have to pay to borrow money for a certain period of time and in a certain currency. The responses are collected by Thomson Reuters, which removes a certain percentage of the highest and lowest figures before calculating the averages and creating the Libor quotes.[1]

There are similar kinds of interbank rates measured elsewhere in the world, such as the Japanese Tokyo Interbank Offered Rate (Tibor) or the Belgium-based Euro Interbank Offered Rate (Euribor).

Concerning the Libor violations—criminal or civil—before, during, and after the Wall Street financial meltdown, these fraudulent rate submissions exceed by orders of magnitude any financial scam in the history of markets. As one of the civil complaints read, "by surreptitiously bilking investors of their rightful rates of return … Defendants reaped hundreds of millions, if not billions, of dollars in ill-gotten gains."[2] In the United States alone, early estimated costs to the states, counties, and local governments came to at least $6 billion in fraudulent interest payments, not counting $4 billion that governments spent to unwind their positions exposed to rate manipulation.[3] In public responses, there were calls for resignations, criminal prosecutions, and stricter regulations of the financial sector. In addition, numerous civil lawsuits were filed by a diversity of plaintiffs, ranging from mutual funds to the city of Baltimore, Maryland, claiming that they had "lost profits on Libor-based securities due to banks' artificial suppression of the rate."[4] Defendants in these legal cases included the Bank of America, JP Morgan, Credit Suisse, HSBC, and Citigroup.

It should be pointed out that before the outrage emerged, in the global world of finance the Libor was considered the "gold standard" for benchmarking interest rates. When the Libor went up, monthly interest payment rates were inclined to go up. When the Libor went down, some borrowers enjoyed lowered interest rates. However, pensioners in general, as well as those who had invested in mutual funds, would lose money or earned less in interest. Like "insider trading" in the stock market, having advance knowledge or information of Libor rates can not only affect the value of a security or a commodity, but its manipulation can also be used to make lucrative profits off of trades. For example, court documents have revealed that at the Royal Bank of Scotland (RBS) it was routine practice among senior traders to make requests to the bank's rate setters as to the appropriate Libor rate. Messages from one Barclays Capital (BCS) trader further revealed that for each basis point (0.01 percent) the Libor was moved, those involved could net a couple of million dollars.[5] On occasions, some hedge funds were also known to request rate information.[6]

In 2012, there was roughly $10 trillion in loans—including credit cards, car loans, student loans, and adjustable-rate mortgages—as well as some $350 trillion in derivatives that were all tied to the Libor.[7] In July of that year, the UK-based investment bank BCS paid $453 million in a settlement with U.S. and UK regulators, admitting that their traders had submitted fraudulent bank rates for their costs of borrowing between 2005 and 2008. These traders had "repeatedly requested that their colleagues in charge of the Libor process tailor the bank's submissions to benefit the firm's trading positions. Barclays staffers also colluded with counterparts from other banks to manipulate rates."[8] Additionally, during the height of the global financial crisis, between late 2007 and early 2009, BCS made artificially low Libor submissions because the bank was afraid that if its submissions were too high, then it would get punished in the markets, as their investors would question the bank's health. As former U.S. Assistant Attorney General Lanny Breuer was quoted as saying regarding a settlement with UBS Financial Services the real reason that Barclays had rigged the Libor rate was "to maximize profits and to hide its weakness during the crisis."[9]

On December 11, 2012, it was announced by the U.S. Department of Justice (DOJ) that HSBC Holdings, a British multinational banking and financial services company headquartered in London—ranking as the fourth largest bank in the world with total assets of $2.67 trillion—had agreed to forfeit $1.25 billion and to pay $665 million in civil penalties for violating the Bank Secrecy Act, the International

Emergency Economic Powers Act, and the Trading with the Enemy Act. The settlement had also agreed not to criminally prosecute HSBC for alleged terrorist financing. One week later, in a global investigation of more than a dozen banks and brokers, UBS, Switzerland's biggest bank, settled with U.S., UK and Swiss regulators for a sum of $1.5 billion for manipulating interest rates and for criminal charges against two former traders.

In fact, regulators found that the Zurich-based bank made "more than 2,000 requests to its own rate submitters, traders at other banks and brokers to manipulate rate submissions through 2010."[10] According to the Financial Services Authority, there were at least 45 bank employees, including some managers, who knew of the persuasive practice and another 70 people who were included in open chats and messages "where attempts to manipulate Libor and Euribor" were discussed.[11] In 2011, Japanese regulators had also temporarily suspended some of UBS and Citigroup's transactions "after finding that both banks had attempted to influence Libor rates and the related Tokyo Interbank Offered Rate."[12]

Besides these multinational banks there were other global banks involved in this kind of collusion and submission of fraudulent Libor rates. Back in March of 2011 the *Wall Street Journal* reported that U.S. regulators were investigating Bank of America Corp. and Citigroup Inc. for manipulating the Libor. Eleven months later, in February 2012, the U.S. Department of Justice announced that it was launching a criminal investigation into widespread Libor abuse. In July of 2012, the UK Serious Fraud Office announced that it too was opening a criminal investigation into Libor. Not only was the UK looking into BCS' fraudulent submission rates but also those of twenty other major banks.

During the same month and year, the Canadian Competition Bureau (CCB) announced that it was carrying out an investigation into the Canadian branches of the RBS as well as HSBC, Deutsche Bank, JP Morgan Bank, and Citibank for "price fixing" around the yen-denominated Libor rate. A federal prosecutor for the CCB stated that "IRD (interest-rate derivatives) traders at the participant banks communicated with each other their desire to see a higher or lower yen LIBOR to aid their trading positions."[13] And, in court documents filed in Singapore, Tan Chi Min, a trader for RBS, told his colleagues that his bank could move global interest rates and that the Libor fixing process had become an interest rate cartel. In his court affidavit, Min claimed that senior traders at RBS were not only aware of the rate manipulation, but that they also supported such actions.

By the end of 2015, more than a half-dozen banks had paid out more than $10 billion to settle charges with regulators for fraudulent rate submissions. However, in the face of all the accusations against dozens of multinational or global banking giants and in the midst of a rate-rigging epidemic in the financial services industry, there were very few traders who were actually indicted and subsequently criminally prosecuted for securities frauds. And there were no CEOs or chairmen of the boards who faced any type of criminal charges, although a number of them bowing to political pressure found it necessary to resign their leadership positions.

Decriminalization, fraudulent libor rates, and victimization

In response to hammering by various politicians in the UK, including the former Prime Minister David Cameron, both the banking chairman Marcus Agius and CEO Bob Diamond of Barclays, for example, resigned over the Libor allegations. When one turns to the number of U.S. criminal prosecutions for globally manipulating Libor rates, there have been eleven individual traders within a handful of banks, such as Rabobank's Anthony Allen (a global head of liquidity and finance) and Anthony Conti (a senior money markets trader who made daily Libor submissions). On November 5, 2015, these two British citizens were the first to be tried and convicted of currency fraud in the District Court of Lower Manhattan, New York. They both appealed their convictions. Previously, in the summer of 2015, Tom Hayes, formerly of UBS and Citigroup, was the very first trader to be convicted in London for conspiring with others to manipulate the Libor.[14] On December 22, 2015 a British appeals court reduced Hayes' sentence from fourteen years in prison to eleven.

Interestingly, in terms of the usual mantra of how difficult it is to prosecute complex financial corporate crimes, one of the prosecutors claimed that trying the two former Rabobank traders had been challenging because of the "arcane technicalities" of how Libor is calculated. On the other hand, one of the other prosecutors in the case had stated that the defendants "left a paper trail a mile long." Similarly, one of the jurors stated, "it was pretty obvious to us something was going on that was interfering with the way the Libor rate was supposed to be" calculated. Another juror agreed, especially because of the emails and text messages presented during the trial as well as the testimony from three former Rabobank traders who had earlier pleaded guilty to participating in the scheme.[15] Significantly, the jurors who spent a little over one day deliberating found the two defendants guilty of all twenty-eight counts; Anthony Allen for nineteen counts of fraud as well as conspiracy and Anthony Conti for nine counts of fraud. Although each of these counts is punishable for up to thirty years in prison, Judge Jed Rakoff in New York sentenced Allen to two years and Conti to one year. Allen, 44, and Conti, 46, both denied any wrongdoing and will remain free on bail pending their appeals.[16]

Despite the lack of difficulty in convicting these multinational financial criminals for their habitual violations of the Libor, pretty much like the history of high finance crimes in general,[17] these have for all intents and purposes been routinized away or decriminalized. Like the state's responses to the epidemic of securities frauds in the financial services industry that led up to and caused the Wall Street meltdown, social control of these criminalities has primarily been subject to conciliatory settlements with the feds or compensatory civil relief for select groups of investors, and rarely have the benefactors of these defrauding schemes been subject to any kind of penal sanction. In terms of victimization and compensation, plaintiff investors and municipalities initially filed a series of class actions in New York. Eventually these lawsuits were joined by homeowners claiming that they too had been victimized by the Libor manipulations, which had, in effect, made their mortgage repayments more expensive than they would have been, and in many instances resulted in foreclosures and repossessions of people's homes.

In the class action suit filed in New York, Annie Bell Adams and her four co-lead plaintiffs explained how their subprime mortgages were securitized in Libor-based collateralized debt obligations and sold by bankers to investors. The class action alleged that traders at twelve of the biggest banks in Europe and North America were "incentivized to manipulate the London interbank offered rate to a higher rate on certain dates when adjustable mortgage interest rates were reset."[18] According to the complaint, the result was that subprime home-owners between 2000 and 2009 ended up paying more. Alabama-based attorney, John Sharbrough, at the time of the filing stated that the number of plaintiffs could be as high as 100,000 and that each of them may have lost thousands of dollars. These plaintiffs held what had been called Libor Plus adjustable-rate mortgages. Moreover, there were at least 900,000 outstanding U.S. home loans indexed to Libor that originated from 2005 to 2009, "with an unpaid principal balance of $275 billion, according to the Office of the Comptroller of the Currency."[19]

Estimates of how much banks were going to end up paying in Libor lawsuits once ranged from a low of $7.8 billion to a high of $176 billion. However, in the spring of 2013, a federal judge dismissed most but not all of the Libor lawsuits against sixteen banks, including JP Morgan Chase and Bank of America, in part, because the plaintiffs "couldn't jump through all of the necessary hoops to show how they had been harmed by violations of U.S. antitrust laws."[20] While Judge Buchwald found that plaintiffs lacked standing to sue the banks either under antitrust laws or the Racketeer Influenced and Corrupt Organizations statues, she let some claims proceed under different laws. For example, she made it possible for big institutional bond investors, including pension funds and money managers like Charles Schwab, to proceed. Similarly, lawsuits by derivative traders were allowed to go forward, which simply resulted in many of the defendant banking institutions settling their cases financially for fractions of what they made from their ill-gotten gains.

As the Managing Editor for Business and Technology at *The Huffington Post*, Mark Gongloff, wrote at the time:

> Regulators, who have more leverage over banks than civil plaintiffs, will keep extracting cash in settlements as the months go forward. But if Libor victims can't make the banks pay more in court, then this whole Libor scandal may well end up being more like the Grenada invasion than World War III.[21]

It turned out that assessment was premature. In May 2016 the Court of Appeals reinstated the private antitrust lawsuits filed against the 16 banks for allegedly rigging Libor interest rates.[22]

The contradictory forces of free-market capitalism and securities law failures to curb Wall Street frauds before and after the financial implosion

State-legal criminalization of security fraud always hangs in the balance of the contradictory forces of free-market capitalism. For example, when similarly dominant interests and behaviors of the political economy are both illegal and highly profitable as numerous financial transactions were in the run up to the Wall Street meltdown, then the capitalist state finds itself in the contradictory positions of trying both to chastise and to excuse these criminal violations. Before and after the recent financial implosion, these contradictions have been reconciled through the selective enforcement of civil and regulatory law rather than criminal law where, for example, in a pre-adjudicated civil case JP Morgan Chase was fined $13 billion to settle state and federal claims of securities fraud. Similarly, five other major U.S. banks agreed to pay some $25 billion to settle alleged claims surrounding their fraudulent and illegal mortgage practices rather than face criminal or civil litigation.

Just as importantly to the history and denial as well as the state routinization of those securities violations perpetrated in all areas of the financial services industry— from investment banking to high-risk mortgage lending to inflated credit ratings to regulatory "failures"—is the cultural narrative of a housing bubble in which only a small group of insightful yet weird short-sellers, the iconoclasts of Wall Street, could see the burst coming. This attractive narrative articulated in Michael Lewis' best selling book *The Big Short: Inside the Doomsday Machine* (2010), and subsequently captured and made into a wonderful, if not, historically accurate depiction of "what people knew, and when did they know it," in the 2015 critically acclaimed film, *The Big Short*, directed by Adam McKay. In the motion picture, a group of hedge fund managers, "through various creative research methods—from reading insanely boring prospectuses that revealed toxic mortgage content of what were seemingly safe bonds to going to Florida and talking to strippers—discovered that housing was primed to crash."[23] Nice story, only Lewis' narrative is problematic for it does not go far enough and never does it explain or describe the actual crimes of Wall Street or what the actual looting was all about.

First of all, contrary to the narrative, a whole lot of ordinary people before the crash, like the Florida strippers who were grinding away at work, were also busy buying and flipping houses in the hot Miami markets. These and other individuals saw the housing bubble and coming real estate crisis years before the market exploded. For example, there were numerous Nevadan consumers who had been complaining about predatory lending since 1999. By 2001, the rate of complaints to the non-profit Nevada Fair Housing Center was 400 per month.

Second, the narrative wrongly explains what was driving the housing bubble because it fails to identify the frauds committed by the biggest banks and hedge fund managers. In brief, the bubble did not occur because a lot of Americans suddenly wanted to buy homes who could not afford them, but rather because Wall Street wanted to supply people with money, including bad credit risks, to increase home purchases. In order to inflate housing market values, all of the necessary components in the financial services industries were incentivized, such as the selling of subprime mortgages or the robo-signing of mortgages. When predictably the money was not paid back, those like Goldman Sachs or hedge fund manager John Paulson (who made $15 billion betting against the housing market) would go short eventually, after first inflating the bubble through securitization of CDOs, derivative instruments, and extreme leverage, while there were still suckers left to bet against them, just before the real estate market finally did go bust.[24]

Theoretically, whether one is talking about the Wall Street meltdown, the Enron-era scandals, or the savings and loan debacle, accounting control frauds have driven each of these system wide epidemics of criminality where company officials used their organization as a "weapon" to defraud others.[25] Thus, the story of the housing crisis was not the story of a regional housing bubble that nobody could see coming nor was it a matter of the stars not lining up correctly. Rather, inflated housing values and debt-driven economies inside and outside of the U.S. were casualties of "market-rigging through derivatives and political corruption, within the confines of a fragile financial global architecture," which victimized hundreds of millions of ordinary people worldwide. Not limited to the United States, and not everywhere, national balance sheets were blowing up.[26] For example, there were simultaneously housing bubbles in Spain, Portugal, and Ireland. While Greece did not have a bubble in housing, it had a bubble in public sector spending. In these and other locales, there were bubbles followed by crashes, insolvent banks, and millions of foreclosed homeowners and unemployed people. The overwhelming majority of these financial crime victims were never compensated for their losses.

Donald Black's holistic method to the study of legal behavior stands apart from most mainstream theorists of the law and punishment. In particular, Black discusses and identifies four styles of law or governmental social control: (1) penal; (2) compensatory; (3) therapeutic; and (4) conciliatory.[27] All but the therapeutic mode, which aspires toward achieving normality for the deviant violator, is applicable to securities fraud. In the case of Wall Street looting and federal regulatory colluding, there were multiple expressions or overlapping exercises in compensatory (i.e., the victim takes the initiative as plaintiff without the assistance of the state) and conciliatory (i.e., the state takes the initiative to negotiate a resolution of the wrongdoing without civil litigation) control. Predictably, according to Black's theory of the law in action, at the very height of the Wall Street pyramid of securities fraudsters, the "high rollers" were not subject to any criminal or penal control. Further down the financial "food" chain, a relatively small number or handful of inside traders and hedge fund dealers were subjected to criminal arrests, indictments, and convictions. Even further down the network of financial illegalities, a few thousand petty mortgage fraudsters were criminally prosecuted and sanctioned.[28]

As Black demonstrates, in the world of criminality both high and low, social control "divides people into those who are respectable and those who are not; it disgraces some, but protects the reputations of others."[29] Within these legal dynamics of social control, at one and the same time criminality and respectability are defined as polar opposites. Black further reveals that social respectability also helps to explain the behavior of the law: "to be subject to law is, in general, more unrespectable than to be subject to other kinds of social control. To be subject to criminal law is especially unrespectable."[30] As one of Black's legal principles maintains, when all else is constant, the amount of criminal law varies inversely with the respectability of the offender's socioeconomic standing.

Black's characteristics of the law's behavior and of social control beg a different and yet related question: How far will agents of law enforcement and academia or policy wonks go to whitewash the financial crimes of Wall Street in order to protect the fraud minimalist reputations of some of the most successful banking cartels in the world? In the summer of 2011, for example, there was the rather alarming and prominent whistle-blowing Congressional testimony of SEC attorney Darcy Flynn about how the state's top financial police had illegally demolished more than a decade's worth of intelligence gathered on some of Wall Street's most conspicuous offenders. These included both insider trading and securities fraud investigations involving such financial heavies as Goldman Sachs, Lehman Brothers, AIG, Deutsche Bank, and many others.

What had transpired shortly after the financial implosion was that the Security and Exchange Commission (SEC) conveniently eliminated the records of some 9,000 investigations of wrongdoing or "matters under inquiry" dating from 1993 to 2008. There were also a cozy number of cases involving high-profile firms that were never graduated into full-blown criminal investigations because of what has been referred to as an "obstruction of justice" by misbehaving attorneys caught up not only in the revolving personnel doors of government regulation and high-stakes banking, but within what has also been described as the Stockholm Syndrome of Wall Street—a condition where investors and regulators alike not only harbor warm fuzzy feelings toward fund managers, but also find themselves hostages of Wall Street where over and over they make fresh capital commitments to the hostage-takers' newest fund.[31]

The problem of controlling securities fraud goes far beyond the revolving doors that are not really conflicts of interests, per se. As Matt Taibbi, formerly of *Rolling Stone*, wrote at the time of Flynn's testimony before Congress, the

> SEC could have placed federal agents on every corner of lower Manhattan throughout the past decade, and it might not have put a dent in the massive wave of corruption and fraud that left the economy in flames three years ago.[32]

Actually, the Federal Reserve (FED) and the SEC have always been embedded throughout Wall Street financial institutions. The same could also probably be said about the widespread use of systems of automated, real-time monitoring of trades and trading patterns that have been around since the 1990s. At the same time, the time is well past due to empower forensic accountants and law enforcement as well as regulatory officials so that they may both "routinely use 'panoptic' surveillance" methods and "digitally mine the online activities of CEOs."[33] After all, banking firms are already "tapping a cottage industry of software companies that use complex algorithms to monitor traders' calls and emails—looking for catch phrases as well as changes in tone—to try to detect signs that traders may be colluding or placing unauthorized bets."[34]

Ultimately, however, the *intent* to pursue is more important than the means used. In the case of the aftermath of the Wall Street implosion, the state's intent was never to criminalize but always to normalize the criminal behavior of the mega financial institutions. For example, a prima facie case was the non-enactment or implementation of the Fraud Enforcement and Recovery Act, signed into law by President Obama on May 20, 2009. This law was designed to "improve enforcement of mortgage fraud, securities and commodities fraud, financial institutional fraud, and other frauds related to Federal assistance and relief programs, for the recovery of funds lost to these frauds, and for other purposes."[35] With respect to the two identical fraud enforcement teams established in 2009 and again in 2012 by U.S. Attorney General Eric Holder to explicitly address the securities and financial institutional frauds of Wall Street, not a single criminal investigation, let alone a criminal prosecution or criminal conviction, ever materialized. "Further on down the fraudulent food chain, however, the Department of Justice [had] been busy busting and prosecuting 'low-level' mortgage fraudsters" that resulted in 1,517 criminal arrests and 525 indictments.[36]

Treating high-risk securities fraud as non-criminal matters

Since the financial meltdown of 2008, people are quick to point out that the Wall Street of today is not your father's Wall Street from a generation ago, let alone your grandfather's Wall Street from the 1930s. In a world of fully digitized trading where super-sized Wall Street firms are enabled by the latest algorithmically based software programs, these insiders can make millions in microseconds from high-volume trades. Moreover, the players of the new Wall Street are in the business of constantly developing innovative instruments and securing advantages over their investors as well as other competitive traders. Whether or not these state-of-the art securities transactions are non-criminal or criminal, civilly legal or illegal, they have not been subject to adjudication, to interpretation, or to differing rules of law. In the case of the recent financial implosion, neither the instruments old or new have been subject to criminal or even civil adjudication, not to mention judicial review on the merits rather than on the settlements. Instead, at the end of the day it is the U.S. banking oligarchy with its capitalist state allies that decides what does or does not constitute a "crime" in the world of securities-based market transactions while the U.S. Department of Justice usually responds in kind.

To recapitulate, by the end of 2016, some eight years after the financial implosion, no senior executives or otherwise from any of the major Wall Street institutions had been criminally charged, prosecuted, or imprisoned for any type of securities fraud, which included providing false information, withholding key information, offering bad advice, and offering or acting on inside information. This is in stark contrast to the savings and loans scandals of the 1980s when special governmental task forces referred some 1,100 cases to prosecutors, resulting in more than 800 bank officials going to prison.[37] Comparatively, some critics have argued that there has been a lack of collective governmental resolve to criminally pursue these offenses. Other critics have argued that a collective governmental resolve not to hold these offenders criminally accountable has succeeded. Both of these claims are sustained by an examination of the available evidence.

The non-prosecution of securities fraud is precisely what the economic elites of Wall Street and the political elites from the Bush II and Obama Administrations as well as from the majorities of both the U.S. Senate and House of Representatives had desired since the Wall Street collapse. The outcome of zero criminal prosecutions is neither by failure nor conspiracy but mostly by agreement. Even before the financial crisis and Great Recession a concerted effort not to prosecute "big time" financial fraud had begun in 2003; a backlash to a short period of "overzealous" prosecution of several corporate fraudsters in the U.S. in the early years of the new millennium. The movement not to criminalize picked up momentum in 2005–2006 when the U.S. Supreme Court overturned the criminal fraud conviction of Arthur Anderson for helping to cook the accounting records of Enron.[38]

From that point on, instead of strategies to "better" control these financial crimes, strategies were developed to control the damage done to the faith of Wall Street investors in the financial system. The outcomes of this non-penal strategy of not controlling financial fraud resulted in: (1) conciliatory efforts by the government, mainly between the SEC and the DOJ, to restore these institutionalized practices rather than to change them; and (2) compensatory efforts by private investors, individual or corporate, to seek damages for their losses. In terms of those conciliatory efforts, these have been pretty successful in reinforcing the "business as usual" relations of Wall Street. It is these structural market relations, unfortunately, that are at the center of the financial securities crisis confronting both the U.S. and the world today. In terms of the compensatory efforts, these have included dozens of successful cases against every major Wall Street investment firm for securities fraud, amounting to hundreds of billions of dollars in corporate fines and payments. Either way, however, these financially respectable crimes of Wall Street remain outside the purview of criminal prosecution and any deterrent value that might represent.

Before turning to an examination of the investment banking fraud case of Goldman Sachs and the contradictory bourgeois legal relations that played out with respect to responding to the epidemic of widespread securities fraud leading up to the Wall Street financial meltdown and the Great Recession that followed, the sparse but representative sample of the number of criminal and civil prosecutions is presented.

Criminal and civil prosecutions[39]

In the world of big-time securities fraud there were three criminal cases pursued. The defendants in each of these cases were pretty far down the financial food chain. In the first case, filed in June 2008 by the U.S. Justice Department in the Eastern District of New York, two former executives, Ralph R. Cioffi and Matthew M. Tannin, from the defunct Bear Stearns, were accused of misleading investors in two of their hedge funds that collapsed concerning the quality of mortgage assets held in those funds. In November 2009, the two defendants were both found not guilty.

In the second case filed against two former Credit Suisse brokers, Eric Butler and Julian Tzolov, but not against Credit Suisse, by the Securities and Exchange Commission and the USDOJ in the Eastern District of New York, September 2008, the brokers were accused of committing securities fraud by misleading clients about their purchases in the auction-rate securities market, thereby gaining higher sales commissions. Butler was found guilty in August 2009. In January 2010, he was sentenced to five years in prison and a $5.25 million fine and disgorgement. Tzolov pleaded guilty in July 2009. In June 2011, he was sentenced to five years in prison.

The third and biggest of these criminal cases, filed in June of 2010 by the SEC and the DOJ in the Eastern District of Virginia, involved a $2.9 billion fraud by Taylor, Bean & Whitaker Mortgage Corp. and its banking partner, Colonial Bank. In the case, several former executives, including Lee B. Farkas, the former chairman of Taylor, Bean & Whitaker, were accused of two fraudulent schemes: one was to issue false mortgages to obtain money from government-related entitles like Freddie Mac, and the other was a failed attempt to help Colonial Bank defraud regulators during the height of the financial crisis and to steal $550 million through the TARP bailouts on the condition that Colonial Bank would also raise $300 million in private money. Six of the former executives plead guilty. In April 2011 Farkas was found guilty of fourteen counts of securities, bank, and wire fraud as well as conspiracy to commit fraud, and he was sentenced in June of that year to thirty years in prison.

In the civil arena, there were twelve cases filed; two were filed in 2009 and five each were filed in 2010 and 2012. Federal regulatory agencies brought forth ten of these and law enforcement agencies two. At the time of the initial announcements of these cases, five had already been settled; the other cases were still pending in the beginning of 2012. As for the settled cases, the charges filed included accounting fraud, breaching fiduciary duties, defrauding investors, disclosure fraud, stealing, misleading investors, misleading statements, and securities frauds.

In the suits with three former executives at American Home Mortgage, their cases were settled in 2009 as follows: Michael Strauss, chairman and CEO, for $2.45 million and a five-year ban from serving as an official at a public company; Stephen Hozie, CFO, for $1.23 million and a five-year ban from acting as an accountant before the SEC; and Robert Bernstein, controller, for $125,000 and a suspension for at least three years from acting as an accountant before the SEC. Similarly, three former executives from the financial giant Countrywide Financial settled in October 2010 as follows: Angelo R. Mozilo, chairman and CEO, for $67.5 million and a lifetime ban from working as an officer of a public company;

David E. Sambol, president, for $5.52 million and a three-year ban from serving as a public company officer; and Eric P. Sieracki, CFO, for $130,000. It should be pointed out that Bank of America, which acquired Countrywide Financial before the settlement, agreed to pay $20 million of Mozilo's settlement and $5 million of Sambol's. In one of the largest Wall Street financial settlements at the time, Goldman Sachs in July 2010 agreed to pay $550 million for making materially misleading statements and omissions related to the creation of a mortgage-backed securities called Abacus.

Structured finance products, investment banking fraud, and the case against Goldman Sachs

In the "years leading up to the financial crisis, large investment banks designed and promoted complex financial instruments, often referred to as structured finance products, which were at the heart of the crisis."[40] These included residential mortgage-backed securities (RMBS), collateralized debt obligations (CDO), credit default swaps (CDS), and CDO contracts linked to the asset-backed securities index (ABX). From 2004 to 2008, financial institutions in the United States issued nearly $2.5 trillion in RMBS and over $1.4 trillion in CDO securities, backed mostly by mortgage-related products. As the underwriters of residential mortgage-backed securitization, banks typically charged $1 to $8 million for each of these types of transactions. To act as placement agents for a CDO securitization, their fees ranged from $5 to $10 million. These fees "contributed substantial revenues to the investment banks, which established internal structured finance groups, as well as a variety of RMBS and CDO origination and trading desks within these groups, to handle mortgage relations securitizations."[41]

In turn, the trading desks of these investment banks participated in those secondary markets, buying and selling RMBS and CDO securities either on behalf of their clients or in connection with their own proprietary transactions. These types of financial products allowed investors to profit off of both the successes and failures of RMBS and CDO securitization. Similarly, the establishment of the ABX index allowed counterparties to wager on the rise or fall in the value of a basket of subprime RMBS securities. Sometimes, the investment banks matched up parties

> who wanted to take opposite sides in a transaction and other times took one or the other side of a transaction to accommodate a client. At still other times, investment banks used these financial instruments to make their own proprietary wages. In extreme cases, some investment banks set up structured finance transactions which enabled them to profit at the expense of their clients.[42]

In the case of Goldman Sachs (GS), among their array of structured financial products, they specialized in "short selling" that allowed them to benefit from the downturn in the mortgage market.[43] In the same way, GS designed, marketed, and sold CDOs that "created conflicts of interest with the firm's clients and at times led to the bank's profiting from the same products that caused substantial losses for its clients."[44] Running up to the crash, circa 2004–2008, Goldman Sachs was a major player in the U.S. mortgage market, buying and selling RMBS and CDO securities on behalf of its clients, while amassing its own multibillion-dollar proprietary mortgage holdings. In 2006 and 2007, GS designed and underwrote 93 RMBS and 27 mortgage-related CDO securitizations totaling about $100 billion. As far back as December 2006 when Goldman Sachs

> saw evidence that the high risk mortgages underlying many RMBS and CDO securities were incurring accelerating rates of delinquency and default, Goldman quietly and abruptly reversed course. Over the next two months, it rapidly sold off or wrote down the bulk of its existing subprime RMBS and CDO inventory, and began building a short position that would allow it to profit from the decline of the mortgage market.[45]

For example, GS twice in 2007 built up and cashed in sizable mortgage-related short positions, reaching a peak of short selling totaling $13.9 billion. By year's end, Goldman's Structured Products Group had purchased record profits totaling $3.7 billion. GS' short positions were "in direct opposition to the clients to whom it was selling CDO securities, yet it failed to disclose the size and nature of its short position while marketing the securities."[46] Four of those 2007 CDO securities were sold as Hudson 1, Anderson, Timberwolf, and Abacus. Those investors lost virtually everything; three investors together lost about $1 billion from their Abacus investments. During the summer of 2008, the SEC started investigating Goldman's marketing of the subprime mortgage deal with Abacus. One year later in July, the SEC sent GS a Wells Notice informing the firm of its intention to file a lawsuit against the company. Goldman's next quarterly financial report, in violation of SEC Rule 10b-5, failed to disclose to the corporation's investors that the firm was under investigation. On a subsequent occasion, Goldman chose not to disclose the SEC's pending enforcement action on its financial statements.

In sum, like other investment banks using loans from subprime lenders known for issuing high-risk and poor quality mortgages leading up to the Wall Street meltdown, Goldman Sachs underwrote and sold risky securities across the United States and around the world. At the same time, GS enabled lenders to acquire new funds to originate still more high-risk, poor quality loans not as the toxic loans that they were but as triple-A rated. Moreover, without full disclosure, Goldman failed to reveal the shorting of the very CDO securities that it was marketing. And, if this risk was not enough, GS came up with some very complex structured finance products, such as synthetic CDOs and naked credit default swaps in which the buyer does not own the underlying debt. These types of instruments further amplified market risk by allowing investors without any "skin in the game" or ownership interests to place unlimited side bets on their performance. Ironically, to have stopped the flow of these high-risk strategies in general or the "CDO machine" in particular at both Goldman Sachs and across the financial services industry would have meant "less income for structured finance units, smaller executive bonuses, and even the disappearance of CDO desks and personnel, which is finally what happened."[47]

Conciliatory collusion, Goldman Sachs, and the costs of doing high finance

So what were the non-criminal legal consequences for Goldman Sachs and for its traders in settling the charges that GS misled investors in a subprime mortgage product just as the U.S. housing market was starting to collapse? One relatively young twenty-eight-year-old trader, Fabrice Tourre, was transferred to its London office while he faced a civil suit filed in 2010 by the SEC. In April of the same year the SEC in a civil complaint accused GS of "duping clients by selling mortgage securities that were secretly created by a hedge-fund to cash in on the housing market's collapse," when its shares were trading near $180, and its investors were "on a roller-coast ride."[48] Three months later on July 15, Goldman settled the case agreeing to "reform its business practices" and to the largest financial penalty— $550 million—assessed up until that time against any firm involved in the Wall Street implosion.[49] Of the monies paid out by Goldman, $250 million went to harmed investors through a Fair Fund distribution and $300 million went to the U.S. Treasury.

In the settlement papers submitted to the U.S. District Court for the Southern District of New York, Goldman acknowledges that

> the marketing materials for the ABACUS 2007-AC1 transaction contained incomplete information. In particular, it was a mistake for the Goldman marketing materials to state that the reference portfolio was "selected by" ACA Management LLC without disclosing the role of Paulson & Co. Inc. in the portfolio selection process and that Paulson's economic interests were adverse to CDO investors. Goldman regrets that the marketing materials did not contain that disclosure.[50]

Remarking on the case's quick resolution, the Director of the SEC's Division of Enforcement, Robert Khuzami, had this say: "This settlement is a stark lesson to Wall Street firms that no product is too complex and no investor too sophisticated, to avoid a heavy price if a firm violates the fundamental principle of honest treatment and fair dealing."[51] Echoing his boss, the SEC's Deputy Director Lorin Reisner added that the

> unmistakable message of this lawsuit and today's settlement is that half-truths and deception cannot be tolerated and that the integrity of the securities markets depends on all market participants acting with uncompromising adherence to the requirements of truthfulness and honesty.[52]

Rhetoric aside, the material compensation amounted to a "slap on the wrist." After all, the fine represented 4 percent of GS's record-setting $13.4 billion in profits for 2009. For more perspective, back in 1989 the investment-banking firm Drexel Burnham was fined $650 million, putting it out of business. One year later its CEO, junk bond king Michael Milken, paid a $600 million settlement fine and served a stretch in prison. As with the other bailed-out financial institutions like AIG or Bank of America that have settled with the government, GS did not have to admit to any wrongdoing with respect to its fraudulent and criminal conduct.

Goldman did acknowledge, however, that it should have been more forthcoming in disclosing some information and in the marketing of some of their financial products. Goldman also promised not to do it again and to better monitor its personnel to ensure that future offerings of mortgage and CDO products would be fully and accurately disclosed. Strangely, while a judge had ruled that there was no finding of willful wrongdoing, he nevertheless issued a permanent injunction from violations of the anti-fraud provisions of The Securities Act of 1993. Did that mean that the next time Goldman commits fraud, federal prosecutors would file criminal charges? Technically or legalistically, it should mean precisely that. Then again, as a repeat offender who has yet to be criminally prosecuted for any previous violations, it suggests that this permanent injunction might be otherwise. Moreover, if the past is any indicator of the future, then the next time Goldman Sachs commits securities fraud it is more than reasonable to assume that this new "solitary" violation will not result in anything more than another fine, more education of their employees, and promises not to do once again what they have never admitted to doing in the first place.

The big banks, SEC waivers, and state financial resources

The repeated granting of nearly 350 exemptions to laws and regulations over the previous decade that could have otherwise acted as a deterrent to securities fraud recidivism and as a protection for investors dwarfs the number of SEC cases in which the waivers were denied. This form of state colluding with big banks like JP Morgan, Bank of America, and GS has helped to keep them in business by extending to these financial institutions market advantages that, if anything, should have been reserved for the most dependable companies, not for those who habitually have been settling fraud cases. For several decades, "wrangling over waivers" has been "an important part of the negotiations when companies accused of fraud discuss a settlement with the S.E.C, and some of it can involve a form of corporate plea bargaining to a lesser charge."[53]

An analysis conducted by *The New York Times* in 2011 counted 91 waivers since 2000 granting immunity from lawsuits and 204 waivers related to raising capital funds. *The Times* also "found 11 instances where companies that had settled fraud cases actually lost the special privilege for fast-track stock or bond offerings, versus 49 times that the S.E.C. granted waivers from the punishment to Wall Street firms since 2005."[54] Between 1999 and 2012, for example, JP Morgan had settled six fraud cases, including a $228 million settlement in the summer of 2011. While JPM had obtained at least twenty-two waivers since 2003, the investment bank had received three waivers alone related to their biggest multimillion-dollar penalty settling civil and criminal charges that the company had "cheated cities and towns by rigging bids with other Wall Street firms to invest money raised by several municipalities for capital projects."[55] In seeking those reprieves, lawyers for JP Morgan had argued in letters to the SEC that despite the record their clients should be granted waivers because the bank has "a strong record of compliance with the securities laws."[56]

During the same period, Bank of America (perhaps the most criminal) had settled fifteen fraud cases and received at least thirty-nine waivers. Similarly, before losing most of its privileges in 2010, Citigroup had settled six fraud cases and received twenty-five waivers in the previous eleven years. By granting these waivers, or exemptions from punishment, the SEC routinizes this criminality as the cost of doing business while allowing these Wall Street firms to maintain their powerful advantages over the competition. In effect, these agreements permit these banks to "continue to tap capital markets without delay (and governmental approval), to manage mutual funds," to help small firms raise money, and to continue "to get certain protections from class-action lawsuits."[57]

The SEC has defended their practices of avoiding trials, especially criminal ones, by stating that they do not have the necessary financial and human resources to take these cases to court rather than settle. If serious about these multinational financial crimes, then the necessary resources would be made available to police Wall Street if only the U.S. Congress and the Presidency were interested in adding, say, another $500,000 million to their annual budget and some 2,500 permanent positions. The SEC budget request for fiscal year 2016 was $1.722 billion in support of 5,205 permanent positions.[58] However, it is not really about the lack of resources, because the real agenda all along has been not to criminally punish these offenses but to normalize them away.

As the SEC has argued, without these exemptions or waivers to settle charges of securities fraud, the negative consequences for these firms (and the ripple effects across the economy) would be enormous. Without these routinized settlements, according to David Ruder, a former SEC chairman, it would be very difficult for these banks to stay in business. Moreover, as Meredith Cross stated when she was still the SEC's corporation finance director, since the purpose of these waivers or exemptions are "to protect investors, not to punish a company," then to deny these waivers is to take away the fast-track offering privileges to capitalize on investments.[59]

Despite the neutralization or rationalization of these securities frauds by way of non-criminal settlements, at least one U.S. Senator, Charles Grassley from Iowa, who had served on the committees that oversee the SEC, was confused by the fact that the agency was not "using all its weapons to deter fraud." The senator went on to say that these practices make already weak punishments "even weaker by waiving the regulations that impose significant consequences on the companies that settle fraud charges. No wonder recidivism is such a problem."[60] Such are the contradictions of bourgeois legality.

Update: "short sellers sold short by Goldman"

On January 14, 2016, Goldman Sachs settled two cases with the Securities and Exchange Commission. In one case, GS agreed to pay up to $5 billion to settle prosecutor's claims that it sold faulty mortgage securities to investors. The other case was part of a more complex or esoteric design of Wall Street plumbing that led to a paltry $15 million fine. But as Gretchen Morgenson has argued, "the smaller settlement merits close study because it sheds light on one of Wall Street's most secretive and profitable arena: securities lending and short-selling."[61] Morgenson is referring to those critically interrelated high-risk services involving the way in which Wall Street firms execute trades for their clients, especially when they want to sell short or bet against a company's stock.

In order for GS clients to do so, these soon-to-become plaintiffs relying on this settlement will seek to recover damages from the firm for its failure to locate the shares they had to borrow and to deliver to a buyer before selling short. In fact, these kinds of omissions in such transactions are known as "naked shorting" and are violations of Regulation SHO, a 2005 SEC rule. Naked shorting, according to the SEC, can be abusive and may drive down company shares. "Therefore, brokerage firms are barred from accepting orders for short sales unless they have borrowed the stock or have 'reasonable grounds' to believe it can be secured. This is known as the 'locate' requirement."[62] Strangely, however, while charging clients for financial services not rendered is securities fraud, in the case of "short selling one's clients of short sellers," GS was not in violation of the rule. It turns out that Goldman's failure to perform "meant that some of its clients were unknowingly breaching this important rule."[63] Go figure.

With regard to habitual violations of securities law, the SEC had charged that between 2008 and 2013, or before, during, and after the market decline, Goldman was "improperly providing locates to customers where it had not performed an adequate review of the securities to be located."[64] Furthermore, the SEC pointed out that not only did GS' responses to their investigation hamper and prolong the inquiry, but that the firm had also falsely "created the incorrect impression" with regulators that it had conducted individualized reviews for all locate requests. Charging for such services not rendered could result in Goldman Sachs paying to its clients hundreds of millions of dollars in compensation, far more than the $15 million the SEC collected because the costs charged for those selling short services run as high as "25 percent or more of the trade's value to secure the shares."[65]

Notes

1 O'Toole, James. 2012. "Explaining the Libor Interest Rate Mess." *CNN Money*. July 10. http://money.cnn.com/2012/07/03/investing/libor-interest-rate-faq/index.htm.
2 Ibid.
3 Preston, Darrell. 2012. "Rigged LIBOR Costs State, Localities $6 Billion." *Bloomberg News*. October 10. www.delawareonline.com/article/20121011/BUSINESS05/310110 056/Rigged-LIBOR-costs-states-localities-6-billion.

4 O'Toole, 2012.

5 Eagle fried. 2012. "Barclays Pays a Heavy Price for Falsifying the LIBOR Submissions." *The Economist*. July 30. www.economist.com/node/21557772.

6 Armstrong, Rachel. 2012. "Ex-RBS Trader Says Brevan Howard Sought Libor Rate Change." *Reuters Business*. March 30. http://uk.reuters.com/article/uk-brevanhowa rd-libor-idUKBRE82T0J920120330.

7 O'Toole, 2012.

8 Ibid.

9 Bruer, Lanny. 2012. "The Real Reason UBS Rigged Libor." *Galactic Connection*. December 12. http://galacticconnection.com/lanny-breuer-the-real-reason-ubs-rigge d-libor/#sthash.Si2KSGrm.dpbs.

10 Brush, Silla and Mattingly, Phil. 2012. "UBS $1.5 Billion Libor Settlement Signals More to Come." *Bloomberg Business*. July 19. www.bloomberg.com/news/articles/2012-12-19/ ubs-1-5-billion-libor-settlement-signals-more-to-come.

11 Ibid.

12 O'Toole, 2012.

13 Beltrame, Julian. 2012. "Canadian Connection to LIBOR Scandal Probed by Compe-tition Bureau." *National Post*. July 15. http://news.nationalpost.com/news/canada/cana dian-connection-to-libor-scandal-probed-by-competition-bureau.

14 Smith, Randall. 2015. "Two Former Traders Found Guilty in Libor Manipulation Case." *The New York Times*. November 5. www.nytimes.com/2015/11/06/business/dea lbook/two-former-traders-found-guilty-in-libor-manipulation-case.html?_r=0.

15 Quoted in ibid.

16 Raymond, Nate. 2016. "Ex-Rabobank Traders Get U.S. Prison Terms for Libor Manipulation." *Reuters*. March 10. http://finance.yahoo.com/news/ex-rabobank-tra ders-u-prison-042434718.html;_ylt=A0LEViyIC_hWlJcAq.wPxQt.;_ylu=X3oDMT BydWNmY2MwBGNvbG8DYmYxBHBvcwM0BHZ0aWQDBHNlYwNzcg--.

17 Barak, Gregg. 2012. *Theft of a Nation: Wall Street Looting and Federal Regulatory Colluding*. Lanham, MD: Rowman & Littlefield.

18 Binham, Caroline. 2012. "U.S. Woman Takes on Banks Over Libor." *Financial Times*. October 15. www.cnbc.com/id/49412365.

19 Ibid.

20 Gongloff, Mark. 2013. "Banks Win Big with Dismissal of Libor Lawsuits, but War is Far From Over." *The Huffington Post*. April 1. www.huffingtonpost.com/2013/04/01/ba nks-libor-lawsuits-dismissed_n_2994198.html.

21 Ibid.

22 Hong, Nicole. 2016. "Banks Dealt Blow in Libor Lawsuits." *The Wall Street Journal*. May 23. www.wsj.com/articles/civil-antitrust-lawsuits-reinstated-against-16-banks-in-libor-case-1464022330.

23 A Washington DC Insider. 2016. "What the Movie Big Short's Brilliant Attack on Wall Street Misses, and Why Michael Lewis is to Blame." *Naked Capitalism*. January 20. www.nakedcapitalism.com/2016/01.

24 Ibid.

25 Black, William. 2005. *The Best Way to Rob a Bank is to Own One: How Corporate Executives and Politicians Looted the S & L Industry*. Austin, TX: University of Texas Press.

26 A Washington DC Insider, 2016.

27 Black, Donald. 2010 (1976). "How Law Behaves: An Interview with Donald Black," reprinted in *The Behavior of Law. Special Education*. Bingley, UK: Emerald Group, p. 105.

28 Barak, 2012.

29 Black, 2010, p. 105.

30 Ibid., p. 111.

31 Deal Journal. 2008. "Mean Street: Stockholm Syndrome Hits Wall Street." *The Wall Street Journal*. May 13. http://blogs.wsj.com/deals/2008/05/13/mean-street-stockholm-syn drome-hits-wall-street/.

32 Taibbi, M. 2011. "Is the SEC Covering Up Wall Street Crimes?" *Rolling Stone*. August 17. www.rollingstone.com/politics/news/is-the-sec-covering-up-wall-street-crimes-201 10817?print=true.

33 Snider, L. 2013. "The Technological Advantages of Stock Market Traders." In *How They Got Away with It: White Collar Criminals and the Financial Meltdown*, edited by S. Will, S. Handelman, and D. Brotherton. New York: Columbia University Press, p. 155.

34 Colchester, M. 2013. "Banks Scan Trader Talk for Trouble." *The Wall Street Journal*. December 6: p. C1–C2.

35 Pub. L. No. 111–121, 123 Stat. 1617.

36 Barak, 2012, p. 14.

37 Calavita, Kitty, Pontell, Henry, and Tillman, Robert. 1999. *Big Money Crime: Fraud and Politics in the Savings and Loan Crisis*. Berkeley, CA: University of California Press.

38 Barak, 2012.

39 The material for this section comes from Barak, 2012.

40 U.S. Senate. 2011. Official Report, *Wall Street and the Financial Crisis: Anatomy of a Financial Collapse*. April 13, p. 10.

41 Ibid.

42 Ibid.

43 In finance, a short selling refers to the practice of selling assets, usually securities, that have been borrowed from a third party, to be sold back at a later date to the lender with the intent of profiting from a decline in the price of the assets between the sale and the repurchase.

44 U.S. Senate, 2011, p. 10.

45 Ibid., p. 11.

46 Ibid.

47 Ibid., p. 13.

48 Craig, Suzanne and Lattman, Peter. 2011. "Goldman's Shares Tumble as Blankfein Hires Top Lawyer." *The New York Times*. August 22. http://dealbook.nytimes.com/2011/08/22.

49 U.S. Securities and Exchange Commission. 2010. "Goldman Sachs to Pay Record $550 Million to Settle SEC Charges Related to Subprime Mortgage CDO." Press Release. July 15. www.sec.gov/news/press/2010/07/15-123.htm.

50 Ibid.

51 Ibid.

52 Ibid.

53 Wyatt, Edward. 2012. "S.E.C. Is Avoiding Tough Sanctions for Large Banks." *The New York Times*. February 3. www.nytimes.com/2012/02/03/business/sec-is-avoiding-tough-sanctions-for-large-banks.html?pagewanted=all&_r=0.

54 Ibid.

55 Ibid.

56 Ibid.

57 Ibid.

58 U.S. Securities and Exchange Commission. 2015. FY 2016 Congressional Justification and FY 2014 Annual Performance Report and FY 2016 Annual Performance Plan. February 2. www.sec.gov/about/reports/secfy16congbudgjust.shtml.

59 Wyatt, 2012.

60 Quoted in ibid.

61 Morgenson, Gretchen. 2016. "Short Sellers Sold Short By Goldman." *The New York Times*. January 31: Sunday Business, p. 1.

62 Ibid.

63 Ibid.

64 Quoted in ibid.

65 Ibid.

4

ENVIRONMENTAL CRIMES

Violations of health and safety

Republican Governor Rick Snyder's appointment of an Emergency Manager to take over the democratically elected duties of the mayor and city council of Flint, Michigan, and the money-saving shortcuts the EM imposed on the residents was, at least partially, responsible for having poisoned up to 8,000 children as well as other residents, mostly African American. From late 2015 to early 2016 a national scandal ensued when the public learned that the state of Michigan, its Department of Environmental Quality, and the Midwest regional offices of the U.S. Environmental Protection Agency were slow, resistant, and/or reluctant to react for almost two years to citizen complaints of sour-smelling, discolored water coming out of residential pipes, to the levels of toxic chemicals in the water, and to the subsequent diagnoses of lead poisoning. In other words, there had been a political period of denial regarding the lead contamination of the Flint drinking water and a dismissal of the environmental needs of the people of Flint.

The economic realities and demographic landscape in Flint provided high-visibility opportunities for two Democratic primary presidential candidates, Hillary Clinton and Bernie Sanders, to condemn the tragedy in Flint. Each campaign produced emotionally televised advertisements of solidarity with the people of Flint and the wider struggles against institutionalized racism and lead poisoning. More fundamentally, however, politicians in the U.S. and elsewhere have, for the most part, been missing in action when it comes to reducing, preventing, and regulating toxic pollution. For example, according to a *USA Today* investigative report, "6 million people nationwide are served by water systems that reported lead levels that exceeded EPA standards."[1] Of the nearly 2,000 water systems in all fifty states with excessive levels of lead—anything above 20 parts per billion (ppb)—350 of them provide drinking water to schools and daycares. One elementary school in Ithaca, New York, tested 5,000 ppb, considered to be "hazardous waste" by the EPA. While children and pregnant women are most at risk from the harmful effects of high levels of lead, adults are not immune from other health issues such as kidney problems. Finally, at "least 180 of the water systems that tested high did not notify their customers as required by federal regulations."[2]

More widely, scientists have already found and identified more than 200 industrial chemicals—from pesticides to jet fuel—as well as neurotoxins like lead in the blood or breast milk of not only Americans, but of people all around the globe. According to Philip Landrigan, a pediatrician and dean for global health at the Icahn School of Medicine at Mount Sinai, New York, "Lead, mercury, PCBs, flame retardants, and pesticides cause prenatal brain damage to tens of thousands of children" in the U.S. annually.[3] The ordinary absence of political concern for these toxic substances is a consequence of the lobbying efforts of chemical companies spending vast sums of money each year—more than $100,000 per member of Congress in 2015. No wonder that almost "none of the chemicals in the products we use daily have been tested for safety."[4]

The city of Flint is not alone or nearly as bad as other places in the United States. Mostly due to older lead-based paint chips and to lead piping that began to be slowly phased out in the 1930s, the Centers for Disease Control and Prevention in Atlanta, Georgia, estimates that there are 535,000 children aged one to five that are suffering with lead poisoning in the U.S. Also, children are more likely to suffer from lead poisoning in Illinois, Pennsylvania, or even in most of New York State than in Flint. Though the data sets are not particularly strong, the comparative rates of elevated lead poisoning in children were 4.9 percent in Flint, 6.7 percent in New York (excluding the city of New York), and 8.5 percent in Pennsylvania. In some parts of Detroit, elevated levels of lead in blood are as high as 20 percent. At the same time, while the victims of lead poisoning and other chemical toxins are mostly poor and people of color who have been subject to the legacies of redlining and other forms of institutionalized racism, it is important to note that underdeveloped brains and diminished IQs are also associated with flame-retardant chemicals used to stuff couches that we all sit on.[5]

In the U.S. race remains the most significant predictor of a person living near hazardous waste or contaminated air, water, or soil. Here are some relevant facts: 56 percent of those living near toxic waste sites are people of color; African-Americans are twice as likely as whites to live in a home with substandard plumbing or without potable water and modern sanitation; people of color have 38 percent higher nitrogen-dioxide exposure than whites; and the EPA has denied 95 percent of the claims filed against polluters by people of color.[6] Much of this environmental racism can be traced to the U.S. discriminatory governmental housing and related insurance policies that existed from the 1930s to the 1960s, which redlined neighborhoods, "locking black people into crowded city centers, while helping white people flee to the more pleasant suburbs."[7] In the case of Flint, redlining exacerbated poverty in the black community as African-Americans were denied the wealth accumulation created by home ownership accessed by whites through cheap mortgage loans. By the mid-1960s, Flint was 94 percent segregated. Over the years, local-level planning and development also facilitated the concentration of low-income communities and communities of color like Flint into "marginal urban geographies."[8] Thereafter, these communities were routinely chosen as dumping grounds for urban sources of pollution and contamination.

In January 2016, residents of Flint filed three different class action lawsuits in the Genesee County Circuit Court against the state of Michigan, Governor Snyder, the Michigan departments of Health and Human Services as well as Environmental Quality, and the city of Flint for their negligence in the town's deadly water crisis. The plaintiffs claim that they have suffered physical injury and financial injustice from drinking and being charged for the contaminated water. Among the different actions, class members are claiming an unjust and unconstitutional taking of their property without fair compensation as well as serious harm (e.g., lead poisoning) resulting from "the prolonged and repeated false assurances" made by public officials that "the Flint River water was safe to drink and use."[9] The suits asked Circuit Court Judge Archie Hayman to "enjoin the City of Flint from water shut-offs and that he declare that the Flint water users are not required to pay past or future bills for useless and harmful water."[10] On April 19, 2016, one of more than a dozen lawsuits filed by Flint residents against the city of Flint and the state of Michigan seeking compensation was tossed from U.S. federal court.

The next day, Michigan Attorney General Bill Schuette announced criminal charges "against two state regulators and a Flint employee, alleging wrongdoing related to city's lead-tainted water crisis."[11] The regulators worked for the state Department of Environmental Quality and the other person was a local water treatment plant supervisor. The "felony and misdemeanor charges include violating Michigan's drinking water law, official misconduct, destruction of utility property and evidence tampering."[12] In a televised statement the attorney general accused those charged with manipulating public records to make the lead levels look lower than they were. He also claimed that more criminal charges would be forthcoming and that nobody would be exempt from prosecution.

Unfortunately, the citizens of Flint have been down similar legal pathways before in their struggles against environmental racism. Back in the 1990s, residents fought against an air permit for a steel "mini-mill," which would operate within the city limits and spew 100 tons of lead and other pollutants into the air each year, adding to existing air pollution generated by the Genesee Power Station.[13]

In this instance, the Environmental Protection Agency ruled against the Flint residents' claims that the combined quantity of pollution would violate their civil rights. Point of information, the EPA has never once made a formal finding of an environmental civil-rights violation.

Green Criminology, environmental crimes, and structural harms

Not unlike the crimes of multinationals in general, environmental crimes in particular are not limited to criminal or civil violations of the law. According to Green Criminology, these crimes may also incorporate those harmful acts that are not necessarily a breach of the law. In effect, this conceptual expansion of the state's legal definition of crime has allowed for encompassing those acts that are just as harmful as or more so than any of the acts that are defined as a breach of either the law or a regulation. In the area of environmental offenses against humanity, the commons, and non-human plant and animal life, the examination of abuse or injury has evolved over the past couple of decades to include those harms organized and committed by multinational corporations, nation-states, military and police apparatuses, the International Monetary Fund, the World Bank, the World Trade Organization, and so on.[14]

For example, Lynch, Long, and Stretesky have examined the viability of non-human animal (as opposed to plant) populations as a function of systemic ecological harm. By "systemic" they are referring to "those ecological harms that are endemic to capitalism as a system of production and which in the current context of global capitalism are also global in their appearance, and therefore are structural in origin."[15] The specific viability issues that Lynch *et al.* were addressing included "the endangerment and extinction of species" and the "relationship of species' viability to the forms of ecological disorganization that are produced by capitalism in its ordinary course of development."[16] Their question became: to what extent does capitalist development produce ecological disorganization, or to what degree is capitalism structurally criminogenic toward the environment?

Theoretically, they began with the well-known observation that "capitalism's primary goal is the promotion of continually expanding profit." In order to meet that goal, "the capitalist system of production must constantly increase production, and hence must also constantly increase its extraction and consumption of raw materials."[17] As a part of this dynamic process of capital accumulation and reproduction, the constantly expanding production and consumption results in both the acceleration and expansion of ecological destruction and disorganization.[18] To illustrate the effects of human economic development on the more general decline of wildlife species, they reviewed the literature on the connection between capitalist expansion and species destruction within and across nations as well as empirical data from the International Union of Conservation of Nature's Red List of threatened species in the U.S. and additional data on species endangerment from the U.S. Wildlife and Fish Service. They concluded "the contemporary expansion of capitalism drives continuous economic development in ways that promote the destruction of nature and facilitate the general decline of species health, vitality, and existence."[19]

As Lynch *et al.* maintain, "The capitalist treadmill of production drives economic development to continually expand in the pursuit of profit regardless of the eco-system consequences."[20] The implications of this kind of structural analysis of environmental crimes are important for several ideological and practical reasons. This kind of structural analysis of capital development, for example, draws attention to the fact that the traditional behaviors of indigenous peoples only become ecologically destructive once capitalism has expanded into developed regions and claims a significant portion of the ecosystem for production, especially through the extraction of raw materials and imposed monoagricultural methods of production that are consistent with the efficiency requirements of capitalism.[21]

Not only do such explanations of ecological destruction depart from those arguments that "blame the poor," but they also provide an alternative perspective to those that argue that "extinction patterns" are caused by population expansion, poaching, and/or wildlife trade.[22]

Exposing West Virginians to toxic substances: DuPont, cover-up, litigation, and decades of chemical pollution

DuPont is one of the most successful science and engineering companies in the world. According to its website, for more than two centuries DuPont, an American chemical company, has been delivering solutions to tackle global challenges. It was first founded in 1802 as a gunpowder mill. During the twentieth century DuPont developed many polymers such as neoprene, nylon, and Teflon. Over time the company has diversified into virtually everything. Today, DuPont's product lines include animal nutrition and disease prevention, crop protection, and seed production. The list of industries that DuPont serves is quite long: agriculture, automobile, building and construction, electronics, energy, food and beverage, government and public sector, healthcare and medical, marine, mining, packaging and printing, plastics, and safety and protection. In 2013 with nearly $36 billion in revenues and $4.848 billion in profits, the company ranked 86th on the Fortune 500. In 2014, DuPont was the world's fourth largest company of its kind based on market capitalization and based on revenue it was eighth.

In December 2015, DuPont and Dow Chemical announced a proposed merger to become DowDupont in an all-stock deal by the end of 2016. Should the merger receive regulatory approval, their combined estimated worth would be around $130 billion. Despite the likelihood that the deal will face antitrust scrutiny in several countries,[23] it is probably safe to assume that the merger will be approved, bringing together two of the historical leaders in multinational toxic contamination. Leading the opposition to the merger was Iowa Republican Senator Chuck Grassley who, in a two-page letter published on June 20, 2016, went on record saying that consumers, small businesses, and industry, and particularly agriculture, could be harmed by a behemoth DowDupont domination of the market. In light of the proposed marriage, it is interesting to note that a decade earlier in 2005, DuPont Dow Elastomers, a subsidiary of both DuPont and Dow Chemical, pleaded guilty and paid an $84 million criminal fine for an "international conspiracy to fix the prices of synthetic rubber."[24] Should the U.S. DOJ approve the merger, DowDupont has plans to split the company into three separate companies within a few years.

DuPont's environmental record is a "mixed bag," which includes such positives as: the company was a founding member of the World Business Council for Sustainable Development in the 1990s; *BusinessWeek* magazine in conjunction with the Climate Group ranked DuPont as the best-practice leader in cutting their carbon gas emissions in 2005; and based on DuPont's performance on sustainability metrics, emissions reduction goals, and environmental transparency, the company was named to the Carbon Disclosure Project Global 500 Leadership Index in 2012.[25] On the other hand, between 2007 and 2014, there were thirty-four accidents resulting in toxic releases at DuPont plants across the United States, with no fewer than eight fatalities. As a result, in 2015 the company became the largest of the 450 businesses placed into the Occupational Safety and Health Administration's "severe violator program." OSHA established the program for those companies with a history of repeatedly failing to address safety infractions.[26]

The story of DuPont's cover-up or "intent to kill" is not merely a story of exposing West Virginians to toxic substances, but it is also a story of DuPont exposing the inhabitants of the world to what the company knew to be hazardous to health and safety. These fraudulent actions by DuPont are not fundamentally any different from those same types of actions performed historically by other multinational killers such as the tobacco, mining, oil and gas, or pharmaceutical industries.

The death of a toxic fluorochemical, or PFOA by another name?

In 2013 DuPont signed an agreement with the U.S. Environmental Protection Agency (EPA) to cease production and use of perfluorooctanoic acid (PFOA).[27] For decades the chemical giant had struggled to keep the highly profitable, chemically toxic substance alive. In the context of the merger with Dow, DuPont in 2015 severed its chemical businesses altogether. These activities have been taken over by a new corporation by the name of Chemours. This company has replaced PFOA with similar fluorine-based compounds designed to more quickly biodegrade. Like PFOA before them, these new substances have not come under any regulation from the EPA. When asked about the safety of the new chemicals for a cover story for *The New York Times Magazine* (January 10, 2016), Chemours in a prepared statement replied: "A significant body of data demonstrates that these alternative chemistries can be used safely."[28]

However, in May of 2015, 200 scientists had signed the Madrid Statement expressing their concern over the production of all fluorochemicals, or PFASs, including those that have replaced PFOA. The problem is that these chemical replacements are suspected of belonging to "a large class of artificial compounds called endocrine-disrupting chemicals; these compounds, which include chemicals used in the production of pesticides, plastics, and gasoline, interfere with human reproduction and metabolism and cause cancer, thyroid problems and nervous-system disorders."[29] The Madrid statement recommended that wherever possible people should avoid stain-resistant, waterproof, or non-stick products that contain or were manufactured using PFASs, such as 3M Scotchgard fabric protector.

When questioned about the Madrid Statement by Nathaniel Rich for *The New York Times Magazine* article, Dan Turner, DuPont's head of global media relations, responded in an email:

DuPont does not believe the Madrid Statement reflects a true consideration of the available data on alternatives to long-chair perflurorochemicals, such as

PFOA. DuPont worked for more than a decade, with oversight from regulators, to introduce its alternatives. Extensive data has been developed, demonstrating that these alternatives are much more rapidly eliminated from the body than PFOA, and have improved health safety profiles. We are confident that these alternative chemistries can be used safely—they are well characterized and the data has been used to register them with environmental agencies around the world.[30]

A PFOA cover-up timeline: what did DuPont know? When did DuPont know it? What did DuPont say about what they knew?

Back in 1951 DuPont started to purchase PFOA, which at the time the company referred to as C8, from the 3M company for its use in the manufacturing of Teflon. 3M had invented PFOA in 1947 for the purposes of keeping coatings like Teflon from clumping during production. At the time of their business transaction, PFOA had not been classified by the government as a hazardous substance. At the same time, DuPont had received recommendations from 3M on how to dispose of PFOA by way of incineration or by being sent to chemical-waste facilities. Moreover, DuPont's own instructions specified that PFOA was not to be flushed into surface water or sewers. Nevertheless, over the decades, through its Parkersburg, West Virginia, facility, DuPont "pumped hundreds of thousands of pounds of PFOA powder through the outfall pipes" into the Ohio River.[31] In addition, in its nearby Washington Works property, DuPont had "dumped 7,100 tons of PFOA-laced sludge into 'digestion ponds'; open, unlined pits … from which the chemical could seep straight into the ground."[32] As a consequence, PFOA entered the local water table that supplied the drinking water to more than 100,000 people from the communities of Parkersburg, Vienna, Little Hocking, Ohio, and Lubeck.

By way of pretrial discovery, in the first of a series of lawsuits that began almost twenty years ago and at least through 2016 still continued, it was revealed that 3M and DuPont had been conducting secret medical studies on PFOA for more than four decades. By 1961 their researchers had found that PFOA could increase the size of the liver in rats and rabbits. One year later, they had replicated the same findings with dogs. What they learned from these studies was that PFOA's peculiar chemical structure made it highly resistant to degradation. PFOA also bound with plasma proteins in the blood, circulating through each organ in the body. During the 1970s DuPont learned that there were high concentrations of PFOA in the blood of factory workers at Washington Works. They did not share this information with their workers.

In 1981, 3M, which was still supplying PFOA to DuPont and other corporations throughout the world, discovered that ingestion of the substance caused birth defects in rats. Soon after receiving this information, DuPont tested the children born to pregnant workers in their Teflon division. A sample of seven births found two with eye defects. DuPont did not make this information public. A few years later in 1984, DuPont became aware that dust vented from their factory chimneys settled well beyond the property line. More disturbing was the fact that they also knew that PFOA was present in the local water. Once again, DuPont declined to share this information with anyone. By the late eighties, concerned enough about ill health affects to its employees, DuPont purchased 66 acres from one of its Washington Works facility employees who did not wish to sell but needed the money.

Most interestingly, in 1991 while discovering that one local water district had contained more than three parts per billion of PFOA concentration, DuPont scientists established an internal safety limit for PFOA concentration of one part per billion for drinking water. Despite internal debate among DuPont employees, the company failed to alert the drinking public. By this time, it was clear that DuPont also knew that PFOA caused cancerous testicular, pancreatic, and liver tumors in lab animals. There was also one laboratory study that suggested that exposure to PFOA might cause DNA damage, and another study of workers that had linked exposure to prostate cancer. A 1993 interoffice memo "announced that 'for the first time, we have a viable candidate' that appeared to be less toxic and stayed in the body for a much shorter duration of time."[33] Discussions were held at DuPont's corporate headquarters about switching to the new compound. However, the decision was made not to because the risks of changing were too great: "Products manufactured with PFOA were an important part of DuPont's business, worth $1 billion in annual profits."[34]

Rob Bilott for the plaintiffs versus DuPont Chemical Company

Shortly before he made partner at Taft Stettinius & Hollister, a large Cincinnati law firm specializing in corporate environmental defense law, Rob Bilott received a phone call on his direct line from Wilbur Tennant, a cattle farmer in Parkersburg, West Virginia. Tennant believed that the DuPont chemical company was responsible for 153 cows of his that had already died on his 600-acre farm, adjacent to a 66-acre plot that his brother, an employee at DuPont, had sold to the company out of financial necessity. DuPont was now using this plot of land for storing PFOA sludge relocated from their Washington Works site. DuPont renamed the property location Dry Run Landfill after the creek that ran through it and flowed on down to a pasture where the Tennants grazed their cows.

Since DuPont owned the entire town, Tennant was at the end of his tether by the time he came around to calling Bilott as he had been rebuffed not only by Parkersburg's "lawyers but also by its politicians, journalists, doctors, and veterinarians."[35] The Parkersburg community would further shun him and his family once they finally sued DuPont, forcing them to change churches three times. Because he knew this woman in Vienna, a suburb north of Parkersburg, whose grandson was a Cincinnati attorney who had spent his summers as a young boy in the area, and as a seven-year-old had enjoyed one weekend at a farm adjacent to the Tennants where the boy had ridden horses, milked cows, and watched Secretariat win the Triple Crown on TV, Tennant reached out to Bilott for assistance. A few weeks later, as requested Tennant and his wife showed up at the Taft headquarters in downtown Cincinnati with cardboard boxes of videotapes, photographs, and documents of their dead, dying and dissected cows. Evidently, shortly after the sale of the land and the dumping of the sludge began, Tennant explained that his cattle started acting deranged. For decades, the cows had always been like pets to the Tennants. "At the sight of a Tennant they would amble over, nuzzle and let themselves be milked."[36] No longer was this the case. Now, when the cows "saw the farmers, they would charge."[37]

The camcorder produced images and the zooming in and out with Wilbur Tennant voiceovers reveal among other things, mounds of soapy froth, dead cattle and deer with blood running out of their noses and their mouths, and a large pipe running from the property into the creek, discharging green water with bubbles on the surface. Speaking in one of the videos Tennant explains that since he could not get any of the local veterinarians to even return his phone calls, he had to dissect some of these cows for himself. The video then cuts to a calf's bisected head, to close-ups of blackened teeth, and other liver, heart, stomach, and gall bladder discolorations that Tennant claimed were due to high concentrations of fluoride in the water. After hours of viewing the videos and stacks of photos, Bilott had seen cows with "stringy tails, malformed hooves, giant lesions protruding from their hides and red, receded eyes; cows suffering constant diarrhea, slobbering white slime the consistency of toothpaste, staggering like bowlegged drunks."[38]

Immediately, Bilott decided to take the law case as "it was the right thing to do" because this was "a bad situation." Keep in mind that Taft was a firm that had established a lucrative practice in the emerging field of environmental law by defending corporate polluters. Thanks to the passage of the Comprehensive Environmental Response, Compensation, and Liability Act (CERCLA) in 1980, otherwise known as the Superfund Act, Bilott's job as an associate was to work with a team of lawyers overseen by one of the senior partners to "determine which companies contributed which toxins and hazardous wastes in what quantities to which sites."[39] His role at the firm also required Bilott to take depositions from plant employees, to peruse public records, and to organize huge amounts of historical data.

In a relatively short time, Bilott became an expert on the Environmental Protection Agency's regulatory framework, the Safe Drinking Water Act, the Clean Air Act, and the Toxic Substances Control Act. Bilott also became a consummate insider, learning "how these companies work, how the laws work, and how you defend these claims" against corporate offenders.[40] Among those clients Bilott had once represented were Thiokol and Bee Chemical. These companies had been carelessly disposing of hazardous waste long before polluting was subject to anything that remotely looked like regulation or environmental protection. In short, who better than Rob Bilott to civilly prosecute these DuPont criminals? Taking on Tennant's case radically changed Bilott's law practice.

Since filing his first federal lawsuit in the Southern District in West Virginia against DuPont in the summer of 1999, Bilott has never again defended another corporation accused of environmental contamination. In fact, for the past seventeen years Bilott has spent all his time doing nothing else besides suing DuPont in relation to violations of health and safety laws in West Virginia. In response to his 1999 filing, DuPont's in-house lawyer informed Bilott that "DuPont and the E.P. A. would commission a study of the property, conducted by three veterinarians chosen by DuPont and three chosen by the E.P.A."[41] Their report did not find DuPont responsible for any of the cattle's health problems. Rather, the report blamed the Tennants for their poor husbandry: "'poor nutrition, inadequate veterinary care and lack of fly control.' In other words, the Tennants did not know how to raise cattle; if the cows were dying, it was their own fault."[42] Never mind the Tennant family history of more than three decades of raising cattle successfully.

Meanwhile, in preparation for the trial, Bilott retained a West Virginia lawyer named Larry Winter, who was a partner at Spilman, Thomas & Battle, just one of the local law firms that represented DuPont in that state. He also retained a chemistry expert to assist with the case, as he would have done in defending any corporate client. Similarly, Bilott engaged in pulling permits, studying land deeds, and in this instance, of course, requesting from DuPont all documentation pertaining to the Dry Run Landfill, which yielded no evidence that could explain what happened to Tennant's cattle. However, he did come across a letter that DuPont had sent to the EPA that referred to a substance at the landfill—PFOA. Despite all of his years of working with chemical companies, Bilott had never heard of the substance. He could find nothing about PFOA in Taft's in-house library, nor did it appear on any governmental lists of regulated materials. However, his chemistry expert vaguely remembered a journal article about a similar sounding compound, PFOS, "a soaplike agent used by the technology conglomerate 3M in the fabrication of Scotchgard."[43] Immediately thereafter, Bilott requested all documentation from DuPont on the substance. DuPont refused to turn over any information they possessed on PFOA.

In early 2000 Bilott requested and was granted a court order forcing DuPont over their strong protests to turn over their documentation of PFOA. As a consequence DuPont turned over a half century of materials, dozens of boxes containing thousands of unorganized documents, including private internal correspondence, medical and health reports, and confidential studies conducted by DuPont scientists, totalling more than 110,000 pages. After spending the next few months on the floor of his office poring over documents and arranging them chronologically, it became apparent to Bilott that DuPont "had known for a long time that this stuff was bad."[44] In another statement, Bilott could not believe the amount of incriminating material that DuPont had delivered to him: "It was one of those things where you can't believe you're reading what you're reading ... It was the kind of stuff you always heard about happening but you never thought you'd see written down."[45]

In August 2000 Bilott made a brief call to DuPont's lawyer letting them know that he knew exactly what had been transpiring all these years. The Tennants quickly settled their claim, and the Taft firm collected its contingency fee.

However, Bilott was not satisfied with the outcome. More than that he was irritated, because these firms were not like those that he had represented in cases resulting from the Superfund Act: "This was a completely different scenario. DuPont had for decades been actively trying to conceal their actions. They knew the stuff was harmful, and they put it in the water anyway."[46] Bilott could not let the whole toxic affair end with the Tennant case. He knew firsthand what the PFOA-tainted drinking water had done to the cattle. With respect to the tens of thousands of humans drinking the water from their taps, he could only wonder what the inside of their brains looked like and whether or not their internal organs were also green.

On March 6, 2001, Bilott sent a 972-page public brief, including 136 attached exhibits, to every relevant regulatory agency, to Christie Whitman, the administrator of the EPA, and to John Ashcroft, the U.S. Attorney General. In "Rob's Famous Letter" as it became known in environmental legal studies, his bottom line was simply: "We have confirmed that the chemicals and pollutants released into the environment by DuPont at its Dry Run Landfill and other nearby DuPont-owned facilities may pose an imminent and substantial threat to health or environment."[47] His demanded remedies consisted of immediate action to regulate PFOA and to provide clean drinking water to the people living near the factory. DuPont reacted quickly, seeking a gag order to block Bilott from sharing the information that he had discovered in the Tennant case and from speaking to the Environmental Protection Agency. A federal court denied the DuPont request and Bilott sent his entire case file to the EPA.

This was another transformative moment for Bilott. In the process of claiming extensive fraud and wrongdoing by a chemical giant, he had now become a highly visible advocate for environmental justice. In effect, Bilott had, according to an internal memo, opened up Pandora's box posing not merely a threat to DuPont, but to "the entire fluoropolymers industry." After all, PFOA is only one of more than 60,000 synthetic chemicals that companies purchase and release into the world everyday without regulatory oversight. As one of Bilott's colleagues has explained, "Rob's letter lifted the curtain on a whole new theater."[48] Up until that time, "corporations could rely upon the public misperception that if a chemical was dangerous, it was regulated."[49] That is to say, Bilott had exposed the arrangement created by the 1976 Toxic Substances Control Act that prohibits the EPA from testing chemicals without first having evidence of the substance's harm. A classic Catch 22 of nonintervention, a case of state-routinized crime where these chemical companies find themselves in the position of self-regulation. This might have something to do with the fact that in forty years the Environmental Protection Agency has restricted only five chemicals out of tens of thousands on the market.

In 2006, DuPont reached a $16.5 million settlement with the EPA, its largest fine at the time, without the company having to admit liability for concealing its knowledge of PFOA's toxicity or for its presence in the environment in violation of the Toxic Substances Control Act. The fine represented less than 2 percent of the profits earned by DuPont on PFOA that year. Still not satisfied, Bilott moved to the next logical step, filing a class-action suit against DuPont, which might possibly set a precedent for suing other corporations over unregulated substances. It was not long afterwards that plaintiffs started materializing, especially those who were currently or had been employed at Washington Works and were familiar with what the workers there referred to as the "Teflon flu" (e.g., fever, nausea, diarrhea, vomiting), a condition that happened after working in one of the PFOA storage tanks. As an unregulated substance, the class-action suit faced an uphill battle, because the health effects of PFOA were unknown. In other words, how could the class prove that PFOA had harmed any of them? Bilott came up with an alternative legal strategy, using in tort law what is called a "medical-monitoring claim," thanks to West Virginia becoming one of the earliest states to adopt this type of tort in the United States.

Without going into any more of the details—especially the scientific ones involved in certifying this class action in 2011, for example, that scientists had to first determine how many parts of PFOA per parts of water was acceptable or unacceptable with respect to human health and safety—the scientific "debate" about where one draws the line runs throughout this legal litigation. Recall the situation when together DuPont scientists and EPA scientists had decided the validity of Tennant's claims. In the context of determining what counts for a relationship between PFOA and harm or injury, there was a team of regulatory scientists that included two former DuPont scientists assigned to this task. It took them seven years to conduct their research, analyzing both the data and the effects of PFOA on the residents of Parkersburg, Their findings met the burden of "probable link" between PFOA and kidney cancer, testicular cancer, thyroid disease, high cholesterol, pre-eclampsia, and ulcerative colitis. Put simply, there was relief owed to these victims or their families in the case of any related deaths.

As of October 2015, 3,535 plaintiffs had filed personal-injury lawsuits against DuPont. The first member of this class to go to trial, a kidney-cancer survivor, Carla Bartlett, received an award of $1.6 million last fall. Of course, DuPont is appealing. Bartlett's case is one of five "bellwether" cases scheduled for trial in 2016. Based on the results of these cases, DuPont "may choose to settle with every afflicted class member, using the outcome of the bellwether cases to determine the settlement awards. Or DuPont can fight each suit individually, a tactic that tobacco companies used to fight personal-injury lawsuits."[50] Using the rate of four trials per year, DuPont would not finish fighting these PFOA cases until the year 2890.

Dow Chemical Company: a trailblazer in multinational criminality

As a trailblazer in "cheminality," Dow has an infamous corporate rap sheet, which includes a history of war crimes and human rights violations, environmental crimes, murder, product safety violations, occupational safety and health violations, union breaking, price-fixing, tax evasion, and violations of due diligence.[51] Dow also has been called the "chemical companies' chemical company" in that most of its sales have been to other industries rather than to end-users. Dow also sells its goods directly to end-users, such as chemicals, plastics, and agricultural products and services to consumer markets in food, transportation, health and medicine, personal care, and construction. With operations in 180 countries, Dow ranked third in chemical production in 2014; its sales were approximately $58.2 billion. In 2015, as already noted, Dow and DuPont announced their desire to become DowDupont.

Dow Chemical Company is an American multinational corporation headquartered in Midland, Michigan. It was founded in 1897 by a Canadian-born chemist Herbert Henry Dow who had invented a method of extracting bromine that was trapped underground in brine. Pretty much from its beginning, Dow's Midland operations were having problems with noxious emissions from the dumping of its initial products, bleach and potassium bromide, which eventually lead to charges of serious environmental health hazards. During this formative era, Dow began diversifying, manufacturing magnesium for incendiary flares, phenol and monochlorobenzene for explosives, and using bromide for medicines and tear gas. By the start of the First World War, Dow was already occupying a significant place in the world market when the chemical company began devoting 90 percent of its production to the war effort. Throughout the two World Wars, Dow was becoming part of the developing military-industrial war complex.

After the Second World War, expansion became multinational with Japanese and Canadian subsidiaries appearing, as well as multiple operations in the United States. The diversification of products continued as well. At Freeport, Texas, Dow's facility produced chlorine, caustic soda, and ethylene as well as bromine from seawater (rather than brine). There was the development of silicone for military, and subsequently, for civilian use, plastics, synthetic rubber, and in 1953 Saran wrap. Flash-forward, throughout the 1980s and 1990s, class-action lawsuits claimed that Dow Corning's (a joint venture between Dow and Corning Incorporated) ruptured silicone breast implants caused all types of health problems, including breast cancer, a range of autoimmune diseases including lupus, rheumatoid arthritis and an assortment of neurological problems. A number of independent reviews of the scientific literature, including the Institute of Medicine in the U.S. determined that silicone breast implants do cause breast cancers and other identifiable systemic diseases. Dow Corning reached a multibillion-dollar class action settlement, placing Dow Corning in bankruptcy protection for nine years, ending in June 2004. On October 6, 2005 the U.S. Court of Appeals for the Sixth Circuit would dismiss the claims filed for personal damages caused by ruptured silicone breast implants.[52]

From 1951 to 1975 Dow managed a nuclear weapons production facility for the U.S. Department of Energy at Rocky Flats near Denver, Colorado, making cores for nuclear bombs and plutonium triggers for hydrogen bombs. Because of secrecy or national security, only the workers in the plant had knowledge about the radioactive contaminants. Dow had informed those residents living in the nearby area that the company was making cleaning products.[53] Before the U.S. Department of Energy transferred management of the plant to Rockwell International in 1975, there had been several fires and instances of radioactive waste leakage and contamination, which should have closed the plant down.[54] Dow had also been illegally storing and dumping its nuclear waste.

In 1957 a fire of burning plutonium dust in the Rocky Flats plant sent radioactive particles into the atmosphere, nearly becoming a catastrophic nuclear meltdown.[55] In 1990, residents in the area filed a class action suit against both Dow and Rockwell for environmental pollution. Almost two decades later, in 2008, the case was litigated in federal court where the two companies were ordered to pay a combined $925 million in damages to the plaintiffs who had claimed that they were harmed by airborne contamination from the facility.[56] However, in 2010 the U.S. Court of Appeals for the Tenth Circuit reversed the decision.[57]

The Appellate Court ruled that the 12,000 property-owning plaintiffs had not proved that their properties had been damaged or that they had suffered from bodily injury from those unregulated radioactive substances where no standards had been established. Recalling the DuPont causality case and the question of the harm done by PFOA, scientists took seven years of research to establish harmful levels standards and to statistically link the harmful health effects of the substance to various bodily organs before class-action litigation could begin. Ironically perhaps, the abandoned weapons facility at Rocky Flats has become the Rocky Flats National Wildlife Refuge, an allegedly environmentally safe and protected area.

By the 1960s Dow was on its way to becoming the world's largest producer of chlorine and chorine-based products, considered to be the largest root source of human as contrasted to natural dioxins, a highly toxic environmental pollutant that can cause cancer, developmental and reproductive problems, damage the immune system, and interfere with hormone activity. During the same period, in its New Plymouth, New Zealand plant, Dow was busy manufacturing Agent Orange, a chemical defoliant containing dioxin. Meanwhile, in its Torrance, California, plant, Dow was fulfilling a governmental contract to produce the incendiary agent napalm B compound.

In an effort to determine the risks of human exposure to dioxin, as many as seventy paid volunteers, mostly black inmates between the ages of 21 and 49 at Holmesburg prison in Philadelphia had dioxins spread on their skin as part of a scientifically commissioned study by Dow in the 1960s. At the same time, another experiment on fifty-one other prisoners was also conducted. These studies came to light by the Environmental Protection Agency investigation in the 1980s. Unfortunately, the identities of tested inmates were never found, so no long-term effects of dioxins were ever obtained. Short-term results indicated that those inmates exposed topically to dioxins (as opposed to the usual route of dioxin exposure by way of consuming the substance in animals and plants subject to herbicides and pesticides), depending on the amounts administered, suffered cases of chloracne, a temporary skin condition, but nothing more serious. Nearly 300 inmates contesting those conclusions filed a lawsuit against Dow and others, but the courts ruled that the statues of limitations had already expired.[58]

During the Vietnam War, the U.S. military was dropping napalm bombs on North Vietnamese, made possible by several chemical companies, including Dow.

Napalm is like jellied gasoline that sticks to skin and often burns its victims to death in great pain. Public protests against the manufacturing and use of both napalm and Agent Orange and the adverse publicity in the 1960s resulted in Dow becoming the sole producer of napalm and one of two makers of Agent Orange. The other was Monsanto Company. At the time, Agent Orange was a defoliant used to deprive guerillas of cover and to pressure peasants to relocate to areas under U.S. military control. Regarding the continued production of napalm, Dow had maintained as a matter of principle, "its first obligation was to the government."[59] Despite the continued boycott of some of their products by antiwar protesters, Dow continued its production of napalm until 1969. The United States did not discontinue dropping napalm bombs on North Vietnam until 1973.

In 2001, Dow Chemical acquired Union Carbide, which had been responsible for the Bhopal, India, poison gas disaster when its pesticide plant exploded on the night of September 2–3, 1984. Considered to be among the world's worst industrial disasters, the explosion released over forty tons of methyl isocyanate gas, immediately killing some 2,250 people and affecting as many as 500,000 more. Subsequently, between 15,000 and 30,000 people have been estimated to have died and that tens of thousands still remain sick as a consequence of this industrial "accident" where safety regulations were inadequate or disregarded.[60] Despite the profitability of Dow Chemical, much of the toxic waste has not been cleaned up and remains in Bhopal. Since its acquisition of Union Carbide, Dow has rejected any responsibility for the survivors and victims of the chemical disaster and has repeatedly failed to respond or appear in Indian courts for legal proceedings concerning the incident. The chemical giant has maintained that it has no liability for the victims injured by Union Carbide, which occurred long before the chemical and polymers company became a subsidiary of Dow.[61] Similar arguments are heard from other corporations that have acquired other corporations facing bankruptcy, debt repayments to investors, and/or compensatory damages such as when Bank of America acquired Washington Mutual Bank or American Insurance Group in the run up to and during the Wall Street financial implosion of 2008–2009.

In 2004 the Vietnam Association for Victims of Agent Orange filed a class action lawsuit against both Dow and Monsanto on behalf of millions of Vietnamese people, who had been exposed to the spraying of nearly 20 million gallons of the substance during the war and to the ongoing horrible health effects of the dioxin still present in the environment. In addition to the vast number of deaths and suffering caused by dioxin poisoning, there were the environmental issues of deforestation that upset the ecological balance of many areas as well as the ongoing contamination of a food chain still affected by the lingering dioxin in the soil and water. In 2005 the case was dismissed and upheld on appeal in 2007. These plaintiffs were unlike the thousands of lawsuits filed by Vietnam veterans against Dow and other Agent Orange producers who settled out of court in 1984. This settlement created a $180 million fund for Vietnam veteran Agent Orange victims. These plaintiffs had charged that the dioxin in Agent Orange caused liver damage, nervous disorders, birth defects, and other health problems.

It was not until the lawsuits were consolidated and documents were discovered that revealed that Dow had known since 1965 that dioxin was exceptionally toxic that Dow finally stopped downplaying the ill health effects of dioxin and settled the class-action lawsuit. Only one year previously in 1983, Dow was running a $3 million advertising campaign to persuade the public that dioxin was nothing to be worried about. When the EPA forced Dow to turn over key documents in preparation for litigation, the 1960s dioxin inmate experiments were revealed for the first time to the public, as was the dioxin contamination at the Midland plant in Michigan and the company's role in having an official EPA report remove the references to Dow's contamination of waterways in Michigan. For decades Dow continued to resist cleaning up the dioxin in Midland.

A 2004 *Detroit Free Press* article, "Battle Rages Over Cleanup of Dow's Toxic Legacy," reported:

> For 16 years, since a federal study said that Dow Chemical Co. dioxin posed substantial health risks, the state [of Michigan] and Dow have bickered over how and when a cleanup should begin, amid charges of Dow foot-dragging and spotty state enforcement.[62]

Subsequently, in 2007 the *Detroit Free Press* obtained a confidential EPA report that described "Dow's efforts to delay a cleanup and mislead the public about the dangers of dioxin."[63] One year later, the EPA's top administrator for the Midwest said that she "had been forced to resign by the Bush Administration because of her efforts to get Dow to finally start dealing with dioxin contamination."[64] The next year, in 2009, Dow and the EPA announced an agreement on a clean up plan. Finally, in 2011 Dow agreed to pay a paltry $2.5 million to the EPA to settle alleged violations of the Clean Air Act, the Clean Water Act, and the Resource Conservation and Recovery Act at its Midland operation and corporate headquarters.

Given the record of Dow's litigation "wins" and "losses" over the past fifty years, the chemical giant has done reasonably well, especially when one considers that the corporation has almost always been culpable, although not usually legalistically, for one reason or another. As the story goes in the United States, if not elsewhere, there are corporations who "dominate and injure individuals because they have powerful legal representation and unlimited resources to crush the little guy in the justice system by drawing out a case for years."[65] Of course, there are also those very rare occasions

> when powerful corporations meet their matches and lose lawsuits because many separate individuals band together to form a class that is able to afford powerful legal representation equal to corporate giants, and with a level playing field, corporations are not guaranteed victory.[66]

Apparently, the rarities of these successful class-action lawsuits over the past several decades in the United States has been too much for the powerful corporations to bear, so they have managed to lobby against the use of class-actions and for the trending of class-action lawsuits not being certified, as increasingly plaintiffs are required to prove substantial portions of their cases on the merits at the time of class certification and because the certification requirements themselves pertaining to class definition, numerosity, commonality and so on, have become considerably more difficult to satisfy today than they once were.[67]

More broadly, it has been argued that the U.S. Supreme Court "has replaced Congress in making laws with no recourse to recall or impeach the corporatist majority," and that "there is little for the American people to do except wait to be poisoned, discriminated against, or deprived of our diminishing freedoms."[68] In eroding away the right to class-action lawsuits, the laws of the land are taking away "the only weapon the little guy has to fight corporations, and when the next toxic spill, bad drug, or oil pipeline explosion occurs, the victims will have to accept responsibility for being in the wrong place at the wrong time. It is unfortunate, but the High Court has made every place in America a danger zone because corporations have no impetus to follow safety standards or protect the environment".[69]

In fact, in 2011 Dow Chemical was allowed to get away with polluting Michigan, when a state judge, Leopold Borello, who had granted class status to hear a case between 100 land owners and Dow, reversed his decision. Although the case met Michigan guidelines for class status, the judge decertified the class action because of the U.S. Supreme Court's decision in the *Wal-Mart v. Dukes* case earlier in the year. The case had disallowed women from suing the retailing behemoth as a class to recoup lost wages due to gender discrimination, creating new rules for what a group must have in common with one another in order to be considered a class. While the federal rules did change, they should have had no bearing on recertifying a class action in the state of Michigan, yet Judge Borello acquiesced accordingly to a motion made by Dow to dismiss the class action.

The Michigan case involved landowners within the vicinity of Dow's Midland facility who had complained that when rivers downstream flooded and sediment laden with dioxin was deposited on to properties in the floodplain, the multinational corporation was spreading dioxin, a highly toxic and cancer-causing by-product of the chemical manufacturing process through the Tittabawassee and Saginaw Rivers and into Lake Huron. The tested soil samples of floodplain properties did reveal

> dioxin contamination thousands of times higher than Michigan allows and prompted health officials to warn property owners to wear masks while mowing their lawns, keep children from playing in dirt near their homes, avoid eating fish and livestock raised in the floodplain, and to take other precautions to keep from being poisoned.[70]

In addition to the ill health effects that the landowners may have experienced, they claimed that because of the dioxin contamination they were not able to make full use of their properties and the value of their property was steadily diminishing. Unfortunately, with Judge Borello's reversal, the property owners in Michigan have had no recourse to ever recoup damages from Dow's negligent actions and they are stuck living on poisoned land that can be neither sold nor reclaimed.

Politically, the Republican side of the American electorate has for many years been in favor of protecting corporate malfeasance with its calls for tort reform to eliminate an individual's collective ability to file class action lawsuits against corporations guilty of causing injury from negligence and discrimination. With the High Court's Wal-Mart decision in 2011 bypassing the state legislative processes to resist passing tort reforms, the Republicans had finally won and corporations are worrying less and less about being sued by class-actions. Individuals, of course, may still file their own lawsuits against corporations if they can afford to hire an attorney, however, they will "hardly be a match for a corporation's legal team, and often, a case will hang on for many years until the plaintiff runs out of money or dies."[71]

Beyond Dow being let off the hook with impunity for poisoning the environment surrounding its chemical plant in Midland, Michigan, this chemical corporation as well as other corporations, chemical or otherwise, can ignore environmental protections, because without the chance of class lawsuits, they will simply keep claiming that they are not guilty of injuring anyone. In other words, without any judgments against these corporations, a corporation will be innocent regardless of how much damage they have caused. And, following the Wal-Mart decision that cost millions of female employees "equal pay" and the tossing out of Michiganders' claims against Dow as precedents, BP began looking for judges to toss out the class-action lawsuits against them for the Gulf of Mexico oil spill.

The year 2013 was not a good one for Dow legalistically. In February a federal court found the company guilty of tax evasion, rejecting two tax shelter transactions entered into by Dow that created approximately $1 billion in tax deductions between 1993 and 2002. In its stated opinion, the Court termed the transactions as "schemes that were designed to exploit perceived weaknesses in the tax code and not designed for legitimate business reasons." Goldman Sachs and the law firm of King and Spaulding (one of the world's largest international law practices with more than 900 associated lawyers and offices located throughout the U.S., Europe, the Middle East, and Asia) created these illegal tax shelters. These forms of tax evasion involved the establishment of a partnership that Dow operated out of its European headquarters in Switzerland. Dow appealed the decision to the U.S. Court of Appeals for the Fifth Circuit where their claims were again rejected. In turn Dow petitioned the Fifth Circuit for an *en banc* hearing arguing that the decision was contrary to established case law. This petition was denied.

Then, in May, U.S. District Judge John W. Lungstrum ordered Dow "to pay $1.2 billion in a price-fixing case involving chemicals used to make foam products in cars, furniture, and packaging."[72] Back in January, the chemical company had gone on trial in Kansas City, Kansas, and in February the federal jury rendered a $400 million verdict against Dow after finding that it had conspired to fix prices of urethane. Three months later Judge Lungstrum denied Dow's appeal of the judgment and a request to overturn the verdict of $400 million in damages, and invoking U.S. antitrust law, he tripled the damage award. According to the plaintiffs' attorney, Joe Goldberg, the "jury found the conspiracy caused approximately $400 million in damages to thousands of businesses" in the United States.[73] Originally filed as a class-action lawsuit in 2005 alleging a conspiracy to fix urethane chemical prices, the three other defendants, without having to admit any wrongdoing, settled as follows: in 2006 Bayer AG agreed to pay $55 million; in 2011 Huntsman International LLC agreed to pay $33 million; and BASF Corp agreed to pay $51 million. Dow has appealed the judgment on several grounds, including the claim that the statistical formula used by the expert to calculate the price-fixing was not reliable.[74]

Monsanto Corporation: masters of fraud, deception, and public relations

In a 2014 Harris Poll measuring the "reputation quotient" of major multinational corporations, Monsanto ranked third lowest, above BP and Bank of America, and just behind Halliburton. In the sociopolitical imagination, the company's name "has become shorthand for corporate villainy, like Standard Oil a century ago or the private military contractor "Blackwater" of Iraq ignominy, whose reputation problems have led the corporation to change its branding name several times.[75] Monsanto has also been a target of ongoing campaigns and protests for some twenty years, especially around issues of genetically modified foods, including those hundreds of cities from around the world that participated in the second annual March Against Monsanto actions on May 24, 2014. On that day in New York City

> a couple thousand protesters gathered in Union Square, next to a farmers market, to hear speakers charge that the company was fighting efforts in states all over the country to mandate the labelling of GM foods; that organic crops were being polluted by GM pollen blown in on the wind, only for Monsanto to sue the organic farmers for intellectual-property theft; that Monsanto had developed a "Terminator" gene that made crops sterile.[76]

With such negative labels as the evil "Mutanto" and the purveyor of Frankenfoods, Monsanto has reinforced what has always been an aggressive lobbying, marketing, and public relations campaign, buttressed by both an offensive and defensive legal strategy. When faced with opposition to its products and policies such as those involving genetically modified organisms, Monsanto has not hesitated to retain high-powered assistance from the federal government:

> In the late 1990s it got members of the Clinton Administration to lobby against possible European restrictions on GMOs. In Washington it made use of U.S. Senator Dennis DeConcini and John Chaffee to promote its interests on issues ranging from patents to taxes. And it made frequent use of the revolving door by hiring former federal bureaucrats to join its army of lobbyists ... Among those was Carol Tucker Foreman, who had served both as assistant secretary of agriculture during the Carter Administration and as executive director of the Consumer Federation of America.[77]

For example, Monsanto has gone into court to sue farmers that it claimed were not following the company's strict rules on how its products can and cannot be used.

Some of their lawsuits have gone to the U.S. Supreme Court, where in 2013 the court strongly affirmed Monsanto's patent rights. The multinational also has its tentacles wrapped around the U.S. Congress that past the short-lived and what critics refer to as the Monsanto Protection Act, "limiting the ability of federal courts to halt the sale of genetically engineered seeds deemed to pose a health risk."[78] Otherwise known as the Farmer Assurance Provision, Republicans slipped this legal rider, or exemption, into a 2013 governmental spending bill that shielded sellers of genetically modified seeds from lawsuits, while it "instructed the Secretary of Agriculture to allow GMO crops to be cultivated and sold even when courts had found they posed a potential risk to farmers or nearby crops, the environment, and human health."[79] Subsequently, after the Monsanto rider had been publicly exposed and was set to expire, the Democrats led by Senator Jeff Merkley of Oregon were able to defeat its extension.

Over a period of several decades, contemporary history has seen Monsanto transform itself from a controversial chemical company into a more controversial biotechnology corporation that holds a dominant position in the herbicide and genetically engineered seed markets. Today, Monsanto Company is a publicly traded American multinational agrochemical and agricultural biotechnology corporation headquartered in Missouri's greater metropolitan area of St. Louis. The worldwide public image of Monsanto is currently that of a company most identified with introducing and producing GMOs into the food supply.

Founded in 1901 by John Francis Queeny, the company initially produced food additives like saccharin and vanillin. By the 1920s, Monsanto had expanded into industrial chemicals like sulfuric acid and PCBs; by the 1940s it was a major producer of plastics, including polystyrene and synthetic fibers. Much of their manufactured products post-World War II are no longer in production, such as the insecticide DDT, PCBs, Agent Orange, and recombinant bovine somatotropin, also known as bovine growth hormone. During the 1980s Monsanto was one of four groups to genetically modify plant cells and to conduct field trials of genetically modified crops. Between 1997 and 2002, the company divested most of its chemical businesses through a process of mergers and spin-offs that ultimately left it focusing on biotechnology. Presently, Monsanto is a leading producer of genetically engineered seeds and Roundup, a glyphosate-based herbicide, used primarily to kill weeds.

From its origins, Monsanto's history has always been contentious, from its role in agricultural change to its application of the biotechnology industry model to agriculture, to the manufacturing of its biotechnology products, to its use and enforcement of biological patents, and to its seed patenting model that has been criticized as biopiracy and as a threat to biodiversity.[80] For example, in 1972, the EPA banned DDT because of its negative impact on the environment and human health, a decade after the publication of Rachel Carson's best selling *Silent Spring* (1962) told the story of how DDT had decimated some bird species including the bald eagle and the peregrine falcon. With some minor exceptions, the Stockholm Convention of Persistent Organic Pollutants eventually banned DDT worldwide in 2004. For the past couple of decades Monsanto has had to contend with the anti-GMO movement in general and the labeling of GMO foods in particular. As far back as the early 1990s when Monsanto introduced the genetically modified seeds,

> it forced farmers to sign contracts prohibiting them from continuing the traditional practice of saving some of the seeds from a harvest for planting the following season. To make sure farmers complied to purchase a new supply of GMO seeds for every season, the company made sure it had the right to inspect and monitor the fields of its customers.[81]

As noted above, Monsanto has filed lawsuits against those farmers it claims have violated those agreements.

A recent history of the growing opposition to GMOs in Europe and elsewhere, includes more than 1,000 poor farmers storming and occupying a Monsanto plant in 2001. The same year that the U.S. Department of Agriculture announced that Monsanto and its research partners had paid a tiny fine of $63,000 back in 2001 for formerly undisclosed violations relating to the testing of genetically modified crops, the Bush Administration also "sought to assist Monsanto and the rest of the GMO industry with the 2003 filing of a World Trade Organization action against the European moratorium against their products," which resulted in the bans later being lifted for some crops.[82] One of the most interesting offensive legal cases was in 2003 when Monsanto sued a small milk producer in Maine for supposedly disparaging its Posilac artificial growth hormone by labeling his milk as being free of the substance. In 2004, bowing to worldwide protests, Monsanto abandoned its GMO wheat project. In 2007, a federal judge in San Francisco ordered the company to suspend sales of genetically engineered alfalfa "because the USDA had approved it without conducting an environmental impact assessment."[83] This was the first time a court had ever taken such an action against an agribusiness. Appealing all the way to the U.S. Supreme Court in 2010, the ruling was overturned on behalf of Monsanto, the same year that the Environmental Protection Agency announced that Monsanto was paying a "cost of doing business" fine of $2.5 million for selling mislabeled bags of genetically engineered cotton seed. In 2011 there was also the adverse publicity linking Monsanto's GMO crops, in combinations with their pesticides and herbicides, to the decline of honeybee populations as well as its Roundup product to the decrease in the population of Monarch butterflies. In 2012, a French court found Monsanto "guilty of chemically poisoning a farmer who reported suffering neurological problems after using one of the company's herbicides."[84]

At its official website, www.monsanto.com, the "Monsanto at a Glance" page describes the multinational corporation as a "sustainable agricultural company" that delivers agricultural products to support farmers all around the world:

> We are focused on empowering farmers—large and small—to produce more from their land while conserving more of our world's natural resources such as water and energy. We do this with our leading seed brands in crops like corn, cotton, oilseeds and fruits and vegetables. We also produce leading in-the-seed

trait technologies for farmers, which are aimed at protecting their yield, supporting their on-farm efficiency and reducing their on-farm costs.[85]

Monsanto financial highlights for the year ending August 31, 2015 were $15 billion in net sales and a cash flow of $2 billion. Nowhere to be found at their website were any references to the company's illustrious history of fraud and deception, false advertising, or environmental degradation. In terms of one public relations chicanery in particular, Monsanto staged a protest outside of an FDA hearing in Washington, D.C. on genetically engineered crops, paying protesters to conduct a counter-demonstration in support of GMOs.[86]

Monsanto has thrice been found to have produced false advertising related to Roundup and its genetically engineered crops. In 1996, the Attorney General of New York State fined Monsanto $50,000 for false advertising regarding claims that Roundup is "environmentally friendly" and biodegradable.[87] In 1999, the UK Advertising Standards Authority condemned Monsanto for issuing "wrong, unproven, misleading and confusing" claims in its advertising.[88] In 2009, France's highest court upheld two lower French courts convicting Monsanto of falsely advertising that its herbicide Roundup is "biodegradable" and that it "left the soil clean."[89] More recently, an interesting exchange took place when an October 20, 2013, *Associated Press* article raised questions about the health risks of Roundup used in Argentina, citing doctors who were "warning that uncontrolled pesticide applications could be the cause of growing health problems" in the region, in which two days later, through the *Associated Press* Monsanto had criticized the *AP* report as lacking in specifics about health impacts, even though the original story had cited "hospital birth records, court records, peer-reviewed studies, continuing epidemiological surveys, pesticide industry and government data, and a comprehensive audit of agrochemical use in 2008–2011 prepared by Argentina's bipartisan Auditor General's Office."[90]

A listing of other consequential crimes against the environment and public safety include:

- In 1986 a federal jury in Galveston, Texas, found Monsanto guilty of negligence and ordered it to pay $108 million to the family of a worker who had died from leukemia after being exposed to benzene at the chemical facility. Monsanto had refused to pay workers' compensation to the family, insisting that the disease was not work related. After the huge award was overturned, the family settled for a reasonable $6 million.
- In 1987 a state court jury found Monsanto liable for failing to warn the residents of Sturgeon, Missouri, about the risks associated with a 1979 train accident that spilled chemicals, including dioxin. Although the residents were granted more than $16 million in damages, the award was later overturned.
- In 1988 Monsanto agreed to pay $1.5 million to settle a lawsuit that had been brought by a group of workers who charged that exposure to a rubber additive at the company's plant in Nitro, West Virginia, had caused them to contract a rare forms of bladder cancer.

- In 2003, Monsanto, still liable for some of its unresolved matters from its older chemical businesses along with Solutia and Pfizer (which had acquired Pharmacia), agreed to pay $700 million to settle a lawsuit over the dumping of PCBs in Anniston, Alabama.
- In 2007 *The Guardian* reported that it was in the possession of evidence that dozens of dangerous chemicals related to dioxin, Agent Orange, and PCBs were leaking from an unlined quarry in Britain that was among various land-fills in the country believed to have been used as dumping sites for contractors working for Monsanto decades earlier.[91]

Spatial limitations prohibit me from going into a number of Monsanto legal cases involving corrupt practices, antitrust violations, and worker discrimination.

In their critical and holistic approach to and overview of key food crimes involved in the production, distribution, and selling of basic foodstuffs, Allyson Gray and Ron Hinch have underscored:

agritech corporations have employed a variety of legal and sometimes illegal methods to promote their business interests. They have used patent laws to overturn traditional farming practices, sometimes penalizing even those farmers who have innocently grown [genetically modified foods]. They have collaborated with governing bodies, including national states and international organizations such as the WTO, whenever they encounter resistance to their products. Thus patent laws are not only poorly framed, virtually allowing the control of life forms and not just the GM process, but they are also poorly enforced, as exemplified by the successful litigation against farmers.[90]

These green criminologists concluded their analyses of food crime and its relationship to agritech companies' pursuit of profit-oriented bottom lines and increase in power or control over the food industry by saying:

Not only are the current laws (if existing) ineffective in providing safe environments, healthy food and healthy people but they are being (re) constructed, neglected and overridden by agritech corporations and agribusiness, often in collaboration with both local and global governing bodies.[93]

Unfettered fracking and the dangers of hydraulic fracturing

Increasingly, a growing number of criminologists, including a former President of the American Society of Criminology, Robert Agnew, are arguing that "the crimes of climate change" are globally positioning the human species for serious risks of extinction.[94] Hyperbolic or not, the potential harm and victimization from environmental crimes to the Earth's ecosystems may ultimately dwarf the combined costs from all the other crimes of the powerful. The diversity of environmental crimes related to climate change and multinational corporations spills over into multiple areas of harm and victimization. For example, take the case of logging.

Logging crimes include an array of offenses, ranging from timber theft to harvesting, transporting, purchasing, or selling timber illegally, to the corrupt means of gaining access to protected forests or the cutting of protected species of forest, and to destroying rain forests and their ecospecies pretty much with impunity. In some places in the world today, like Vietnam, "illegal logging is demolishing forests at appalling speed, largely for the United States and European markets."[95] In 2016, for example, a U.S. federal judge approved a settlement in a logging case involving the forests of Russia's Far East, the one remaining home to some 450 wild Siberian tigers and fifty wild Amur leopards. Nobody went to prison, but Lumber Liquidators, the largest retailer of hardwood flooring in the United States was fined pocket change of just $13.1 million. The felony was for importing and selling flooring via China that was illegally logged in the forests of Russia's Far East. Probably Lumber Liquidators is more notorious for a 2015 CBS *60 Minutes* program that exposed the company for having sold laminated flooring, also from China, that contained dangerous levels of a carcinogen: formaldehyde.[96]

In the case of greenhouse gas emissions, there are the contemporary crimes of hydraulic fracking carried out by multinational oil and natural gas industries. These "fracking crimes" are being carried out all around the globe from beneath the farms of Midland, Texas, or near the rivers and streams that empty into the Great Lakes of the northern United States, to the southern edge of the Sahara Desert in Timbuktu, Mali. Despite the efforts of powerful oil and gas lobbies to prevent the accumulation of scientific knowledge as well as the push back against the negative impact of fracking on global warming from an industry-funded MIT report, the anti-fracking movement has attracted the attention of scientists at Cornell and Harvard who have shown that the methane gas that escapes into the atmosphere from fracturing is more efficient than carbon dioxide in trapping heat. Thus, rather than fracking, for example, being a safer and cleaner alternative to coal, it turns out to exacerbate global warming and climate change.[97]

In their examination of "unfettered fracking," criminologists Jacquelynn Doyon and Elizabeth Bradshaw attempted to get a handle on both the regulatory practices of the industry and on the environmental and human health effects of fracking. In the United States, however, this cannot be reasonably accomplished because contrary to decades of fracking, there is still not a federal framework in place for regulating the hydraulic fracking industry. Hard to believe, the government has not performed any kind of comprehensive or uniform examination of the effects of fracking on water contamination, seismic activity, and workplace safety. Making matters worse, calls for transparency of the chemicals used in fracking fluids are shielded by "trade secrets" where "some 84 percent of the registered wells in the USA claim exemption from full disclosure."[98]

As for the presence of any federal regulations of fracking, they do not exist because the Energy Policy Act of 2005, otherwise known as the Halliburton Loophole, exempts oil and gas companies from several environmental protections laws, including both the Clean Water Act and the Safe Drinking Water Act. As a consequence, a hotchpotch of locally established policies currently exists within and between states, allowing for enormous latitude in implementing environmental protections and standards. At the same time, while there have been some grassroots political successes in banning fracking in certain communities and regions of the country, for the most part, big oil and gas have been able to stymie these "not in my backyard" efforts. Doyon and Bradshaw concluded their study by saying that without some type of uniform legislation based upon independent scientific research the prevailing economic logic of capital accumulation and the harmful effects of industrial fracking will continue unabated.[99]

In addition to the dangers posed to global warming from methane emissions, the evidence of pollution and environmental harm continues to mount in heavily fracked regions across the United States, accounting for ground and surface water contamination, dead livestock, and an array of cancer and respiratory illnesses on the rise.[100] So far, the fracking pursuit of "cheaper energy" appears to be endangering humans, animals, and the environment in five basic ways. First, in the Midwest and Eastern portions of the U.S. where underground acquifers supply much of the water that pours from folks' taps, the injection and explosion of hundreds of unnamed chemicals below ground is polluting the water and causing taps to light on fire. The "tons of toxic wastewater that results from the fracking process is either being left in newly created ponds, injected back below earth, or in some instances dumped straight into nearby creeks and streams, endangering both humans and wildlife."[101]

Second, in post-fracking areas such as Pittsburg, Pennsylvania, "inexplicable levels of radiation are appearing in the wastewater," and "radon, which happens to be the number one cause of lung cancer among non-smokers, has even traveled through pipes to spew out of kitchen stoves."[102] Speculation, if not explanation, surmises that well below the earth's surface the fracking process is now unleashing a variety of potential poisons, including radon, radium, and uranium from tightly packed detritus rock that dates back to a time before dinosaurs. Third, air quality levels near hydro-fracked gas wells in Wyoming have measured worse than New York City and Los Angeles. Wherever fracking wells are drilled into the ground, there are wellheads on the surface for ventilation. And, significantly, high levels of benzene—a cancer-causing pollutant proven to cause birth defects and leukemia—have been measured venting from these wellheads. Fourth, there are the toxic diesel fumes associated with the industries that are accompanying fracking, such as processing plants, thousands of miles of pipeline built to deliver the gas, not to mention the fleets of heavy duty trucks that deliver all that water and sand. These diesel fumes "are affecting ozone and smog levels near drilling sites, upping smog levels and increasing asthma."[103] Finally, not only are humans at risk but so too are animals and the land. For example, in Louisiana "migrating birds have changed centuries-old flying patterns to avoid poisoned water, and ranchers have reported herds losing hair and fish dying in ponds."[104] Moreover, what were once pristine rural areas of America are now on their way to becoming industrial wastelands.

Climate change, power plant regulations, and the U.S. Supreme Court stay as a potential unraveling of the Paris Agreement?

In December 2015, 195 nations adopted the first ever universal, legally binding global deal, subject to the signing and ratification that occurred by April 22, 2016, by at least fifty-five countries that accounted for at least 55 percent of global emissions at the time. In February 2016 the U.S. Supreme Court temporarily blocked the Obama Administration's effort and the EPA plan issued in the summer of 2015 to combat climate change by regulating emissions from coal-fired power plants. The Paris Agreement to avoid dangerous climate change by limiting global warming to well below 2 degrees centigrade was predicated upon the EPA's requirement that the states cut their greenhouse gas emissions created by electric power plants one third by 2030, compared to a 2005 baseline.

The arguments surrounding the litigation over President Obama's executive order are politically and ideologically illuminating, and they underscore the contradictions of sustainable capital accumulation. The implementation of the EPA plan requires the closing of hundreds of heavily polluting coal-fired plants as well as for the increased production of wind and solar power. The first deadline for power plants to reduce their emissions is in 2022, with full compliance not required until eight years later. The regulation also requires that the states were to submit their plans to comply by September 2016, though they could seek a two-year extension. As a consequence of the Supreme Court's unprecedented action in which a "generally applicable regulation pending initial judicial review in the court of appeals" was stayed, the new power plant regulations have been put on hold until after the appeals court "considers an expedited challenge from 29 states and dozens of corporations and industry groups."[105]

The states challenging the regulation, led mostly by Republicans and many "with economies that rely on coal mining or coal-fired plants, sued to stop what they called 'the most far-reaching and burdensome rule the E.P.A. has ever forced onto the states.'"[106] In a second filing seeking a stay, coal companies and trade associations represented by Laurence H. Tribe, a "liberal" law professor at Harvard, stated that they should act to stop a "targeted attack on the coal industry" that would "artificially eliminate buyers of coal, forcing the coal industry to curtail production, idle operations, lay off workers and close minds."[107] Well, that's the whole point of the plan and what 195 nations have allegedly agreed to pursue. Eighteen states, mostly led by Democrats, opposed the request for a stay, saying that they were "continuing to experience climate-change harms firsthand—including increased flooding, more severe storms, wildfires and droughts."[108] Such harms are "lasting and irreversible," they said, and "any stay that results in further delay in emissions reductions would compound the harms that climate change is already causing."[109]

The three-judge panel of the U.S. Court of Appeals for the District of Columbia Circuit in January 2016 unanimously refused to grant a stay; however, the court agreed to expedite the case and that it would hear arguments on June 2. A month later, the U.S. Supreme Court ruled 5–4 to grant the unprecedented stay. The two sides disagree about whether or not the current declines in coal mining and coal-fired power generation, including the declaration of bankruptcy by some of the nation's largest coal companies, are attributable to the administration's plan as the plaintiffs articulate or, as a coalition of environmental groups and companies that produce and rely on wind and solar power have maintained, due to changes stemming from an "abundant supply of relatively inexpensive natural gas, the increasing cost-competitiveness of electricity from renewable generation sources such as solar and wind power, the deployment of low-cost energy efficiency and other demand-side measures, and increasing consumer demand for advanced energy," not to mention "the rising costs of coal production and high costs of maintaining very old coal-fired plants."[110]

Regardless of the decision of the Court of Appeals, the losing side will undoubtedly bring the case back to the U.S. Supreme Court, which hopefully by that time will have replaced the late Justice Antonin Scalia, who died one week after the Supreme Court granted the stay (5–4) with his vote, leaving the esteemed body with eight justices and one vacancy. Although a potential solution to global warming and climate change may very well depend on a ruling by the Supreme Court, it now appears that the big banks are pulling out of the financing of new coal-fired power plants in the U.S. and in other wealthy nations. Allegedly they are looking to finance ventures that produce less carbon emissions, a trend that might signal a cleaner future. These changes, coincidentally, are occurring as coal companies are being squeezed by competition from less expensive energy sources like natural gas or wind turbines and by stiffer regulations. For example, three of the largest oil companies in the United States by the end of 2015 had already filed for bankruptcy protection. Most significantly, on March 20, 2016, Peabody Energy, the world's largest private sector coal company with operations in twenty-six countries spread out over six continents, announced that it too might have to file for bankruptcy protection in the near future.[111]

Notes

1 Richter, Greg. 2016. "USA Today Investigation: Excessive Lead in 2,000 Water Systems in Every State." *Newsmax*. March 16. www.newsmax.com/Newsfront/lead-flint-water-usa-today/2016/03/16/id/719477/.
2 Ibid.
3 Kristof, Nicholas. 2016. "Are You a Toxic Waste Disposal Site?" *The New York Times*. February 14: Sunday Review, pp. 1 and 9.
4 Ibid.
5 Ibid.
6 Covert, Bryce and Konczal, Mike. 2016. "Environmental Racism." *The Nation*. March 7: p. 5.
7 Ibid.
8 Christian-Smith, Juliet and Gleick, Peter. H. 2012. *A Twenty-First Century US Water Policy*. New York: Oxford University Press.
9 Pitt McGehee, Palmer & Rivers. 2016. "New Class-action Lawsuits Filed by Flint Residents." January 19. http://pittlawpc.com/2016/01/new-class-action-lawsuits-

filed-by-flint-residents-seek-compensation-for-injuries-damages-caused-by-legionella-bacteria-and-lead-tainted-water/.

10 Ibid. On March 19, 2016 the Mayor of Flint, Michigan announced the city is stopping its billing of residents for the city lead contaminated water.

11 Tribune News Services. 2016. "Flint Water Crisis: Criminal Charges to Be Announced, Government Officials Say." *Chicago Tribune*. April 20. www.chicagotri bune.com/news/nationworld/midwest/ct-flint-water-crisis-criminal-cha rges-20160419-story.html.

12 Ibid.

13 Covert and Konczal, 2016.

14 See, for example, Beirne, Piers and South, Nigel (eds.). 2007. *Issues in Green Criminology*. Devon, UK: Willan; Rothe, Dawn and Friedrichs, David. 2015. *Crimes of Globalization*. London and New York: Routledge; Stretesky, Paul, Long, Michael, and Lynch, Michael. 2013. *The Treadmill of Crime: Political Economy and Green Criminology*. London and New York: Routledge.

15 Lynch, Michael, Long, Michael, and Stetesky, Paul. 2015. "Anthropogenic Development Drives Species to Be Endangered: Capitalism and the Decline of Species." In *Green Harms and Crimes: Critical Criminology in a Changing World*, edited by Ragnhild Aslug Sollund. New York: Palgrave/Macmillan, p. 117.

16 Ibid.

17 Ibid., p. 123.

18 Stretesky *et al.*, 2013.

19 Lynch *et al.*, 2015, p. 119.

20 Ibid., p. 133.

21 Ibid., p. 134.

22 Ibid., p. 135.

23 Mulvany, Lydia, Forden, Sara, and Gower, Patrick. 2015. "Dow-DuPont Merger Likely to Face Antitrust Scrutiny Worldwide." *Bloomberg Business*. December 11. www.bloomberg.com/news/articles/2015-12-11/dow-dupont-merger-likely-to-face-antitrust-scrutiny-worldwide.

24 Ruskin, Gary. 2015. *Seedy Business: What Big Food is Hiding with Its Slick PR Campaign on GMOs*. Chapter 15. http://usrtk.org/seedybusiness.pdf.

25 Because of space limitations, I will not attempt to highlight in my following discussions of Dow and Monsanto the similar kinds of accolades that these two multinational corporations have received for their various efforts to become "greening" or "sustainable" enterprises.

26 DuPont. *Wikipedia*. https://en.wikipedia.org/wiki/DuPont.

27 The five other companies in the world that produce PFOA are also phasing out production.

28 Quoted in Rich, Nathaniel. 2016. "Rob Bilott v. DuPont." *The New York Times Magazine*. January 10: p. 59.

29 Rich, 2016, p. 61.

30 Ibid.

31 Ibid., p. 41.

32 Ibid.

33 Ibid., p. 42.

34 Ibid.

35 Ibid., p. 38.

36 Ibid.

37 Ibid.

38 Ibid., p. 39.

39 Ibid.

40 Quoted in ibid., p. 40.

41 Rich, 2016, p. 40.

42 Ibid.

43 Ibid.

44 Quoted in Rich, 2016, p. 41.
45 Ibid.
46 Ibid., p. 42.
47 Ibid.
48 Quoted in Rich, 2016, p. 43.
49 Ibid.
50 Rich, 2006, p. 59.
51 Mattera, Philip. 2016. "Dow Chemical: Corporate Rap Sheet." *Corporate Research Project*. January 7. www.corp-research.org/dowchemical.
52 Frontline. 1999. "Chronology of Silicone Breast Implants." *Breast Implants on Trial*. www.pbs.org/wgbh/pages/frontline/implants/cron.html; Miller, Henry I. 2015. "The Sad Saga Of Silicone Breast Implants." *Forbes*. March 4. www.forbes.com/sites/henrym iller/2015/03/04/infuriating-titbits-about-silicone-breast-implants/#267e0bd 518d6.
53 Iversen, Kristen. 2012. *Full Body Burden: Growing Up in the Nuclear Shadow of Rocky Flats*. New York: Random House.
54 Buffer, Patricia. 2003. "Rocky Flats History." Office of Legacy Management. U.S. Department of Energy.
55 Cohen, Andrew. 2015. "A September 11th Catastrophe You've Probably Never Heard About." *The Atlantic*. September 10. www.ocnus.net/artman2/publish/Resea rch_11/A-September-11th-Catastrophe-You-ve-Probably-Never-Heard-About.shtml.
56 AP. 2008. "Rocky Flats: Dow Chemical and Rockwell International Billed $925M for Contamination at Nuclear Site." *The Huffington Post*. June 11. www.huffingtonpost. com/2008/06/03/rocky-flats-dow-chemical_n_104974.html.
57 *Denver Post* staff and wire reports. 2010. "Appeals Court Tosses Jury Award in Rocky Flats Case." *The Denver Post*. September 4. www.denverpost.com/ci_15989514.
58 Robbins, William. 1983. "Dioxin Tests Conducted in 60s on 70 Philadelphia Inmates, Now Unknown." *The New York Times*. July 17. www.nytimes.com/1983/07/17/us/ dioxin-tests-conducted-in-60-s-on-70-philadelphia-inmates-now-unknown.html.
59 Donaldson, Thomas. 1982. *Corporations and Morality*. Englewood Cliffs, NY: Prentice Hall, p. 183.
60 Ruskin, 2015.
61 Ibid.
62 Quoted in Mattera, 2016.
63 Mattera, Phillip. 2015. Monsanto: Corporate Rap Sheet. *Corporate Research Project*. October 25. www.corp-research.org/monsanto.
64 Ibid.
65 Rmuse. 2011. "The Supreme Court Allows Dow Chemical To Get Away With Polluting Michigan." *Politicus USA's Archives (2008–2011)*. July 26. http://archives. politicususa.com/2011/07/26/supreme-court-dow-michigan.html.
66 Ibid.
67 Klonoff, Robert. 2013. "The Decline of the Class Actions." 90 Wash. U. L. Rev. 729. http://openscholarship.wustl.edu/cgi/viewcontent.cgi?article=6004&context= law_lawreview.
68 Rmuse, 2011.
69 Ibid.
70 Ibid.
71 Ibid.
72 Sullivan, Casey. 2013. "Judge Orders Dow Chemical to Pay $1.2 Billion in Price-Fixing Case." *Reuters*. May 15. www.reuters.com/article/us-dowchemical-urethane-judgment-idUSBRE94F03R20130516.
73 Quoted in ibid.
74 Sullivan, 2013.
75 Bennett, Drake. 2014. "Inside Monsanto, America's Third-Most-Hated Company." *Bloomberg Business*. July 3. www.bloomberg.com/bw/articles/2014-07-03/gmo-factory-monsantos-high-tech-plans-to-feed-the-world.

76   Ibid.
77   Ibid.
78   Mattera, 2015.
79   Jeff Merkley quoted in Alman, Ashley. 2013. "Monsanto Protection Act To Expire, Won't Be Part of Continuing Resolution." *The Huffington Post.* September 24. www. huffingtonpost.com/2013/09/24/monsanto-protection-act-expire_n_3985673.html.
80   Fernandez-Cornejo, Jorge. 2004. "The Seed Industry in U.S. Agriculture: An Exploration of State and Information on Crop Seed Markets, Regulation, Industry Structure, and Research and Development." *Agricultural Information Bulletin.* USDA. February. www.ers. usda.gov/publications/aib-agricultural-information-bulletin/aib786.aspx.; Shiva, Vandana. 2012. "The Seed Emergency: The Threat to Food and Democracy." *Al Jazeera.* February 12. www.aljazeera.com/indepth/opinion/2012/02/201224152439941847.htm l; Parsai, Gargi. 2012. "Opposition to Monsanto Patent on Indian Melons." *The Hindu.* February 5. www.thehindu.com/news/national/article2861063.ece; Vidal, John. 2000. "Biopirates Who Seek the Greatest Prizes." *The Guardian.* November 14. www.thegua rdian.com/science/2000/nov/15/genetics2?INTCMP=SRCH.
81   Mattera, 2015.
82   Ibid.
83   Ibid.
84   Ibid.
85   "Monsanto at a Glance" Accessed December 2016 www.monsanto.com/investors/ documents/pubs/2007/ar_2007_glance.pdf
86   Petersen, Melody. 1999. "Monsanto Campaign Tries to Gain Support for Gene-Altered Food." *The New York Times.* December 8.
87   Attorney General of New York. 1996. "In the Matter of Monsanto Company." Consumer Frauds and Protection Bureau, Environmental Protection Agency.
88   Arlidge, John. 1999. "Watchdog Slams Monsanto Ads." *The Guardian.* February 27. www.theguardian.com/news/1999/aug/11/food.foodanddrink.
89   *BBC.* 2009. "Monsanto Guilty in 'False Ad' Row." October 15.
90   Excerpt quoted from Seedy Business, Chapter 15. No date. "A Few Other Things the Agrichemical Industry Doesn't Want You to Know About Them: Crimes, Scandals And Other Wrongdoing." *U.S. Right To Know.* http://usrtk.org/a-few-other-things-the-agrichemical-industry-doesnt-want-you-to-know-about-them-crimes-scandals-and-other-wrongdoing/#_ftn37.
91   Mattera, 2015.
92   Gray, Allyson and Hinch, Ron. 2015. "Agribusiness, Governments and Food Crime: A Critical Perspective." In *Green Harms and Crimes: Critical Criminology in a Changing World,* edited by Ragnhild Aslug Sollund. New York: Palgrave/Macmillan, p. 111.
93   Ibid., p. 112.
94   Agnew, Robert. 2012. "Dire Forecast: A Theoretical Model of the Impact of Climate Change on Crime." *Theoretical Criminology* 16 (1): 21–42.
95   Conniff, Richard. 2016. "For Logging's Crimes, Tougher Punishment." *The New York Times.* February 21: Sunday Review, p. 4.
96   Ibid.
97   McKibben, Bill. 2016. "Global Warming's Terrifying New Chemistry." *The Nation.* April 11/18, pp. 12–18.
98   Doyon, Jacquelynn and Bradshaw, Elizabeth. 2015. "Unfettered Fracking: A Critical Examination of Hydraulic Fracking in the United States." In *The Routledge International Handbook of the Crimes of the Powerful,* edited by G. Barak. New York: Routledge, pp. 235–246.
99   Ibid.
100   Bowermaster, Jon. 2012. "5 Ways Fracking Can Make You Sick." *Takepart.* May 24. www.takepart.com/photos/5-ways-fracking-can-make-you-sick/how-fracking-making-you-sick.
101   Ibid.

102 Ibid.
103 Ibid.
104 Ibid.
105 Liptak, Adam. 2016. "Supreme Court Deals Setback to Obama's Power Plant Regulations." *The New York Times*. February 9. www.nytimes.com/2016/02/10/us/politics/supreme-court-blocks-obama-epa-coal-emissions-regulations.html?_r=0.
106 Ibid.
107 Quoted in ibid.
108 Quoted in ibid.
109 Quoted in ibid.
110 Quoted in ibid.
111 Corkery, Michael. 2016. "As Coal's Future Grows Murkier, Banks Pull Financing." *The New York Times*. March 20. www.nytimes.com/2016/03/21/business/dealbook/as-coals-future-grows-murkier-banks-pull-financing.html?_r=0. See also, Smith, Yves. 2016. "The Oil and Gas Fire Sale: How Bad Will Losses to Banks and Investors Be?" *Naked Capitalism*. March 22. www.nakedcapitalism.com/2016/03/the-oil-and-gas-fire- sale-how-bad-will-losses-to-banks-and-investors-be.html.

5

COLLUDING CRIMES OF STATES AND CORPORATIONS

Violations of the community

The contemporary global economy is primarily driven by asset and debt economies rather than by production and consumption economies. In those earlier production and consumption economies, producers made goods and services by paying labor to produce them so that they could turn around and consume goods and services with their pay. Banks and related financial institutions invested a greater share of their capital (i.e., lent money) to businesses to make goods and deliver services. By contrast, asset and debt economies are part of the global orbits of finance, insurance, and real estate (FIRE), which are dominated by financial leverage markets over capital. For perspective, in North America and Europe today, 70 to 80 percent of bank loans are for mortgages against real estate rather than for the production of goods and services. These changing relations in the production of capital are reflective of the transition away from manufacturing economies and toward post-industrial and service economies. These new means of production also reflect the rise of digital technologies that are surpassing the older analog ways of doing business. Digital applications, for example, have the ability to make money by creating value that can both improve the way customers are served and facilitate the agility and speed of enterprises to conduct business.

Financialized economies are debt-leveraged economies, which means that a larger proportion of assets are represented by debt, whether real estate, insurance, education, transportation, or just ordinary living rather than by capital or equity. Since the 1980s, as debt to equity ratios have increased, this financialization of capital has meant that more and more income as well as corporate and government tax revenue are paid to private creditors. By the turn of the twenty-first century the revenue flow was moving from the production and consumption economy to the FIRE economy. As a consequence of these new economics, the existing austerity programs are "making budget deficits even worse, driving governments further into debt, further into reliance on the IMF" and World Bank, which necessitates nation–states paying off their debts by way of privatization.[1] This type of "money supply system" or monetarism forces "countries to have such self-defeating policies that they end up having to privatize their natural resources, their public domain, their public enterprises, their communications and transportation" as in the case of the recent Greece selloffs.[2] As Michael Hudson expounds, this leads to an empire where

> [e]verything that the classical economists saw and argued for—public investment, bringing costs in line with the actual cost of production—that's all rejected in favor of a *rentier* class evolving into an oligarchy. Basically, financiers—the 1 percent—are going to pry away the public domain from the government. Pry away and privatize the public enterprises, land, natural resources, so that bondholders and privatizers get all of the revenue for themselves. It's all sucked up to the top of the pyramid, impoverishing the 99 percent.[3]

In political economy, the public domain or "the commons" refers to resources and amenities not owned privately that are to be enjoyed by all people, rich and poor alike. Those commons include the cultural and natural wherewithal including the air, water, and ecosystem as well as a habitable earth for all creatures to share. The eighteenth-century utopian philosopher Jean-Jacques Rousseau once wrote:

> The first man who having enclosed a piece of ground, bethought himself saying *This is mine*, and found people simple enough to believe him … Beware of listening to this imposter, you are undone if you once forget that the fruits of the earth belong to us all, and the earth itself to nobody.[4]

Moreover, it was Senator John Sherman when introducing the bill that would become the Sherman Anti-Trust Law of 1890 who famously declared: "If we will not endure a king as a political power, we should not endure a king over the production, transportation, and sale of any of the necessaries of life."[5] However, it was seventeenth-century utilitarian philosopher John Locke's social contract and his theory of the rights of private property, along with the legitimation of the accumulation of capital in Adam Smith's *The Wealth of Nations*, first published in 1776, which assisted ideologically to undermine the communal spirit and to guarantee that there would "not be enough, and as good, left in common for others."[6]

When the commons, resources of the earth, or communities have been "partitioned and divided up as private property rights guaranteed by the state" in order for the environment to be monetized or made tradable—thus facilitating the extraction of social wealth from the ownership of a commodified nature as well as from the monopolization, securitization, and lack of regulation of these geopolitical economic relationships—then the contradictions of capitalism and the likelihood of global financial crises are heightened, portending to the ultimate departure of the unsustainable political economy.[7] In these matters, as with amoral investments, environmental damage, labor exploitation, and the harms of multinationals more generally, the colluding violations of states and corporations represent symbiotic assaults on the cultural and natural resources that were once accessible to all people and that have now become the institutionalized subjects of austerity, contraction, neoliberalism, and privatization.

For example, even though civilization "is at last turning green, albeit a pale green," our attention still "remains focused on the physical environment—on pollution, the shortage of fresh water, the shrinkage of arable land and, of course, the great, wrathful demon that threatens all our lives, human-forced climate change."[8] The problem of concentrating almost exclusively on the physical environment is that the Earth's living environment, including all of the species and all of the ecosystems that they constitute, continues to be all but neglected. As the biologist Edward O. Wilson argues, this is a huge mistake: "If we save the living environment of Earth, we will also save the physical, nonliving environment, because each depends on the other."[9] In terms of the Earth's sustainability, its biological diversity and stability and saving the planet's species from extinction, the global conservation movement has raised awareness of nature's plight. At the same time, research also reveals that human intervention to resist extinction, such as the increase in natural refuges, has only slowed the hemorrhaging for a relatively few species.

For context, there are about 2 million species that have been discovered, described, and given a Latinized scientific name. Conservation efforts have targeted roughly one-fifth of some 63,000 endangered species of the vertebrates (e.g., birds, mammals, reptiles, amphibians, and fish) and a far smaller percentage of the approximately 270,000 species of the flowering plants, leaving millions of fungi, algae, insects, and other invertebrate animals unaccounted for in the race to extinction. Bottom line: if humans have been slow to react to global warming and climate change, we have been comparably much slower to react to species extinction.

As Wilson underscores, the "disappearance of natural habitat is the primary cause of biological diversity loss at every level—ecosystems, species and genes, all of them."[10] Accordingly, humans preserving significantly more natural habitats might bring extinctions close to a sustainable level:

> The only way to save upward of 90 percent of the rest of life is to vastly increase the area of refuges, from their current 15 percent of the land and 3 percent of the sea to half of the land and half of the sea. That amount, as others and I have shown, can be put together from large and small fragments around the world to remain relatively natural, without removing people living there or changing property rights.[11]

Unfortunately, a potential solution to species extinction, namely the expansion of the commons, runs smack into the contradictions of capitalist expansion and commons contraction. Together, collective actions and the commons could represent a "system for the long-term stewardship of resources that preserves shared values and community identity,"[12] the antithesis of what the contemporary corporate state represents. At the same time, there "is no master inventory of commons because a commons arises whenever a given community decides it wishes to manage a resource in a collective manner, with special regard for equitable access, use and sustainability," as well as with "minimal or no reliance on the Market or State."[13]

Routinizing collusion between and within nations: the neutralization of crime and the rise of securitization

Through the reproduction of acts of commission and omission, dismissal and normalization, suppression and surveillance, and neutralization and deception, states and corporations collude when both powerful entities benefit by reinforcing the other in the facilitation and routinization of their complementary forms of deviance, further concentrating their state-corporate power. Whether discussing the criminalizing processes of Mexico, Central America, and the U.S. toward migrants later in the chapter, or the securitization as well as the state-routinization of human smuggling in undocumented migrants, and access to as well as acquisition of oil in the Middle East discussed here, for example, these "criminal undertakings" are often realized in commonly established policies and/or practices that facilitate the interests of both capitalist states and multinational corporations.

Two geopolitically related examples of oil, securitization, and state-routinized collusion involving bribery, economic crime, multinational corporate wrongdoing, and international relations underscore how invisible these financial crimes are, even when they are not successfully covered up. In case one, the punishment amounted to far less than a slap on the wrist given the magnitude of the financial crime. In case two, there have yet to be any criminal indictments even though the number of countries East and West as well as the number of high profile multinational corporations involved is large. Indictments and prosecutions could be forthcoming (or not) as at least one investigation has officially begun in the United Kingdom.

In the first case, after seven years of pretrial litigation a wealthy and politically connected U.S. businessman James H. Giffen was eventually indicted on sixty-five counts in the Southern District of New York for allegedly giving more than $84 million dollars in payments to the President of Kazakhstan and other senior officials in his government. It was also alleged that during the time period covered in the indictment that Mr. Giffen personally cleared more than $30 million. Finally, on November 19, 2010, the Court sentenced Giffen to time served (one day) and to a fine of $25,000.[14]

Although the payoff scheme allegedly "involved the use of sham contracts, Swiss bank accounts, and off-shore corporate shells—all designed to provide a legitimate cover to private bribes," the trial was actually about the geo-politics of oil in central Asia.[15] Not only did these transactions involve the states of Kazakhstan, China, Russia, and the United States, they also involved such "noteworthy oil corporations as Mobil, Amoco, Texaco, and Phillips Petroleum."[16] In this particular case, there was circumstantial evidence that "the CIA, State Department, and even the Clinton White House knew what Mr. Giffen was doing in Kazakhstan, and looked the other way—so as to favor American, multinational oil companies seeking low-cost oil leases from the Kazakhstan government."[17] Some of the commentary of U.S. District Court Judge William H. Pauley III is worth sharing and provides some of the important background material involved in this prosecution:

> Suffice it to say, Mr. Giffen was a significant source of information to the United States Government and a conduit for secret communications with the Soviet Union and its leadership during the Cold War. He undertook that effort as a volunteer and was one of the only Americans with sustained and reliable access to the highest levels of Soviet officialdom. For example, in 1980, Mr. Giffen helped to facilitate the emigration of thousands of Soviet Jews to the West. Following the collapse of the Soviet Union, Mr. Giffen focused on the new Republic of Kazakhstan. He became a trusted advisor to Kazakhstan's President Nazarbayev. In that capacity, he helped Kazakhstan invest foreign investment and provide advice on economic development .... In doing so, he advanced the strategic interests of the United States and American businesses in Central Asia. Throughout this time, he continued to act as a conduit for communications on issues vital to America's national interest in the region.[18]

While these cooperative or negotiated payoffs may have benefitted an array of allied and adversarial interests, these collusions of transgression by some very "strange bedfellows" does not mean to imply that these power players do not also have serious conflicts or disagreements within and between these power-yielding relations that work on behalf of various multinational corporations and security state apparatuses worldwide. Think of the contradictory interests of Russia and the U.S. generally and more recently to those conflicting interests between Syria, Russia, and the United States.

In the second case, a joint investigative exposé by Fairfax Media and *The Huffington Post*, in a series of articles in late March 2016 revealed the depth and reach of a massive looting scheme involving bribery in Iraq orchestrated by a family-owned oil company (Unaoil) based in Monaco, which failed to gain any mainstream media attention in the U.S., even though one of the alleged perpetrators, Rolls-Royce, was already being investigated by the Serious Fraud Office of the United Kingdom. Otherwise, what should have been a major scandal in the world of multinational corporate corruption, especially considering that the bribery and graft exposed, shone light on the wide extent to which fraud pervades the oil industry and strikes at the very essence of the Foreign Corrupt Practices Act. Literally, there were dozens of multinational oil companies, bureaucrats, and politicians engaged in a complex web of bribery and graft. As a direct result of the millions of dollars of bribes paid on behalf of many MNCs from such countries as Germany, Italy, the Netherlands, and involving such giant firms as Halliburton in the U.S., Australia's Leighton Holdings, Korea's Hyundai, and Britain's Rolls-Royce, billions of dollars of government contracts were awarded involving companies doing business with Unaoil's Middle East operations.[19]

One has to speculate about why this story never developed any "media legs," as they say. It is not likely that the three different days the series ran in late March 2016 just happened to be very busy news days. More likely, the "black out" by the mass media might be attributed to a combination of the long list of major oil and other multinational firms from the West linked hand-in-hand with officials and businesses from Middle Eastern countries such as Iraq, Iran, Libya, Syria, and Kuwait? The "black out" may also have had something to do with the rise of the new security states.

Whatever the reason that these stories never found their way to prime-time or gained any mass media traction, post 9/11 and subsequent to the U.S. formation of its Department of Homeland Security in 2003, there have been developing transnational security communities and expanding responsibilities for security activities involving both the private for-profit sector and nation-states themselves. For example, during the second term of the G.W. Bush Administration, private contractors working with Israel and the U.S. committed numerous cybercrimes against Iran when they jointly developed the Stuxnet computer viruses used to repeatedly sabotage Iran's nuclear reprocessing plants.[20] By May of 2009 President Obama had announced that he was appointing "the nation's first cyber security czar to help protect the nation's telecom infrastructure and information systems that have grown so crucial to industry, the military and individual citizens."[21] During the same period of time, the Pentagon publicized its formation of a new Cyber-Command "to both defend against cyber attacks and wage cyber warfare against our enemies."[22] These techno-geopolitical changes reflect the emergence of a growing security interdependence between foreign policy and national and local security and vice versa.

The recent developments in "securitization" have generated all kinds of arguments, discussions, and questions regarding the governance arrangements within contemporary world politics, raising concerns about the adequacy of current accountability and oversight mechanisms, which help comprise legitimacy for current political and law enforcement and security relationships.[23] For example, several scholars from security studies argue that there is competition over not only security control, but also security discourse, as both have become "powerful political tools influencing policy decisions and the agendas of ministers and senior law enforcement and security leaders."[24] In particular, Paul Williams contends that the ability to control security discourse determines "who gets to decide what security means, what issues make it onto security agendas, [and] how those issues should be dealt with."[25]

For nearly a decade, Didier Bigo has been arguing that an international "security consensus" already exists, which focuses its primary attention on and cooperation around transnationally organized crime, human trafficking, genocide, and terrorism.[26] However, what is conspicuously omitted from this consensus of potential victims and security risks are all of the habitual crimes and undertakings by multinational corporations against workers, consumers, and the environment. And, so opportunistic crimes of the powerful march on and on to the "capitalist beat" of corporate reproduction.

Transparency, surveillance, whistleblowing, and drone warfare

For nearly a decade both new and amended whistleblowing laws have appeared in countries as diverse as Ghana, Malaysia, and Australia. This legislation has also responded to numerous issues and raised as many questions about transparency, surveillance, and the absence of the rule of law in the negotiations between these contradictory objectives. As the editors of *Whistleblowing and Democratic Values* (2011) have written:

> Empirical research in the USA and UK has shown that employers are increasingly recognising both the need and desirability of having effective whistleblowing policies and procedures in place. Of course, some will be responding in order to comply with the law, for example the requirements of the Sarbanes-Oxley and Dodd-Frank legislation in the US, but others may have acted out of enlightened self-interest. Another development has been the disclosure of information by WikiLeaks. This has led to questions being asked about the relationship between whistleblowing and leaking and about how people could be persuaded to raise their concerns internally rather than internationally. One particular problem for organisations is that many individuals have come to realise that if whistleblowers are not protected by law it might be wiser to leak information anonymously than to use official channels.[27]

Despite the differences of perspectives on these issues, there does seem to be a growing consensus that whistleblowing is an important tool in the fight against state and/or corporate fraud and/or governmental corruption.

There also seems to be a consensus that without protective and enforceable legislation whistleblowers will remain vulnerable and subject to all kinds of adverse effects on their careers, most notably to blacklisting and concealed retaliation. As Sawyer, Johnson, and Holub conclude from their examination of corporate culture and whistleblowing:

> In recognizing the negative correlation between the actions of the organization and the whistleblower it becomes clear that the continuing legitimacy of the organization necessitates the illegitimacy of the whistleblower. This helps explain the continual blacklisting of the whistleblower and their vilification resulting in the destruction of both their professional career and their reputations.[28]

Adding to the complexities of securitization and establishing protections for whistleblowers is the fact that these activities are occurring in both the state and corporate sectors. Ordinarily, for example, "policing and its associated surveillance and intelligence practices have been associated mostly with governmental authority, i.e. the state."[29] In other words, when one thinks of surveillance, monitoring, or the tracking of people one usually thinks of the Government or of George Orwell's Big Brother.

Put differently, one of the world's leading whistleblowing-advocacy groups, the Washington based NGO, Government Accountability Project, which currently provides legal representation for the National Intelligence Agency whistleblowers Thomas Drake (former executive who discovered that the U.S. President had ordered warrantless wiretapping of everyone in the country) and Edward Snowden (who now resides in Russia after successfully revealing the massive surveillance program of the National Security Agency (NSA) and who is willing to come home and face trial in the U.S. for his unlawful behavior if he would be allowed to use a "public interest" defense) as well as U.S. Defense Department whistleblower John Crane (former Assistant Inspector at the Pentagon, from 2004 until 2013 when he was forced out for standing up for abused whistleblowers at the Pentagon who had become the subjects of repeated obstructions and denials of justice), is not by chance identified as the Corporate Accountability Project. Such a project would of course be a good idea, if it does not already exist, because one needs increasingly to think not only in terms of state violations of privacy and public surveillance but also in terms of corporate violations of the public trust and private surveillance as well as the coordinated efforts of states and corporations carrying out jointly sponsored ventures.

When combined, these activities of states and corporations may be directed at both the internal whistleblowers and the external critics who narrowly constitute the world of those people who blow the whistles on these frauds and illegalities. For example, researchers have found that "fraud detection does not rely on standard corporate governance actors (investors, SEC, and auditors), but takes a village, including several non-traditional players (employees, media, and industry regulators)."[30] Groups such as Anonymous, a loosely associated network of activists and hacktivists, are also useful actors in checking, exposing, and/or resisting the misbehavior of states and corporations. These groups are valuable as well in the larger struggles surrounding those policies, laws, and controls of digital technology, information, and surveillance, especially as these are related to the more general and indiscriminate collecting and monitoring of communication.[31] Hence, in relation to changes in globalization, technology, and securitization, including those MNCs engaged in the practices of policing, surveillance, and intelligence, researchers have begun to investigate the role of non-state actors as well as political elites and the news media in the creation of public panics as covers for state crimes.

In the case of multinational corporations, they

> are increasingly under fire and challenged by indigenous peoples, local communities and others affected by the detrimental consequences of corporate activity for their local environment and livelihoods. The oil industry in particular constitutes a site of controversy, with civil society groups exposing companies' misconduct to public scrutiny.[32]

Just as the response of the oil companies has been to monitor the activities of its critics, the same is the case of other MNCs. Moreover, as Hans Krause Hansen and

Julie Uldam have pointed out, it is important to appreciate how corporate surveillance (CS) is carried out in relation to private forms of self-regulation (SR), corporate social responsibility (CSR), and global governance. As they suggest:

> CSR and corporate surveillance may be usefully understood in relation to wider social changes, including the proliferation of private hybrid forms of policing to protect new sites of private authority within global governance. While in various ways drawing on intelligence gathering, these forms of policing both contribute to and thrive on the emergence of global information markets where various forms of risk is produced and commodified ... This intelligence is valuable to corporations as they seek to protect the reputational benefits of their CSR activities with efforts to anticipate and contain civil society criticism.[33]

In the case of a digitizing world the home has become the new frontier where virtually every household item has been (or could be) technologically upgraded and rendered "smart," meaning that they can perform their respective mechanical tasks while also connected to the Internet. When applied to the latest consumer gadgets, "smart" performs an ideological slight of hand because "what is presented as an upgrade is actually a stealthy euphemism for 'surveillance'."[34] While a "smart" lighting system, for example,

> promises to adapt to an owner's preferences or help the environment by lowering electricity bills, what it also does is provide a company with a permanent foothold in a person's home from which he can be monitored. That smart-lighting company knows when the owner of its product comes home, when he goes, and when he dims a light for a date and when he leaves them on.[35]

Not only can these "smart" devices be used to collect information to sell to advertisers for huge profits to these companies, but they may also be used as tools of control, "tracking user habits, trying to anticipate and shape their owners' behaviors and reporting back to the corporate mother ship."[36]

When it comes to monitoring fraud and surveillance, democratic values, and whistleblowers as a group, there are problems of national sovereignty and of the lack of legal protection for persons that would elect to use official internal channels rather than to leak information externally. In the case of sovereignty, for example, after Edward Snowden's leaks of NSA spying went viral, linking the United Kingdom's involvement in wide-ranging and illegal surveillance practices to the NSA's PRISM program, "including the routine mass interception of communications data and cyber-hacking of foreign companies and diplomats," the European Parliament on September 26, 2013, invited Sir Ianin Lobban, Director of the UK's intelligence-gathering agency GCHQ, "to testify before the LIBE Committee inquiry on the electronic surveillance of EU citizens."[37] On behalf of the UK government, Lobban declined the Parliament's invitation by maintaining: "National security is the sole responsibility of Member States. The activities of intelligence services are equally the sole responsibility of each Member State and fall outside the competence of the Union."[38] Some nations have agreed with Lobban. Several other EU member states such as Sweden, France, and Germany are also running their own smaller secret interception programs. In 2014 the Centre for European Policy Studies in Brussels made a case for why covert, large-scale surveillance programs of member states should not be beyond the scope of EU intervention.

In response to the European Parliament's Inquiry on the Electronic Mass Surveillance of EU Citizens, launched in July 2013, a CEPS Commentary, authored by Carrera, Guild, and Parkin, provided four legal rationales for why the EU should not abdicate its responsibility for monitoring transnational secrecy, surveillance, and whistleblowing. These rationales included:

> First, the EU is competent to regulate and protect the fundamental rights of data protection and privacy, and any derogation member states wish to apply to those rights must be overseen by European institutions and courts. The EU's competence over data protection is regulated by a raft of data protection directives, which are currently being updated and extended under the so-called "data protection reform package." Furthermore, the EU is charged with protecting the privacy rights of Union citizens and the privacy of everyone falling within the scope of EU law, as enshrined in the European Charter of Fundamental Rights. Any interference with privacy rights and data protection obligations—and the larges-scale surveillance of an individual's communications data cannot constitute anything but—must be justified under EU law.
>
> Second, secret surveillance is not only subject to EU oversight, but it also falls under strict judicial control by the European Court of Human Rights. It is highly uncertain that the large-scale surveillance as alleged to be practiced by the UK and others would be deemed lawful within the judicial system governed by the European Convention on Human Rights. In its jurisprudence the Strasbourg court has established detailed criteria with which to determine the legality of a state's secret interception of communications.
>
> Third, to what extent can we distinguish these practices from acts of cybercrime? The Council of Europe's 2001 Convention on Cybercrime identifies illegal access and illegal interception as an offence against the confidentiality, integrity and availability of computer data and systems under criminal law. The EU has taken the Council of Europe Convention as a legal reference point, and building on this foundation is developing a substantial body of policy to boost cybersecurity and enhance its operational capacities with the establishment of the European Cybercrime Centre within the EU's law enforcement agency Europol.
>
> Fourth, member states' large-scale surveillance practices blur the lines between national security and matters relating to EU competence when they threaten to spill over into the security activities of the EU institutions and its agencies. Member states may have the main competence in relation to national

security, but the Union has shared competence with the member states when it comes to the Union's internal security, particularly as regards the policy areas of terrorism and crime.[39]

Let's now explore transparency and accountability of drone "warfare" during the Obama Administration's eight years. In 2013 the administration adopted stricter guidelines for the use of drones, currently run by the Central Intelligence Agency and the U.S. Military Pentagon. The guidelines

> instruct intelligence and military personnel to determine with "near certainty" that their target is present at the location of an intended strike, that non-combatants will not be hurt or killed, that capture is not a feasible option and that local government is not equipped to address the threat.[40]

However, without transparency or more detailed data, including the identity of targets, dates, locations, and the assessment of collateral damage, it is impossible to know whether or not these ambitious goals of "drone warfare" are being realized on the ground, or even if they are not in violation of domestic and international law.

Thus, in 2015 the American Civil Liberties Union filed a lawsuit in Federal District Court in Manhattan, New York, to obtain records about the legal basis for the use of force outside of conventional war zones as well as the evidentiary standards the administration uses to authorize drone airstrikes. As the director of the National Security Project of the ACLU stated:

> There is great damage to the rule of law and human rights law when the United States, of all countries, engages in killings based on secret interpretations of the law, or entirely new and unilateral frameworks outside the agreed-upon international framework that places important constraints on the use of lethal force and protects the right to life.[41]

At the start of the 2016 Fourth of July holiday weekend, late on a Friday afternoon, despite the President's opposition in the federal lawsuit to prevent the disclosure of documents that would offer substantive information about the legal underpinnings of the program and the criteria the government uses to authorize strikes, the Office of the President released the estimated number of civilian bystanders killed by 473 drone airstrikes conducted during his administration outside of conventional war zones like Afghanistan, Iraq, or Syria to be between sixty-four and 116 and that the number of terrorists members killed was about 2,500. Most of these strikes had occurred in Libya, Pakistan, Somalia, and Yemen. This allegedly transparent revelation of the "death toll" tried to somewhat lift "the secrecy that has cloaked one of the United States' most contentious tactics for fighting terrorists," however, its

> official civilian death count is far lower than estimates compiled by independent organizations, such as the London-based Bureau of Investigative Journalism

with its estimates ranging from 200 to 800 civilians killed by American airstrikes outside of war zones since 2009.[42]

As Bill Roggio, editor of the *Long War Journal* at the Foundation for the Defense of Democracies, who has been tracking civilian deaths for a decade has stated, "nobody's data is accurate, everyone is guessing to a certain extent."[43]

Although critics welcomed the administration's efforts as a first step toward transparency, they were also disappointed by the limited data. For example,

> "the government should be releasing information about every strike—the date of the strike, the location, the number of casualties, and the civilian or combatant status of those casualties," said Jameel Jaffer of the American Civil Liberties Union.[44]

After all, "without the locations and dates of strike … the administration's numbers are impossible to compare with independent accounts."[45]

Moreover, pointing to attacks on Somali training camps involving Shabab's top terrorist leaders or to targeting of Al Qaeda in Yemen, critics have wanted to know whether or not the U.S. was or is at war, anywhere, anytime. The administration has responded that these attacks are covered by the fifteen-year-old Authorization for Use of Military Force (AUMF) against the sponsors of the September 11, 2001, terrorist assault upon the U.S.

So it appears that within the context of the global war on terrorism and without any type of "checks and balances" or legal objections or even posing of questions by domestic governmental bodies such as the U.S. Congress with its various armed services and foreign relations and intelligence committees in both the House and Senate, or by international bodies such as the United Nations or the International Criminal Court, then in the U.S. anyway:

> We can wake up on a given morning and discover that America is already at war with yet another Islamist group in yet another part of the world—based not on Congressional deliberation but on an executive branch decision that such a group is an *associated force* of Al Qaeda or ISIS.[46]

At the same time these official narratives, explanations, and rationalizations can be used legalistically to "boot strap" any type of executive deployment of Special Forces, the C.I.A., or paramilitary contract workers into direct combat roles with lawful cover.

Crimmigration and privatization: cashing in on refugee desperation

In North America crimmigration has two popular meanings that are not mutually exclusive. One refers to the more technical intersection of criminal law and immigration law with its emphasis on enforcement, deportation, criminal sanctions, and incarceration. The other refers to criminalizing some forms of migration and turning those violators of these forms into criminals. In the early 1990s, for example, illegal border crossings were usually treated as civil offenses, punishable by deportation alone. Although the U.S. Congress began changing this practice a decade earlier, it was not until 1996 that simply crossing the border after once having been deported became a criminal offense, punishable by years of imprisonment. The classification of this type of behavior resulted in a federally privatized prison system for "crimmigrants." As part of the U.S. Bureau of Prisons, twelve facilities are operated and owned by private companies. All but one of these prisons, the District of Columbia facility, exclusively houses non-citizen-only crimmigrants.

For over a decade "hundreds of thousands of people [every year] from Guatemala, El Salvador, and Honduras attempt to cross Mexico, where they regularly encounter rape, dismemberment, and death."[47] Since 2014 the U.S. and Mexico have been colluding to endanger refugee minors often running for their lives from their neighborhood gang violence, including some of the highest murder rates in the Global South. During the last three years of Obama's second term as President, he and Mexican President Enrique Pena Nieto had been cooperating to intercept desperate young Central American refugees traveling in Southern Mexico long before reaching the borders of the United States. In a May 2016 *New York Times*' editorial column, Nicholas Kristop points out that by the U.S. providing $86 million for the interdiction program, it had effectively "pressured and bribed Mexico to do our dirty work, detaining, and deporting people fleeing gangs in Honduras, El Salvador and Guatemala. This solved a political crisis that Obama faced with refugees," however, the program betrayed "some of the world's most vulnerable people."[48] In fact, Kristop says that the President has blood on his hands and has called Obama out when he writes: "Although Obama portrayed his action as an effort to address a humanitarian crisis, he made the crisis worse. The old routes minors took across Mexico were perilous, but the new ones adopted to avoid checkpoints are even more dangerous."[49] An already flawed refugee and immigration policy was simply made worse.

Integral to the journeys across Mexico heading toward the U.S. is the commodification of undocumented Central American migrants, according to an ethnographic study by Wendy Voigt that explains how "migrants' bodies, labor, and lives are transformed into commodities within economies of smuggling, extortion, and humanitarian aid."[50] She concludes that "everyday violence along the journey is produced by historical trajectories of political and criminal violence and by local and global economies that profit from human mobility," including the likes of organized crime, law enforcement, and energy exploration.[51] Beyond the locale and the journey itself, "migration is crucial to capital accumulation, as the movements of Central Americans are circumscribed by demands for labor and drugs in the United States and for weapons, military funding, and remittances in Mexico and Central America."[52]

Whereas Central Americans have experienced abuse in Mexico since they started "migrating in substantial numbers during the civil wars of the 1980s, direct violence and exploitation in recent years has become far more systematic and inescapable."[53] While Voigt focuses on the sites of violence along the migrant journeys, she acknowledges that human mobility has always been linked to processes of violence, "from the transatlantic slave trade to asylum seekers fleeing genocide or war."[54] She also underscores that the "effects of policing, militarization, and racism are particularly salient in spaces associated with migration, such as border regions, factory work zones, and immigrant enclaves."[55] The rest of this section outlines the continued victimization as well as the criminalization of those migrating workers who cross the borders into the United States and are often incarcerated before they are eventually subject to deportation and returned to their countries of origin.

Although the U.S. Immigration and Customs Enforcement (ICE) may refer to the detention site in Dilley, Texas, as a "family residential center," Yancy Maricela Mejia Guerra, a detainee from Central America, says: "It's a prison for us and a prison for our children, but none of us are criminals."[56] The Dilley center holds people detained by ICE, a governmental agency, but the facility is run by Corrections Corporation of America (CCA), the largest private prison and detention company in the United States. In recent decades, many Western governments have increasingly outsourced prisons to private companies, part of a global trend and multimillion-dollar revenue-generating industry for warehousing immigrants and asylum seekers. Three examples include the following:

- The company Hero Norway that runs ninety refugee centers in Norway and ten in Sweden.
- The Australian contracted company Broadspectrum to manage two detention camps in Nauru and Papua New Guinea for asylum seekers.
- The British award of a seven-year contract to the security firm Serco worth over $100 million for running the Yarl's Wood Immigrant Detention Center.[57]

Comparatively, these private facilities cannot hold a candle to public facilities, the former plagued by scandals, abuse, and killings:

- The CCA has a long history of ignoring detainee safety and federal laws.
- Serco has been accused of inadequately training its guards and overcharging the British government for substandard work.
- One doctor who worked at a site run by Broadspectrum in Nauru told *The Guardian* that the detention center was "reminiscent of Guantanamo Bay."[58]

It is not that state-run facilities guarantee more respect for human rights, per se. However, a 2014 report by the American Civil Liberties Union "found that private immigration detention centers in the United States were more crowded than state-run ones, and detainees in them had less access to educational programs and quality medical care."[59] And public centers, while still flawed, were more transparent than private centers. "Opacity is a common denominator in the privatized detention system around the world. In Australia, Europe, and the United States journalists have less access to private prisons than they do to public ones; governments maintain less oversight."[60] Finally, making profits from incarceration not only drives the costs up, but it also requires keeping beds filled, so the CCA and other companies are continually lobbying politicians to keep more people behind bars rather than in the community or deporting them. Companies can and do, of course, make more profits by reducing or skimping on services and facilities. Hence, mental health care, outdoor activities, and healthy food are far less available in private detention centers than at government-run centers.[61]

For-profit charter schools and the privatization of public education: looting the public purse at the expense of the public interest

According to the National Alliance for Public Charter Schools, there were 3 million children enrolled in charter schools across forty-two states and the District of Columbia in 2016, representing about 5 percent of student K-12 enrollment. The examination and evaluation of charter schools, the privatization or loss of public education, and the democratic control of this fiscal issue is typically marketed falsely as one of "school choice." However, when public school systems, from Miami to New Orleans to Los Angeles to Chicago to Detroit and geographical locales between those cities, are having to close down their neighborhood schools because of insufficient public funding, and students are having, as a direct result, to travel long distances to a growing number of government funded but privately operated for-profit charter schools by way of private or public transportation, then K-12 learning is more about economic inequality, class, and ethnicity, making money not in the public interest, and the slow demise of a U.S. public education system and its privatized charter replacements rather than the quality of academic choices or the reconstruction (re-establishment) of democratic, public education in America.

Since 1992, the Walton Family Foundation (WFF) has acknowledged supporting a quarter of the 6,700 charter schools established across the United States. Numerous hedge fund millionaires and philanthropic billionaires led by the Walton family, as well as the Bill and Melinda Gates Foundation, have been heavily invested in the charter school movement and industry, as have politicos and operatives from both the Democratic and Republican parties. In the beginning of 2016, Wal-Mart announced the closing of 269 of its stores in small towns and suburban neighborhoods across America. In those same areas where this MNC had previously driven most locally owned small "mom and pop" businesses out of business, Wal-Mart has now been abandoning these same communities and their thousands of underpaid associate workers. While Wal-Mart's business model was helping to "bankrupt" these population sites, or at least significantly reduce the tax revenue for public funding of education there, the WFF was also announcing that it would be "doubling down on its investments in school choice with a $1 billion plan to help expand the charter school sector and other choice initiatives over the next five years."[62]

Regardless of their ideological, political, and educational differences, the Gates ("liberals") and the Waltons ("conservatives") without any known expertise in the fields of education, are able as best they can, with and without assistance and against their critics and resisters alike, to shelter as much of their wealth from taxation as possible in order to "socially engineer" the future of public education in America, subject to little or no democratization of education input. They have done so one way or the other by buying into and advancing the educational ideas of the libertarian economist Milton Friedman and his wife Rose Friedman. To advance their ways to improve K-12 educational systems, the couple established the Friedman Foundation in 1996, which to this day is still a large recipient of millions of dollars from the Waltons for promoting school choice. Back in 1995, calling for a radically restructured elementary and secondary educational school system, M. Friedman argued that "reconstruction can be achieved only by privatizing a major segment of the educational system—i.e., by enabling a private, for-profit industry to develop" a wide variety of learning opportunities to offer effective competition to public schools, which had become monopolized by the "professionalization and unionization of teachers."[63] As Friedman saw it, the only solution to

> fixing the nation's education monopoly was "through a system of vouchers." As long as public schools were essentially free, and private schools charged tuition, most parents would keep sending their kids to the local public school. But introducing a voucher that could be "redeemed" by parents at a private school would break that dynamic, and in turn, break up the public education monopoly.[64]

Among the Walton family's early ventures into school choice was a 1998 pledge coupled with a pledge by the New York City financier Theodore J. Forstmann for a total of $100 million "to launch a national privately financed voucher program that would offer scholarships to as many as 50,000 poor students."[65] After a brief time future scholarships disappeared and a transition began away from vouchers to charters. The WFF continues to expand the number of charter schools today as they are creating "a constituency of parents and others who will have a direct stake in the continued funding and expansion of these schools."[66]

Putting aside the financial scandal—the malfeasance and corruption—that has become commonplace in states where these schools have proliferated like Ohio, Michigan, Florida, and Pennsylvania, including the series of reports from the Center for Popular Democracy in 2014 and 2015 that "uncovered many hundreds of millions in 'alleged and confirmed financial fraud, waste, abuse, and misman-agement' committed by charter schools around the country," the movement is still growing in the U.S. Moreover, the charter school system is able to more routinely skim money legally from the larger funded state coffers because its blend of public and private players and the outsourcing of managing services to for-profit manage-ment firms, allows for a variety of financial slights of hand.[67] In *The Business of Charter Schooling: Understanding the Policies that Charter Operators Use for Financial*

Benefit published in 2015 by the National Education Policy Center (NEPC), Bruce Baker and Gary Miron identified four policy concerns that revolve around the ways that individuals, companies, and organizations secure financial gain and generate profit by operating and controlling charter schools. These include the following:

1. A substantial share of public expenditure intended for the delivery of direct educational services to children is being extracted inadvertently or intentionally for personal or business financial gain, creating substantial inefficiencies.
2. Public assets are being unnecessarily transferred to private hands, at public expense, risking the future provisions for "public" education.
3. Charter school operators are growing highly endogenous, self-serving private entities that are built on funds derived from lucrative management fees and rent extraction, which further compromises the future provision of public education.
4. Current disclosure requirements make it unlikely that any related legal violations, ethical concerns, or merely bad policies and practices are not realized until clever investigative reporting, whistleblowers, or litigation brings them to light.[68]

One of the fundamental flaws related to charter school for-profit operations has to do with the "business model" underlying how these schools are funded based on the idea that "money should follow the child." In other words, when students exercise their "choice" and transfer to a new or existing charter school from a public school because the latter school system has abandoned a particular neighborhood altogether or has insufficiently funded schools if they remain, the per-pupil funding to educate that child transfers when s/he does. This financial model, however, drains money and harms the education of public school students even before we address the quality of that education, because

> [a]s a public school loses a percentage of its students to charters, the school can't simply cut fixed costs for things like transportation and physical plant proportionally. It also can't cut costs of grade-level teaching staff proportionately. That would increase class sizes and leave the remaining students underserved. So instead, the school cuts a program or support service—a reading specialist, a special education teacher, a librarian, an art or music teacher—to offset the loss of funding.[69]

Ultimately, these underfunded fiscal realities translate into the closing down of neighborhood schools and the consolidation of the public education system as a whole, in exchange for for-profit charter schools of dubious merit. This "zero-sum" game may or may not benefit any individual students, but it is certainly harmful to some neighborhoods, especially those ethnically poor ones that have become, in effect, "school deserts" much like those "food deserts" found in many low-income communities across America.

As for the "verdict" on the value or performance of charter schools and the real costs to taxpayers, parents, students and the traditional public schools, research has shown that on average

> Charters don't outperform traditional public schools, and not infrequently fare worse. They accept public funds, but in many cases give day-to-day oversight to private, for-profit organizations. They're exempt from many regulations that govern traditional public schools, which, depending on the sate, can include "minimum standards" covering such things as training and qualifications of personnel, public disclosure of instructional materials, equipment, and facilities; organization, administration, and supervision of schools; and "reporting requirements."[70]

Significantly, the very ability to "opt out" of those rules that make public education accessible to all exacerbates already existing issues like racial segregation and the achievement gaps between white and minority students.

For a long time, school privatizers have promoted the idea that putting more money into traditional public education K–12 is a bad idea, echoed recently by New York Democratic Governor Andrew Cuomo and the hedge fund financial community. However, if one still doubts that this education is not about the money to be made or the quality of education not delivered, consider in May of 2015 the Waltons held a symposium to help hedge funders and other wealthy investors learn how best to get a crack at the $500 billion spent each year on K–12 public education. On the other hand, short of abolishing for-profit charter schools and in the spirit of addressing and responding to the concerns raised by the National Education Policy Center, Baker and Miron made eight recommendations to reign in these charter schools for profit. The first and second of these were, respectively:

- States should include in their charter statutes a broad declaration that charter schools are "public" and that all remaining provisions should be read to ensure that charter school students, parents and taxpayers waive no rights in their choice to attend a charter school or as a citizen whose tax dollars are allocated to a charter school.
- Districts or other local public and government authorities should maintain control over public lands and facilities and should serve as centralized managers and stewards of facilities space to be used by both district and charter schools.[71]

As good as these two recommendations are against expensive for-profit charter schools, the bottom line is that democratic school choice still does not exist: "many parents choose charters not because they want to, but because without fully funded, high-functioning local public schools, they feel they have to."[72] If one is living in Detroit, for an obvious example, and the community schools are riddled with problems and often lack the basic provisions, then one is more likely to "choose" a charter rather than a parochial school. After all, what other choices are there? Once again, this is neither free choice nor does it recognize that if public education was funded across the board for every student, then there would be no need for charters in the first place. Then again, advocating for special interests and the privatization of public education is apparently easier than talking about the structural inequality in school funding and addressing the poverty, racism, and other socioeconomic factors that have led to the bankruptcy of many public school systems in the United States.

Notes

1 Interview of Michael Hudson by Long, Gordon T. 2016. "The Wall Street Economy is Draining the Real Economy." *Naked Capitalism.* April 29. www.nakedcapitalism.com/2016/04/michael-hudson-the-wall-street-economy-is-draining-the-real-economy.html.
2 Ibid.
3 Ibid.
4 Quoted in Bollier, David. 2014. *Think Like a Commoner: A Short Introduction to the Life of the Commons.* Gabriola Island, BC: New Society Publishers, p. 107.
5 Quoted from the Congressional Record—Senate, 1890 by Senator Elizabeth Warren, June 29, 2016. "Reigniting Competition in the American Economy." Keynote Remarks at New America's Open Markets Program Event, p. 5.
6 Bollier, 2014, p. 107.
7 Harvey, David. 2014. *Seventeen Contradictions and the End of Capitalism.* New York: Oxford University Press, pp. 250–251.
8 Wilson, Edward O. 2016. "The Global Solution to Extinction." *The New York Times.* March 13: Sunday Review, p. 10.
9 Ibid.
10 Ibid.
11 Ibid.
12 Bollier, 2014, p. 175.
13 Ibid.
14 Yeager, Matthew. 2012. "The CIA Made Me Do It: Understanding the Political Economy of Corruption in Kazakhstan." *Crime, Law and Social Change* 57 (4): 441–457.
15 Ibid., p. 455.
16 Ibid.
17 Ibid., p. 441.
18 Quoted in ibid., p. 454.
19 Bauman, Nick, Blumenthal, Paul, and Grim, Ryan. 2016. "There's A Huge New Corporate Corruption Scandal: Here's Why Everyone Should Care." *The Huffington Post.* April 11. www.huffingtonpost.com/entry/unaoil-bribery-scandal-corruption_us_56fa2b06e4b014d3fe2408b9.
20 Arthur, Charles. 2013. "Symantec Discovers 2005 U.S. Computer Virus Attack on Iran Nuclear Plants." *The Guardian.* February 26. www.guardian.co.uk/technology/2013/feb/26/symantec-us-computer-virus-iran-nuclear.
21 *Denver Business Journal.* 2009. "Obama's Cyber Czar an 'Important 1st Step' to Security, Says Qwest CEO." May 29. http://bizjournals.com/denver/stories/2009/05/25/daily77.html.
22 ChattahBox. 2009. "Pentagon to Create New Cyber-Command: Turf War with NSA Looming." May 29. http://chattahbox.com/us/2009/05/09/pentagon-to-create-new-cyber-command-turf-with-nsa-looming/.
23 Laverick, Wendy. 2016. *Global Injustice and Crime Control.* London and New York: Routledge.
24 Ibid., p. 19

25 Williams, Paul. 2013. *Securities Studies: An Introduction*. Abingdon: Routledge, p. 2.

26 Bigo, Didier. 2008. "International Political Sociology." In P. Williams (ed.), *Securities Studies: An Introduction*. Oxford and New York: Routledge, pp. 116–129.

27 Vandekerckhove, Wim and Lewis, David (eds.). 2011. *Whistleblowing and Democratic Values*. International Whistleblowing Research Network, p. 4. http://ssrn.com/abstract=1998293.

28 Sawyer, Kim R., Johnson, Jackie, and Holub, Mark. 2010. "The Necessary Illegitimacy of the Whistleblower." *Business and Professional Ethics Journal* 29 (1): 85.

29 Hansen, Hans Krause and Uldam, Julie. 2015. "Corporate Social Responsibility, Corporate Surveillance and Neutralizing Corporate Resistance: On the Commodification of Risk-Based Policing." In G. Barak (ed.), *The Routledge International Handbook of the Crimes of the Powerful*. Oxford and New York: Routledge, p. 191.

30 Dyck, I.J. Alexander, Morse, Adair, and Zingales, Luigi. 2008. "Who Blows the Whistle on Corporate Fraud?" October 1, 2007. AFA 2007 Chicago Meetings Paper; Chicago GSB Research Paper No. 08–22; CRSP Working Paper No. 618; First Annual Conference on Empirical Legal Studies; ECGI—Finance Working Paper No. 156/2007. http://ssrn.com/abstract=891482 or http://dx.doi.org/10.2139/ssrn.891482

31 Steinmetz, Kevin and Gerber, Jurg. 2015. "Hacking the State: Hackers, Technology, Control, Resistance, and the State." In G. Barak (ed.), *The Routledge International Handbook of the Crimes of the Powerful*. Oxford and New York: Routledge, pp. 503–514.

32 Hansen and Uldam, 2015, p. 186.

33 Ibid., pp. 187–188.

34 Silverman, Jacob. 2016. "All Knowing." *The New York Times Magazine*. June 19: 14.

35 Ibid.

36 Ibid.

37 Carrera, Sergio, Guild, Elspeth, and Parkin, Joanna. 2014. "Who Will Monitor the Spies?" *CEPS Commentary*. January 8: 1.

38 Quoted in ibid.

39 Ibid, pp. 2–3.

40 Editorial. 2016. "The Secret Rules of the Drone War." *The New York Times*. July 10: Sunday Review, p. 8.

41 Quoted in ibid.

42 Savage, Charlie and Shane, Scott. 2016. "U.S. Reveals Death Toll From Airstrikes Outside War Zones." *The New York Times*. July 1. www.nytimes.com/2016/07/02/world/us-reveals-death-toll-from-airstrikes-outside-of-war-zones.html.

43 Quoted in ibid.

44 Quoted in ibid.

45 Ibid.

46 Jackson, William E. 2016. "Unaccountable Power: Drone Warfare Under the Obama Administration." *The Huffington Post*. April 4. www.huffingtonpost.com/news/drone-warfare/.

47 Voigt, Wendy. 2013. "Crossing Mexico: Structural Violence and the Commodification of Undocumented Central American Migrants." *American Ethnologist* 40 (4): 764.

48 Kristop, Nicholas. 2016. "Blood on Obama's Hands." *The New York Times*. June 26: Sunday Review, p. 11.

49 Ibid.

50 Voigt, 2013, p. 764.

51 Ibid.

52 Ibid., p. 765.

53 Ibid., p. 764.

54 Ibid., p. 765.

55 Ibid.

56 Quoted in Loewenstein, Antony. 2016. "Private Prisons are Cashing in on Refugees' Desperation." *The New York Times*. February 25. www.nytimes.com/2016/02/25/opinion/private-prisons-are-cashing-in-on-refugees-desperation.html.

57 Ibid.
58 Ibid.
59 Ibid.
60 Ibid.
61 To learn how the U.S. has let dozens of immigrants die in segregated, private prisons, see Wesller, Seth Freed. 2016. "Separate, Unequal, and Deadly." *The Nation*. February 15: p. 12–21.
62 Quoted in Bryan, Jeff. 2016. "How the Cutthroat Walmart Business Model Is Reshaping American Public Education." *Alternet*. March 13. www.alternet.org/education/how-cutthroat-walmart-business-model-reshaping-american-public-education.
63 Quoted in ibid.
64 Ibid.
65 Ibid.
66 Ibid.
67 Ibid.
68 Baker, B. and Miron, G. 2015. *The Business of Charter Schooling: Understanding the Policies that Charter Operators Use for Financial Benefit*. Boulder, CO: National Education Policy Center. http://nepc.colorado.edu/publication/charter-revenue.
69 Bryan, 2016.
70 Holloway, Kali. 2016. "Campbell Brown: The New Leader of the Propaganda Arm of School Privatization." *Alternet*. May 28. www.alternet.org/education/campbell-brown-new-leader-propaganda-arm-school-privatization.
71 Baker and Miron, 2015.
72 Holloway, 2016.

PART III
Halting corporate harm

6

CHECKING CORPORATE POWER AND STATE-ROUTINIZED CRIME IN AN AGE OF GLOBAL CAPITALISM

In 1973 the political sociologist and labor historian John C. Leggett wrote in the preface to *Taking State Power* that the evolutionary break was clear, referring to the inventions of private property and the state some 6,000 to 7,000 years ago, when a small minority of persons declared "their commitment to coerce a majority and to justify minority use of force in the name of the common good."[1] During that time a relatively small number of people had

> moved successfully to acquire the vast bulk of societal strategic resources—the land, the flora and fauna, the minerals, and the water—and to use them to insure a working relationship with a government that could normally and effectively claim a monopoly of violence within a territorial union in question, be it a community or a society.[2]

Subsequently, the "owners of private property and the state thereby developed relations that proved to be reciprocal for the few, as private property holders and state wielders subordinated the majority."[3]

Historically, "the vast bulk of the nonpropertied masses have never rebelled or revolutionized against their earthly lords."[4] On the other hand, despite the conservatizing power of culture and social institutions, on occasion the powerless have fought back, to the chagrin of the powerful. Over the past 7,000 years, development has included many social movements—pre-agrarian, agrarian, and industrial—which have certainly "challenged a small minority of persons who have mobilized land, labor, and capital to produce and sometimes export commodities at the expense of the overwhelming majority of the earth's inhabitants."[5] For example, back in the 1930s the Cooperative Commonwealth (CC) movement and its vision were very much alive during the heyday of the New Deal. Although in line with the New Deal of its time and with Bernie Sanders' espoused progressive political campaign of 2016, the agenda of the CC went much further in its advocacy for another social structure of economic organization.

The CC called for the elimination of corporate personhood and unchecked speculation, provided preferences for worker-owned cooperatives and local living economies, and was committed to the long-time health of the ecological commons. The CC's popularity during the 1930s stemmed, in part, from the older populist farmer and labor alliances reaching back to the late nineteenth century and, in part, from the successful Farmer-Labor Party in Minnesota with its new model of the economy and radical platform. The party's famous 1934 Cooperative Commonwealth Statement pronounced:

> We declare that capitalism has failed and that immediate steps must be taken by the people to abolish capitalism in a peaceful and lawful manner, and that a new, sane, and just society must be established, a system in which all the natural resources, machinery of production, transportation, and communications shall be owned by the government and operated democratically for the benefit of all the people, and not for the benefit of the few. Palliative measures will continue to fail. Only a complete reorganization of our social structure into a cooperative commonwealth will bring economic security and prevent a prolonged period of further suffering among the people.[6]

The CC was advocating for new a economic system with three layers:

1. The largest industries, banks, national transportation systems, utilities, and natural resources would be run by government or strictly regulated as monopolies—this was the socialist part of the system. They would be jointly administered by representatives of workers, consumers, and the communities wherein they operated. As part of the transition to public ownership, a state bank would compete with private finance while stock market speculation would be sharply curtailed.
2. A far greater number of large, but not monopolistic, enterprises would be run as cooperatives, with decisions made by workers and consumers. These might include major retail outlets, supermarkets, farmers' markets, manufacturers, health service providers, and so forth.
3. The third layer of the economy would be made up of small private businesses—cafes, small shops, local banks, service stations, etc.—and small, privately owned farms, providing plenty of room for entrepreneurship.[7]

A twenty-first-century adaptation of this model, figuring in globalization and post-industrialism, provides an alternative framework for managing more sustainable, democratic, and green economies.

Of course, the idea of the English commonwealth or a political community founded for the general welfare dates from the fifteenth century onwards. Historically, commonwealths are also as American as Massachusetts, Kentucky, Pennsylvania, or

Virginia. Each of these commonwealths emphasized a set of relationships for those things that we all hold in common like natural resources, as well as conveying the sense not only that we are all in this together, but that we'll do better when we all do better. In an age of global capital and its disproportionate benefits going to the wealthy or super rich and to multinational corporations, the expansion of worker-owned cooperative businesses could very well serve as one countervailing force among many others to redistribute those benefits as well as some power on behalf of worker-citizens. Presently, in the context of global warming and climate change, there has been a slowly emerging and developing post-industrial, worldwide social movement rallying against and trying to resist the unchecked corporate power of the multinational few who are continuing to engage in unsustainable capitalist expansionism at the expense of the many and the environment, too.

The myriad of movements today, local and global, that challenge corporate abuse have their roots in the 1960s when insurgent international actions were taken against the old forms of imperialism and on behalf of the new forms of environmentalism. For example, since 1977, Corporate Accountability International (CAI) has been one type of organization that has worked to protect human rights as well as the environment from corporate abusers. Born out of the idea that by stopping "the deadly marketing practices of the world's largest food corporation, Nestlé," they "could save the lives of millions of newborns," its motto became: Challenging Abuse, Protecting People. By 2016, CAI was powered by tens of thousands of members, volunteers, activists, and allied organizations. For many years now it has been regarded as a force for change among national decision makers and global governing bodies such as the United Nations.[8] CAI's two primary goals are: (1) *stop corporate abuse* not only by challenging irresponsible and dangerous life-threatening actions of global corporations, but also, at the same time, increasing multinational corporate accountability to public institutions and people around the world; and (2) *create a more just and sustainable world* whereby all people have their basic human needs for food, water, shelter, and health met as well as the opportunity to pursue their full human potential within the thriving contexts of democratic institutions and civil society, and where people are unthreatened by corporate power and hegemonic influence in policy-making.[9]

Corporate Accountability International's historic victories include changing the corporate practices of both Nestlé and General Electric (GE). In the case of the former, they led the Nestlé boycott to force the world's largest food corporation to make major changes in its life-threatening marketing of infant formula to women in the Global South. In the case of the latter, they exposed GE's abuses of millions of people around the world and led the boycott that helped to stop the world's leading nuclear weapons manufacturer from making weapons of mass destruction. More recently, CAI successfully partnered with organizations and governments from around the world to secure the World Health Organization's global tobacco treaty, the world's first public health treaty, now in effect in 179 countries. CAI's work today continues in this area as the not-for-profit is currently challenging tobacco giant Philip Morris International to stop marketing tobacco to young people around the world and manipulating public policy to the detriment of human health.

For more than a decade, CAI has been exposing and reporting on corporate abuse and corruption that threatens public health at the expense of human rights and the environment with its annual identification and listing of the Corporate Hall of Shame. Many of the recipients of this infamous designation have been multiple "winners" including: Koch Industries "for lavishing untold millions of dollars on politicians, lobbyists, and front groups to mislead the public about climate change"; Monsanto "for recklessly promoting genetically engineered seeds that exacerbate food scarcity globally"; and Chevron "for dumping an estimated 18.5 billion gallons of highly toxic chemicals into the Ecuadorian Amazon."[10] The ten Corporate Hall of Shame nominees for 2016 included:

- *Chevron:* For suing those who speak out about its toxic dumping in the Ecuadorian Amazon—where it hid details of its pollution—and for spending millions to elect industry-friendly candidates to local office.
- *Citigroup:* For drafting legislation to use taxpayer-backed money for banks' high-risk trading while committing felony collusion to fix currency prices with other banks in a price-fixing scheme.
- *Dow Chemical:* For heavily lobbying for its toxic products, including the herbicide used in Agent Orange and spending millions to defeat GMO labeling laws.
- *Halliburton:* For merging with Baker Hughes (maker of the shameful pink drill bit) in order to dominate U.S. fracking, and driving devastating environmental consequences including water contamination and increased earthquake activity.
- *Koch Industries:* For flooding U.S. elections with millions of dollars to undermine environmental protections and enrich giant corporations, and for denying climate change while being the top foreign leaseholder of Canadian tar sands.
- *McDonald's:* For driving a public health crisis, sourcing ingredients high in pesticides and other dangerous contents, and lobbying (both individually and with the National Restaurant Association) to continue paying poverty wages to its workers.
- *Monsanto:* For mass-producing toxic chemicals, threatening the livelihoods of small farmers, and suing states and individuals who attempt to label or regulate GMOs.
- *Nestlé:* For extracting and bottling hundreds of millions of gallons of water in California on expired permits while residents suffered through one of the worst droughts in decades.
- *Nike:* For aggressively lobbying to fast-track the Trans-Pacific Partnership while earning record profits from the sweatshop conditions in which its products are made.
- *Shell:* For pursuing drilling in some of the world's most biologically sensitive areas, from tar sands to the Artic, while aggressively lobbying to block progress on climate policy.[11]

In one unregulated industry—advertising—in relationship to the world's largest pharmaceutical companies that have not received their due or been among these nominees of shame, in rank order are: Pfizer (USA), Novartis (Switzerland), Sanofi-Abentis (France), Merck (USA), and GlaxoSmithKline (UK). In 2012, their combined net incomes exceeded $50 billion.[12] Perhaps this is the case because among developed countries only the U.S. and New Zealand allow for the marketing of healthcare products or services without having to prove their actual worth. In 2014, the marketing of pharmaceutical drugs, nutritional products, and hospital services spent $14 billion (up nearly 20 percent from 2011) aimed at tiny niche markets and wealthy consumers. Slightly more than one third of that total, or nearly $5 billion, was spent by prescription drug manufactures with marketing campaigns that health economists and doctors are concerned about because their advertisements not only help to increase the prices of drugs overall, but they also promote unnecessary expensive treatments. And, if medical conditions do warrant treatments, these products might not even work or there may be less expensive alternatives that work better. Some of these drugs cost as much as several thousand dollars per month to fill or $5,000 per single injection.[13]

It seems that the other nations without this type of unregulated marketing as well as the American Medical Association understand that advertising tends to drive patients to the latest expensive and patented treatments. Furthermore, in the U.S. federal regulations do not require that these advertisements mention how much a medicine costs, how well it works, or if there is a cheaper option. Worse yet, there are no regulations whatsoever when it comes to advertising the quality of hospital services. Consequently, many of these well-marketed procedures or services tend to revolve around emotional rather than scientific, factual, or evaluative stories.[14]

Educational debt and the need for collective bargaining, not collective punishment: implications for resisting state-routinized debtors

In March 2014 there were roughly 37 million Americans straddled with more than $1.2 trillion in student debts. While two-thirds of contemporary students graduating from U.S. colleges and universities today do so with some level of debt, the average borrower owed $26,000 in federal student loan debt at the end of 2013, accounting at the time for almost 7 percent of the $16.7 trillion federal debt. Behind home mortgage debt, educational debt ranks second as the highest form of consumer debt. At an average interest rate of 6 percent compounded yearly using the standard ten-year payback plan for federal loans, the total cost for that debt comes to about $44,000 or $500 per month for 120 months going toward student loan payments for that $26,000. Of course, educational debt costs former students time in savings as well as in interest. It also pushes back when and whether former students can buy a home, start a family, open a small business, or have access to capital. When parents have co-signed to secure these loans and their children may have defaulted for whatever reasons, Mom's or Dad's social security retirement checks may be garnered as repayment for their children's outstanding debt. As Andrew Ross argues in *Creditocracy and the Case for Debt Refusal* (2014), for these casualties of mass default it amounts to a form of collective punishment.

Rising rates of default—more than a million in 2013—and rising rates of delinquencies—more than 30 percent of all borrowers in 2013—suggest that many student debts cannot, and never will, be repaid. One could argue that the current financial arrangements of student loans are not only unsustainable, but that they are depraved. While most people agree that the cost of college for the average student in the United States is too high, most people do not understand how inexpensive it would be for the federal government to cover the cost of tuition for every student at every 2- and 4-year public college or university, estimated to be as low as $15 billion annually hardly amounting to a line item in the defense budget. Perhaps this is why many other DCs offer "free" (e.g., government supported) college enrollment to their citizens; besides the fact that it is considered to be a wise social investment in the future. In the U.S. by contrast, access to this essential "social good" has been turned into a transactional commodity financed through debt and the governance or holding of power in the interests of a creditor class. Only those students from well-off families are able to escape these debt traps of access to higher education. The hardest hit of course are low-income students, minorities, and first generation immigrants whose relative lack of information and financial advisers can make them easy prey for unscrupulous lenders and admission officers.

So what could be done to resist these prevailing debt financial arrangements for students in the United States? Strike Debt, the nationwide movement of debt resisters who fight for economic justice and democratic freedom, has taken one response or first step. An outgrowth of the Occupy Student Debt Campaign, the home page of strikedebt.com reads:

> Debt is a tie that binds the 99 percent. With stagnant wages, systemic unemployment, and public service cuts, we are forced to go into debt for the basic things in life—and thus surrender our futures to the banks. Debt is a major source of profit and power for Wall Street that works to keep us isolated, ashamed, and afraid. Using direct action, research, education, and the arts, we are coming together to challenge this illegitimate system while imagining and creating alternatives. We want an economy in which our debts are to our friends, families, and communities—and not to the 1 percent.

Originally started in 2013, the goal of Strike Debt's Rolling Jubilee Initiative was to highlight the injustice of ordinary people having to go into debt for access to vital goods like education and healthcare, arguing that these should be commonly provided. After a short period of time the Rolling Jubilee morphed into buying and cancelling people's debt for pennies on the dollar. Strike Debt does so not for the purposes of collecting individual debt like most debt collectors but for the purposes of abolishing debt. By the end of 2014, in less than one year some 3,000 students were off the hook and $18,591,436 of debt had been abolished through

Debt Strike's mutual support and collective refusal, and because the "new world" is to be based on the common good, not on Wall Street profits. Expanding beyond student loans and debt, Debt Strike has now launched the Debt Collective, a debtor's union project.

Ross argues that debtor unions are necessary because elected politicians are unable to check the power of the creditor class. Not only have these officials failed to protect citizens from financial harms, but in many cases, they have enabled the most deceitful lenders associated with various private and for-profit educational college chains, such as the Corinthian network with fifty-six campuses across the United States. This routinization of abuse of the federal loan program extends well beyond the for-profit sector as very reputable universities, public and private, are also complicit in the nexus that exists between the U.S. Department of Education and the Wall Street banks. In fact, debt liberators argue that generations of students are now in the process of being driven into a condition of "indentured servitude," and with some 40 million student debtors, if organized, they could potentially become a twenty-first-century variant of the industrial labor movement. Thus, the reference to labor is far from rhetorical as it actually describes the need to go into debt in order to labor. In other words, for most of these borrowers, debts become the wages of the future that creditors far in advance lay claim to. As Ross contends, educational debt may be thought of as a form of "premature wage theft." Ross also believes that those debtors who organize to resist this theft and who defend the common interests of student debt could ultimately be in a position to engage in a form of collective bargaining over the "costs" of higher education.

Reclaiming the older and newer commons

The "commons" as used here refers to the vesting of "all property in the community and organizes labor for the common benefit of all" and "must exist in both juridical forms and day-to-day material reality."[15] Drawing its roots from the "two charters forced on King John at Runnymede," the commons encapsulates both "juridical rights of the accused and the extraction of hydrocarbon energy resources."[16] There is the Great Charter of Liberties that most people are familiar with, concerning mostly political and legal rights. There is also the less familiar Charter of the Forest with its emphasis on the importance of the *estovers* or the necessities of life allowed by law. As Peter Linebaugh has written, the message of the two charters is plain: "political and legal rights can exist only on an economic foundation. To be free citizens we must also be equal producers and consumers."[17]

For more than 500 years. capitalists (and companies or corporations) have been taking (legally or illegally) public property or stealing the "older" commons for private use and profits. Less traditionally and reflecting the changing relations in the U.S., for example, between, on the one hand, taxable public services (e.g., police, emergency services, fire and safety, corrections, education) and, on the other hand, the privatization of these same services for corporate use and profits, these exchanges of ownership may be thought of as shrinking those newer forms of what had become modern expressions of the commons. Another newer type of twenty-first century commons includes the digitized world of intellectual property. This form of appropriation is more subtle and covert than the traditional forms. It is also expansive and all encompassing because digital technologies and "smart" applications in particular have produced a virtual world "where we no longer exert control over the objects we've bought from corporations, but corporations exert control over us through things we pay for the privilege of using."[18] Moreover, when the notions of smart are "crudely applied to the cities we live in—to our crumbling infrastructures and militarized police forces—we give into forces of privatization, algorithmic control and rule by corporate contract."[19] As Jacob Silverman has perceptively noticed with respect to the "digitized" commons and its relation to the older "brick and mortar" commons:

> It seems an indelible symbol of the time that New York City neglects essential but mundane services like public restrooms while promoting other putative municipal innovations, like the mass conversion of pay phones to Wi-Fi kiosks. As with other smart devices, which subsidize their costs with data collection, these kiosks are free—provided you submit to the collection of your information and location data. The commons becomes simply another site for private companies to spy on people.[20]

In more than a few words, the problems of losing and reclaiming the spirit, social property, and democratic power of "the commons" are complex because the terrain, literal or virtual, is located at the social intersections of where the "private" and the "public" as well as the "private" versus the "public" converge offline and online, complicated further because these different landscapes are each dynamic and subject to change over time. This is also the case with respect to the people versus the government rather than a government of, by, and for the people. Parallels at the same time exist between markets and governments as well as markets versus governments. Historically, the social products of these governing political–economic relations have yielded to varying degrees of "mixed" if not "balanced" or "sustainable" economies.

Part of losing or taking the commons involves framing the narrative on what the commons of the twenty-first century global economy looks like or is. Part of reclaiming or taking back those commons—locally and globally—involves reframing when necessary the narratives on the practices of economics, politics, ecology, and living. In the case of the U.S., those new or different or alternative or resurrected narratives include the viewpoint that democratic governments actually can be of value—efficient and functional—not only at the local levels of governing but also at the federal level of governing. Once upon a time, circa 1910 to 1970, before the U.S. government and related politics would become hijacked by an ideology of deregulated markets, by associations like the Business Roundtable and the U.S. Chamber of Commerce, and by the federal government itself, the central government was not viewed negatively by ordinary Americans. The government was not regarded as the fundamental problem or as an "enemy of the people." On the contrary, at least the overwhelming majority of Caucasian Americans regarded it favorably or in a positive light.

However, by the 1980s, aided by the stagflation of the 1970s, Ronald Reagan and the Republicans had not only declared that government was "too big," but also that government was "the problem" and needed to get out of the way so "free" markets could work at their unimpeded best. Only one decade later, the "new" centrist leaning Democratic party, acquiescing to the not-for-profit Democratic Leadership Council (DLC) was essentially on board with the "neocons" as well as with their neoliberal agendas. Accordingly, Bill Clinton found himself announcing that "the era of big government was over" even though by 1989 there was only one federal government worker for every 110 Americans compared with one for seventy-eight in the 1950s (and around one for 150 today).[21] In other words, the number of federal government employees in the United States today is about half the size that it was some sixty years ago based on population size. Nevertheless, over the past couple of decades Americans have come to dislike, if not hate, "big government" as part and parcel of the changing hegemonic view of the respective proper roles of the state, markets, government, and the private sector. Over the course of some thirty-five years of post-Keynesianism, deregulation, and free trade policies of global capitalist development, the government and the Congress have become the problem rather than expressive symptoms of the prevailing relations of the political economy.

For an excellent illustration of the ill effects of privatization and one type of newer commons loss are in the areas of emergency medical services, such as those involving Emergency Medical Technicians (EMT) and ambulance companies. These public emergency services may be provided by for-profit or by not-for-profit corporations. The latter are usually in some kind of legal relationship with hospitals or fire departments. However, since the implementation of the stricter Dodd-Frank financial regulations went into effect in 2010, which required more capital and less proportional debt by the TBTF Wall Street banks, the "corporate raiders" of an earlier era, private equity firms, with less limitations have increasingly taken over a wide array of not only financial services but also civil services like ambulance and EMT services. Today, people engage private equity firms and their incessant fees, charges, add-ons, and so forth not just to pay their home mortgages, but also when they play a round of golf on publicly or privately owned courses, when they turn on the kitchen tap for a glass of water, and when they dial up 911.

An extensive investigative study by *The New York Times* found that while private equity firms are primarily skilled in making money, they did not have much experience in providing non-financial services. The newspaper discovered that these firms were applying "a sophisticated moneymaking playbook: a mix of cost cuts, price increases and litigation."[22] The bottom line was: "Squeezed for Profit by Private Equity, Emergency Services Fail to Deliver."[23] When pitting care against costs, here are some real life examples of what happened when people dialed 911:

- A Tennessee woman slipped into a coma and died after an ambulance company took so long to assemble a crew that one worker had time for a cigarette break.
- Paramedics in New York had to covertly swipe medical supplies from a hospital to restock their depleted ambulance after emergency runs.
- A man in the suburban South watched a chimney fire burn his house to the ground as he waited for the fire department, which billed him anyway and sued him for $15,000 when he did not pay.[24]

Under private equity ownership, in addition to these anecdotal stories, local governments and their citizens experienced a few unnecessary deaths, some slower ambulance response times, failing heart monitors, and companies slipping into bankruptcy. For regulatory context, part of the reason private equity firms are subject to less restrictions today than the big banks—even though they are now doing more or less the same thing that big banks were doing before the financial crisis—is because unlike banks that take deposits and borrow from the government, private equity firms invest money from wealthy individuals and from pension funds "desperate for returns at a time of historically low interest rates."[25] For perspective, since the financial crisis, private equity firms with relatively little scrutiny have gone from managing $1 trillion to managing $4.3 trillion, more than Germany's GDP.

Another twenty-first century global or international "commons" loss are taxation revenues, accounting for an estimated 6 percent of the world's assets being hidden away.

> Over the last two decades, the growing volume of international financial transactions has allowed more and more taxpayers to escape domestic taxes by hiding their income and wealth abroad, particularly in offshore centres with strict banking and financial secrecy rules. Links and transactions with counterparts and subsidiaries located in tax havens provide individuals and business entities with channels to avoid or evade taxes or transfer funds abroad.[26]

Today, it is estimated that tax havens result in unreported financial assets amounting to between $6 and $7 trillion. Based on such figures, "the related tax evasion is between $19 and $38 billion a year on capital income, and between $2 and $2.6 trillion on personal income."[27] As Bernie Sanders has argued, "We need to end the international scandal in which large corporations and the wealthy avoid paying trillions of dollars in taxes to their national governments."[28]

In an age of global capital, the paradigmatic shift away from liberalism and Keynesian "mixed" economics to neoliberalism and private or "free" market economics occurred in less than twenty years. In the case of the U.S., the shrinking ratio of federal employees to the general population as well as cutbacks in other areas of the public sector such as higher education, welfare, and social security benefits are reflective of these ideological changes. So too are the efforts to privatize public services whenever possible. Coupled with the fastest rising rates of inequality among the richest developed nations and a weakening central government that increasingly subjects federal lawmakers to the dictates of lobbying and political contributions, to financialization, and to policies of austerity and contraction. All of these developments are related to zero-sum politics of Washington, D.C. As political scientists Jacob S. Hacker and Paul Pierson have argued in *Winner-Take-All Politics* (2011) and *American Amnesty* (2016), antipathy toward the federal government in the United States has been a rather successful product of manipulation and sabotage initiated by conservative foundations and rich libertarians such as Charles and David Koch, reaching as far back as the 1970s. What ties these two books together is Hacker and Pierson's three-prong analysis of the strategies used by Republican political players to limit and weaken government by: (1) denouncing crony capitalism while catering to narrow business interests; (2) feeding political dysfunction while railing against it; and (3) undermining the capacity of government to perform its vital functions while decrying a bungling and corrupt public sector.

Perhaps no better example of orchestrated political "dysfunctionality" was more self-evident than when President Obama nominated U.S. Court of Appeals (DC Circuit) Chief Judge Merrick Garland on March 16, 2016, to the United States Supreme Court to replace the late Justice Antonin Scalia. With neither grounds nor precedent, the Republican-controlled Senate refused to even hold confirmation hearings, let alone carry out its constitutional duty to vote the nominee up or down. In effect, they blocked any appointment of the next Justice until after the next President takes office on January 20, 2017. Such dereliction of duty by a political party in the Unites States marks an historical first. More importantly, it means that the Supreme Court would have worked for about one year without a full complement of nine justices, an unprecedented court condition as well.

As a consequence of this unique vacancy on the highest court several major decisions during the 2015–2016 season resulted in 4–4 split decisions, including a Texas Higher Education Affirmative Action case as well as Obama's Executive Action to spare some 4 million undocumented immigrants living in the U.S. from being subjected to deportation. Lower courts, in effect, have decided these cases at least temporarily. In the latter case, also brought in Texas regarding deportation deferral, this went down to defeat based on a 2015 U.S. District Court ruling that a financial burden would be placed on the state because of the additional expenses involved in issuing these immigrants driving licenses. Ordinarily, these and other deadlocked 4–4 decisions would have been resolved one way or the other by a vote of 5–4, assuming that the U.S. Senate would have taken its customary time (less than two months) between nomination and confirmation. In other words, the ninth Supreme Court Justice should have been in place at least six weeks before the end of the 2015–2016 season to cast the deciding votes in each of those deadlocked cases.

Fundamentally, reclaiming the commons means redistributing economic, political, and social power from the 1 percent to the 99 percent so that all people could be made sustainable, as in a Universal Basic Income (UBI) discussed in the final section of this chapter and checking corporate power by nationalizing or turning the oligopolistic multinationals into public utilities as discussed in the concluding chapter. In the meantime, among those efforts to reclaim the commons are two related political actions—the enactment of disclosure or accountability and anti-corruption laws—across the U.S. that are gaining footage into confronting the power of "dark money," corruption, and the Citizens United decision, which, among other things, made it constitutional without any type of donor disclosure to spend unlimited amounts of money on campaign contributions and political advertising.

To measure the effects of election spending post-Citizens United, the Brennan Center for Justice in 2015 analyzed outside spending from before and after the 2010 Citizens United decision in Alaska, Arizona, California, Colorado, Maine, and Massachusetts as well as in dozens of state and local elections where particular interests could be linked to dark money. The Brennan Center found that, compared to what was known with respect to federal spending during the same period of time between 2006 and 2014, on average dark money spending had increased at the state and local levels thirty-eight times and at the federal level thirty-four times. There are at least three other related matters to keep in mind when thinking about special interests and secrecy. First, the rise of dark money probably matters less in presidential or congressional elections than it does, for example, in a race for the utilities commission in a particular area of a state. In these political races, voters typically know less about those candidates, which also receive

> little news coverage but whose winner will have enormous power to affect energy company profits and what homeowners pay for electricity. For a relative pittance—less than $100,000—corporations and others can use dark money to shape the outcome of a low level race in which they have a direct stake.[29]

Moreover, the "ability to dominate a race with high stakes at low cost and with no oversight can facilitate corruption."[30]

Second, the growth in dark money does not take into account "the growth in 'gray money' spent by organizations that are legally required to disclose their donors but receive their funding through multiple layers of PACs that obscure its origins."[31] Third, according to the data complied by the National Institute on Money in State Politics for those same six states identified above, the percentage of outside spending that was fully transparent in 2014 was 29 percent compared to 76 percent in 2006. During this period several cases of corruption came to light from Utah to Wisconsin to California to Arizona.

As a consequence, until quite recently it was virtually impossible for voters to know which dark or gray money groups were fueling and influencing their elections, thanks once again to Citizens United. However, that has begun to change for the better through the passage of strong disclosure and enforcement laws in some states that have made it very difficult for spenders to conceal their identities from the public. For example, in California where disclosure laws are tough, there was "remarkably little increase in dark money over the cycles" that the Brennan Center examined, especially given the high levels of outside spending there.[32] In fact, only because of California's long history of rigorous (and getting tougher) disclosure laws, could the Brennan Center or anybody else even study this subject matter.

Unless more states follow the lead of California—closing non-profit loopholes, requiring the names of top donors, and making reasonable and enforceable laws—like Delaware, Maine, and Montana that have recently passed transparency laws, or Citizens United is overturned, then dark and gray monies alike will continue to skew the outcome of elections that hit closest to home without voters even knowing about it. Turning from dark money or "amoral corruption" to the more traditional forms of illegal corruption, local and state anti-corruption and governmental accountability laws have recently been enacted across the United States.

These anti-corruption laws are diverse and include felonies, misdemeanors, and civil penalties for the "usual suspects" including: influencing a public officer, accepting gratuities or gifts, official misconduct or abuse of public trust, official oppression or extortion, embezzlement or misuse of public property, misuse of official or confidential information by a public officer, and fraudulent or unlawful interest in a public contract. A summary of the provisions and spirit of model legislation is found in The American Anti-Corruption Act as follows:

1. *Stop political bribery* by making it illegal for politicians to take money from lobbyists, by banning lobbyist bundling, and by closing the revolving door.
2. *End secret money* by mandating full transparency of all political money.
3. *Give voters a stronger voice* by changing how elections are funded, by preventing politicians from fundraising during working hours, by empowering small donors over traditional PACs.
4. *Enforce the rules* by cracking down on super PACs, by eliminating lobbyist loopholes, and by strengthening anti-corruption enforcement.[33]

The sustainable paradigm and changing the political culture

Developing and spreading sustainable practices and policies is about more than changing political cultures, if this was not enough. Sustainability is also about resisting the contemporary tendencies of sustainability to become market driven rather than eco-systemically based. As Mark Halsey has shown with forestry, climate change, and the dark figure of carbon emissions, the power of capital accumulation or the force of economic rationalist logic "tightly constrains what counts as an appropriate response to climate change" or "indeed whether climate change is perceived as a problem" in the first place. Thus, one speaks "not of capitalism but of the free-market, not of pollution but carbon credits, not of fossil fuels but of green coal, not of forest or biodiversity but of carbon sinks."[34] This discourse of "ecological modernization" in other words becomes one way that the techno-capitalist state hopes to "have its cake and eat it too." Or what the oil and gas industry advertises as "balanced" rather than "less polluting" energy as a means of forestalling or slowing down the inevitable transition to renewable or clean energy.

Sustainability is also about the enabling of a new kind of post-consumption *gemeinschaft* or at least nurturing some kind of ecological mindset of new norms for transitioning to environmentally responsible lifestyles as well as improving the use of land and the design of urban space and buildings. Of course, this level of environmental consciousness begs the question of how can we achieve "just" societies that value the work of ecological reproduction or recognize that the activity of ecosystems keeps the earth viable for human life, and that these need to be cared for while we are still relying on fossil fuels or exacerbating other forms of environmental destruction? One answer involves what socialist-feminists have long emphasized, the recognition of and attention to the labor of social reproduction. Referring to the activities necessary to replenish wage laborers both individually and across generations, such as education, childcare, housework, and food preparation.

The various struggles over social reproduction have focused on the demands and possibilities of life outside of work. These efforts have much to teach us about organizing new ways of living and about creating societies that emphasize quality of life over quality of things:

> We need to find ways to live luxuriously but also lightly, aesthetically rather than ascetically. Instead of an endless cycle of working and shopping, life in a low-carbon socialist future would be oriented around activities that make life beautiful and fulfilling but require less intensive resource consumption: reading books, teaching, learning, making music, seeing shows, dancing, playing sports, going to the park, hiking, spending time with one another. Robust provision of public goods makes it possible to enjoy communal luxuries while decreasing wasteful forms of private consumption. That means public housing that's affordable for all; free, extensive transportation systems both within and between cities so that people can get around without owning a car; spacious parks and gardens that offer respite from daily life; support for arts and culture of a variety of forms; and plentiful spaces for public educational and recreational use, like libraries, basketball courts, and theatres.[35]

The story of Portland, Oregon as a "sustainable utopia" in Box 6.1 represents one of several dozen cities around the world that are "cutting-edge" leaders in sustainability. What Portland (population 619, 360 in 2010 census) has accomplished after more than twenty years of working on sustainability is a testimony to the Portland *gemeinschaft* and to what organized communities are capable of doing to change their collective human footprints when they have a mind to and set agendas accordingly. In the case of Portland's optimal geography, it also helps the city that biking is a year-round option as there are rarely freezing winters and the summers are mild, reducing the general need for heating and cooling in the respective seasons. Nevertheless, benchmark accomplishments are based on previous baselines, so reductions and improvement on the usage of resources, energy, and so on is always worth pursuing in terms of sustainability.

In the case of Portland's community *gemeinschaft* or sustainability mindset, these have been building as social forces since the 1970s. That was the time within the state of Oregon when local governmental bodies developed a penchant for what we in criminology refer to as evidenced-based policy and research. I know this to be the case from personal experience. For a short period of time, from the end of the 1979 summer to the end of the 1980 winter I lived in Portland and worked for the City's Office of Justice and Planning Evaluation. As an independent contractor I carried out a six-month study of Youth Development and Delinquency Prevention in Multnomah County involving the schools and the juvenile and human service systems.

At the time Portland as well as the other larger cities of Oregon had already established the practice of creating policy statements for all areas of community development, from transportation to energy to waste management to healthcare to education to crime prevention, and so on and so forth. Both the qualitative and quantitative data that I collected as well as the recommendations of my final report became input for an updated and broader citywide Youth Policy statement that was being rewritten at the time. One of the purposes of these policy statements is that they were to shape the rationales of the city's future development. When business people or service providers, private or public, wanted to pursue their particular interests with the appropriate local governmental bodies, they had to make the case that their proposals were conforming to the guidelines and priorities identified in the respective policy statements. This helped Portland to develop and shape the type of "geist" necessary for evolving into the Pacific Northwest's sustainable city.

BOX 6.1 "PORTLAND IS A SUSTAINABLE UTOPIA"

The following is an excerpt from *Can a City Be Sustainable?* (State of the World) by the Worldwatch Institute: "City View" (2016, pp. 292–296). Reproduced by permission of Island Press, Washington, DC.

"Portland is a sustainable utopia—how it happened" (title from a nakedcapitalism.com posting, June 2016)

The City of Portland has created and implemented strategies to reduce greenhouse gas emissions for more than 20 years. In the early 1990s, it became the first city in the United States to adopt a comprehensive carbon dioxide reduction strategy. In 2001, Multnomah County (the most populous of Oregon's 36 counties) and the City of Portland (which is the seat of Multnomah County and Oregon's largest city) passed their joint Local Action Plan on Global Warming.

In 2009, Multnomah County and Portland adopted an updated climate action plan (CAP) with expanded categories for actions and more-rigorous reduction targets. The plan identifies 93 action steps in 8 categories to reach its emissions reduction goals, ranging from curbside pickup of residential food scraps to expanding the city's streetcar and light rail system.

Thanks to strong government leadership, science-informed policy making has long been practiced in Portland. To avoid the catastrophic consequences of climate change, the city set its latest emissions reduction target by referring to current science from the Intergovernmental Panel on Climate Change (IPCC). Portland adopted an 80 percent emissions reduction target by 2050, with an interim goal of 40 percent by 2030. In line with IPCC recommendations, 1990 was set as the baseline year for the reduction target.

Expanding transit and biking options

Portland has developed a broad set of policies and programs to achieve its ambitious emissions reduction targets. Some measures far predate the concern about the changing climate but offer important tools in this fight. As early as the 1970s, Oregon adopted a statewide land-use policy to prevent urban sprawl by establishing urban growth boundaries. Guided by this policy, cities were encouraged to develop more-dense urban neighborhoods while preserving farmland and wilderness. This successful policy set the stage for a series of effective greenhouse gas emissions reduction programs in Portland.

With a focus on development that aims to provide accessible transportation options to people within its city limits, Portland has made the expansion of streetcar and light rail systems a priority in the past several decades. Since 1990, Portland has added four major light rail lines (with a fifth under construction) and the Portland Streetcar. Construction is nearing completion on the nation's first multi-modal bridge that is off-limits to private automobiles, which will carry bikes, pedestrians, and public vehicles over the Willamette River.

In addition, Portland now has 513 kilometers of bikeways, including 95 kilometers of neighborhood greenways; 291 kilometers of bike lanes, cycle tracks, and buffered bike lanes; and 127 kilometers of dedicated bike paths. Portland received the League of American Bicyclists' highest rating for being a bicycle-friendly community. In addition, *Bicycling* magazine designated Portland as the number-one bike-friendly city in the United States.

As a result of these efforts, Portland drivers travel fewer vehicle miles than those in most other similarly sized cities. Transit ridership has more than doubled in the past 20 years (totaling 100 million rides in 2013), and, today, at least 12,000 more people bike to work daily in Portland than in 1990. Six percent of Portlanders commute to work by bike, nine times the national average. Although the population of Portland has increased 31 percent, gasoline sales have decreased 7 percent compared to 1990.

Building greener and smarter

In addition to providing more transportation options, Portland has implemented a series of clean energy and energy efficiency programs. A strong focus on green buildings has led to more than 180 certified green buildings. Data for

2012 show that Portland had more LEED Platinum-certified buildings than any other city in the United States. The city also is expanding the use of solar energy in its facilities and neighborhoods; the number of solar energy systems has increased from only 1 in 2002 to 2,775 today.

Portland's energy efficiency program, Clean Energy Works (CEW), was started in 2009 with 500 pilot homes. Aimed at reducing energy consumption by 10–30 percent, CEW provides long-term, low-interest financing to homeowners for whole-home energy upgrades, with on-bill utility repayment of the loan. Because of its innovation and success, CEW attracted $20 million from the U.S. Department of Energy to scale up the pilot into a statewide effort.

The program has realized multifaceted benefits. As of April 2014, more than 3,700 homes in Oregon had been upgraded for energy efficiency. These upgrades help avoid more than 5,000 tons of greenhouse gas emissions each year, equal to powering nearly 500 homes for one year. Meanwhile, the program has generated $70 million in economic activity and created some 428 jobs.

Stormwater, the runoff created by rainfall, is another challenge faced by modern cities. Like many older cities, Portland has a combined stormwater and wastewater system, which has resulted in the pollution of local rivers and streams when high storm volume causes the system to overflow. To protect rivers and natural systems, Portland voted to enforce a series of policies that promote green infrastructure, including requiring all new construction to manage 100 percent of stormwater on-site through structures such as green streets and green roofs.

Thanks to these new policies and the city's ongoing promotion of green roofs, a number of buildings and structures in Portland now have living, vegetated roof systems that decrease runoff and offer aesthetic, air quality, habitat, and energy benefits. Portland is now home to more than 390 green roofs, covering nearly 8 hectares of rooftops. The city also has invested heavily in green infrastructure, such as rain gardens and bioswales (landscaping elements designed to remove silt and pollution from surface runoff water), with more than 1,200 such facilities in the public right-of-way. Portland uses green infrastructure to manage millions of liters of stormwater each year.

Recycling, saving energy, and creating jobs

Portland also is a national leader in recycling efforts. It has a 70 percent overall recycling rate for residential and commercial waste. Due to the addition of a weekly food scrap composting service and a shift to every-other-week garbage collection in 2011, residential garbage taken to the landfill has decreased by more than 35 percent, and collection of compostable materials has more than doubled.

Leading by example, Portland also has been setting more-aggressive emissions reduction targets for its own operations. Through efficiency improvements, including traffic lights, water and sewer pumps, and building lighting systems, the city has realized energy savings of more than $6.5 million a year, which adds up to around 30 percent savings in Portland's annual electricity costs.

Contrary to the widely held assumption that pursuing emissions reduction goals will likely slow down the local economy, the experience in Portland shows that climate actions have reduced the cost of doing business and created more-equitable, healthier, and livable neighborhoods. The number of green jobs is growing in Portland. More than 12,000 jobs in the city can be attributed to the clean technology sector, including green building, energy efficiency, and clean energy. Portland is also a national leader in innovative bicycling product manufacturing and services.

Portland's emissions reduction programs have been successful. Local greenhouse gas emissions in 2013 were 11 percent below 1990 levels (equal to a 32 percent per capita reduction), and Portland homes now use 11 percent less energy per person than in 1990. With all of these efforts and achievements, the City of Portland became one of the 16 local jurisdictions across the United States to receive recognition as a Climate Action Champion from the White House in 2014. In the same year, Portland was among ten cities worldwide to receive the C40 Cities Climate Leadership Award for its Healthy Connected City strategy. The award honors cities all over the world for excellence in urban sustainability and leadership in the fight against climate change.

Moving forward

Multnomah County and the City of Portland are in the process of reviewing and revising their 2009 climate action plan. Building on previous successes and lessons learned, the 2015 update incorporates recommendations for action and social equity into the development process.

For the energy program, the city is planning to advance net-zero energy buildings and to require energy disclosure for large commercial buildings. The focus on solar and low-carbon fuel sources will remain, and efforts to encourage the adoption of electric vehicles will be enhanced.

Portland has adopted a set of Sustainable City Principles to guide daily operations by city agencies, officials, and staff. In addition to promoting greener choices in city procurement, these principles seek to balance environmental quality, economic prosperity, and social equity, and to encourage thinking beyond first costs and consideration of the long-term, cumulative impacts of policy and financial decisions. They encourage innovation and cross-bureau collaboration; engage residents and businesses in the promotion of more-sustainable practices; and include measures in favor of a diverse city workforce and ensuring equitable services to communities of color and other underserved communities.

The city now is seeking reductions in global lifecycle emissions from consumption. Lifecycle emissions are those created by the production and use of products, from furniture to computers to appliances. For this, Portland has taken the innovative step of measuring lifecycle emissions generated through consumption by households, public agencies, and businesses. The consumption-based inventory revealed that Portland's global greenhouse gas emissions are double the in-boundary emissions traditionally measured.

Portland is planning to increase its efforts in this area and to find an effective way to communicate these findings to the local community. There also is a need to help businesses and residents better understand that their consumption choices contribute significantly to global emissions.

Portland recognizes that cities around the country and the world need to collaborate more in order to succeed in their efforts to reduce urban climate impacts. In June 2014, Portland was one of seventeen cities worldwide to launch the Carbon Neutral Cities Alliance, which is committed to achieving aggressive long-term carbon reduction goals. The Alliance aims to strategize how leading cities can work together to attain emissions reductions more effectively and efficiently.

Part of changing local and other political cultures involves not only a coalescing of multiple social movements, but importantly, it also requires changing or altering the political narratives and mindsets. In the aftermath of the 2016 Presidential election in the United States, for example, time will tell whether or not Bernie Sanders' political revolution—both in terms of his critique of a "rigged system" and his vision of a people's democracy—becomes a springboard for substantive change. In other words, will what resonated so well during the primary campaign season, especially with millennials, a narrative that interweaved the attitudes and sentiments of the Occupy Wall Street movement with anti-fracking or environmentally conscious and climate conserving folks, and with those who recognize the harmful effects of legalized corruption by way of billions of dollars in lobbying, in Super Pac contributions, and by individual political donors buying elections up and down the municipal, state, and congressional ballots, have legs that will significantly change those political realities in the future remains to be seen.

People must understand that while "a host of current technologies, from clean energy sources to biotechnologies, promise to be part of a more sustainable future," as long as these are privately owned, controlled, and produced "only when profitable, and accessible only to those who can pay, their potential will be exploited only as it serves capitalists."[36] State-owned MNCs would make decisions about producing and implementing new technologies based on scientific research and democratically chosen objectives and goals to comport with environmental and health benefits and social needs, "rather than producing and consuming wastefully in order to keep various industries profitable."[37] For example, "deregulation and privatization of electric utilities in the neoliberal era has crippled the public's ability to build the new interconnected electric infrastructure [at least in the United States] that would make a major clean-energy transition possible" on an affordable and large scale for all.[38]

Recall that capitalism began by appropriating the means of production and enclosing public and common resources for private benefit while dispossessing previous indigenous users. Under neoliberal economizing, this type of dispossession continues into the global present. By contrast, collective ownership of the means of production would include common ownership of the land, oceans, and atmosphere. This would mean not only sharing in the resources that those spaces generate, but also democratically deciding how these should be used in the first place.

From manufacturing to post-industrialism and services: building a sustainable global economy

In *The Entrepreneurial State*, Mariana Mazzucato accomplishes many things. For one, she debunks the myth that the state is some kind of slacker and bureaucratic apparatus naturally at odds with the dynamics of the private market: "Despite the perception of the U.S. as the epitome of private sector-led wealth creation, in reality it is the State that has been engaged on a massive scale in entrepreneurial risk to spur innovation."[39] For another, Mazzucato describes several key examples of the successful entrepreneurial state, including the U.S. government's Defense Advanced Research Project, its Small Business Innovation Research venture, and the National Nanotechnology Initiative as well as the Orphan Drug Act passed by the U.S. in 1983 and the European Union in 2001. She argues that what these projects all have in common is the proactive role taken by the state to shape markets and drive techno-innovation. In each of these cases, the state "provided early-stage finance where venture capital ran away, while also commissioning high-level innovative private sector activity that would not have happened without public policy goals backing a strategy and vision."[40]

Most importantly perhaps, Mazzucato makes it clear among the multiple purposes for state investment that providing taxpayer subsidized research to spare the private sector from the expenses and the risks should not be one of those purposes. On the contrary, she maintains that the government and the private sector should "take the risks together" and that we should all "enjoy the rewards." The problem is that during the transition away from a manufacturing and toward a services economy, in the U.S. and elsewhere there has also been an ideological obsession with cutting public spending, austerity economizing, and privatization, which have all contributed to the disinvestment from market innovation. The lessons drawn here and applied to the rest of the twenty-first century are simple: the state, and better yet, state-owned multinational corporations, should be investing and reinvesting in sustainable R & D that could drive global markets so that all people on earth could benefit.

Unlike the turn of the twentieth century when there was an even larger transition from agriculture to industry, the contemporary transitioning from a manufacturing to a services economy is occurring in a global world where both demand and consumption are declining and global warming is demanding a radical change in energy production and distribution. Comparatively, over the course of the last century, "farm employment in the United States dropped to 2 percent of the work force from 41 percent, even as output soared. Since 1950, manufacturing's share has shrunk to 8.5 percent of nonfarm jobs, from 24 percent."[41] Similarly, the loss of manufacturing jobs locally and globally still has a way to go before it bottoms out. Thanks to automation and robotization, the "return of manufacturing" is not going to happen because of these technological developments. Moreover, the zero-sum nature of manufacturing jobs worldwide means that those jobs will continue to chase the cheapest costs of labor. Also, as long as debit is up, then demand will be down. Even by transforming both locally and globally the maldistribution of wealth, resources, and services into productively sustainable economies that respect the limitations of both the earth and climate change, manufacturing jobs inside of factories will continue to decline around the world. As Nobel-winning economist Joseph Stiglitz has pointed out: "Global employment in manufacturing is going down because productivity increases are exceeding increases in demand for manufactured products by a significant amount."[42] This cannot change without some fundamental modifications in both monetary polices and in the ownership of mega multinational corporations.

The shrinking of manufacturing jobs globally is already having its negative effects on the developing countries (DCs), emerging countries (ECs), and lesser developed countries (LDCs), especially those developing economies that are suffering from premature deindustrialization. In these emerging (e.g., India, China, and Brazil) and lesser developed (e.g., countries in Asia, Africa, and Latin America) nations, for example, peaks in manufacturing job demands are setting in earlier or at much lower levels of income than they did with respect to those DCs that benefitted from earlier industrialization. As Eduardo Porter explains:

> The richest countries today started deindustrializing when they were already well off and benefitted from fairly skilled and productive workforces that could make the transition into well-paid service jobs, as increasingly affluent consumers devoted less of their incomes to physical goods and more to leisure, advanced health care and other services. Poorer countries have more limited options. If the demise of manufacturing jobs in the United States forced many workers into low-paid retail jobs and the like, imagine the challenge in a country like India, where factory employment has already topped out, yet income per person is only one twenty-fifth of what it was in the United States at its peak.[43]

Of course, the same could be said of China in relation to Japan or Taiwan. With respect to the poorest countries of the Global South the forecast is even gloomier as they have come, if they did, to manufacturing relatively late in the age of industrialism.

"Fall out" from these global relations of capitalist development has intensified inequalities across all economies. These inequalities are expressed in Latin American drug cartels, Middle Eastern conflicts, hundreds of thousands of migrating refugees worldwide, millions of homeless people, heightened xenophobia, ethno-nationalism, the Brits leaving the EU, and American workers rebelling against the politics of neoliberalism and "free" trade. The "bottom line" is that promises to recapture industrial-era greatness are hollow ones and should be abandoned. Instead full employment of meaningful work and benefits should be available for all folks who need them. At the same time, because of the surplus number of laborers in work forces worldwide, those who want to pursue other forms of community, artistic or other socially valuable pursuits, should be provided with some kind of a universal basic income (UBI). In the United States and in other developed economies, emphasis should be focused on clean energy, healthcare, education, and infrastructure, to name some of the most obvious areas critical to sustainability. A significant problem is that financial inequality, expressed in the declining median net worth of U.S. families (see Table 6.1) from 1998 to 2013, will also not occur without some kind of radically pragmatic change in the distribution of goods and services.

One "commonwealth response" to the growing inequality in wealth and purchasing power could be the adoption of a UBI, or the guaranteeing that all people will have a minimum number of dollars to participate in the marketplace to acquire and consume goods and services, which would sustain the net worth of the bottom 20 to 30 percent of U.S. families enabling them to provide for their basic needs. The UBI would potentially be a more efficient and effective system for balancing supply and demand markets especially around the basic distribution of food, shelter, and healthcare. With all people able to avail themselves of their basic needs for life, a more democratic power would be voiced with respect to what is created and how much is actually needed.

Building a sustainable global economy depends upon rooting out contradictory sources of the sustainability problem as well as defining the parameters of sustainability as an economic, social, and environmental hybrid. For measures and definitions of "sustainability," economic or otherwise, to be viable ones, they need

TABLE 6.1 Median net worth, 1998 vs. 2013 (figures in 2013 dollars)

	1998 ($)	*2013 ($)*	*Percentage change (%)*
All families	102,500	81,000	−20.8
Lower class★	8,300	6,100	−26.5
Working class★★	47,400	22,400	−52.7
Middle class★★★	76,300	61,700	−19.1
Top 10%	646,600	1,130,700	74.9

Source: U.S. Federal Survey of Consumer Finances (2013). www.federalreserve.gov/econresdata/scf/scfindex.htm.

Notes: ★Bottom 20 percent of incomes; ★★second lowest 20 percent of incomes; ★★★middle 20 percent of incomes. Median is the halfway point with half of incomes below and half of incomes above. Net worth is what you own minus what you owe.

to be able to answer two questions affirmatively: (1) Is the measure used to document sustainability a sustainable one? (2) Is the definition commensurate with a global perspective on sustainability such as the optimization of the long-term quality of life for all living organisms and their descendants? Spoiler alert: no models of sustainability—economic, global, or environmental—are able to answer both of these questions in the affirmative without the viability to modify the current trajectories of both climate change and global warming, ergo, the Paris Agreement of 2015–2016 that was set in motion to avoid dangerous climate change by limiting global warming to below 2 degrees centigrade. In the case of the U.S. that means by 2030 cutting its greenhouse gas emissions created by electric power plants by one-third, using 2005 for the baseline.

Whether locally or globally, sustainability has been defined in both economic and ecological terms. Economic sustainability generally implies the ability of nations to support a level of economic production indefinitely; however, there are different measures used to calculate economic sustainability. The most common measure includes the use of the Gross Domestic Product (GDP), or the total amount of production created within a nation, typically for a one-year period. According to the Central Intelligence Agency's World Factbook, GDP for 2010 varied from $16 trillion for the European Union, $15 trillion for the U.S., and $6 trillion for China to $16 billion for Afghanistan, $7 billion for Haiti, and $105 million for the Falkland Islands.

Sustainability, in turn, becomes what nations want to happen indefinitely to growth in relation to their Gross National Product (GNPs). Hence, they annually establish GDP growth targets. Typically these rates of growth are not less than 2 percent per year (see total annual target, Table 6.2) except following periods of economic recession or depression, like they still are globally in 2016. Tautologically, steady growth in total national GDP above the target rate of growth becomes the de facto definition of sustainability.

The problems with this definition of economic sustainability are many. For example, national GDPs do not calculate how much the average person's income

TABLE 6.2 GDP data for selected countries for 2010

Country	Total annual target (%)	Average GDP per person in US$	% below preferred minimum standard of living level
India	9	3,500	76
China	8	7,600	36
Vietnam	7	3,100	48
United States (implied target)	2	47,200	15
Japan	2	34,000	16
England or UK	1.7	34,800	14

Source: "Finding and Resolving the Root Causes of the Sustainability Problem." *Thwink.* www.thwink. org/sustain/glossary/EconomicSustainability.htm is, nor do they reveal how many people are at the low end of the distribution of income or are starving (see average GDP per person, Table 6.2). The GDP per person is more important than the GDP per nation, because the former measure reveals the large gaps between the average persons living in developing economies and living in developed economies. They also help to explain the higher and unrealistic growth targets of the LDCs and ECs as efforts to catch up in average GDP per person. Globally, however, a model of forever expanding GDPs is not reasonable in general or in particular, given the persistent worldwide slowdown in contemporary economic growth. On the other hand, the GDP per person may be a better and more reasonable or sustainable measure or path to pursue toward sustainability, especially when comparisons are also made in relationship to the quality of lives. This is rendered possible when one accounts for the poverty threshold or poverty line, referred to in Table 6.2, as the percent below preferred minimum standard of living level.

The poverty thresholds, lines, or minimum living standards refer to "the minimum level of income deemed necessary to achieve an adequate standard of living in a given country."[44] In poor countries the poverty threshold or minimum standard of living may be as low as $1.25 per day, which is considered enough money to avoid malnutrition, and frequently, death. In the United States, it is $30 a day. In the scheme of global monetary dollars it is reasonable to use this index as a measure of economic sustainability that occurs when a political unit or nation has a very small percentage—say, 5 percent or less—of its population below its preferred minimum standard of living. It is also reasonable to imagine that these preferred minimum standards of living could be raised for all people in all nations with some sustainable redistribution of the concentrations of globalized wealth.

The problem with these economic models of sustainability, however, is that they have still not factored in climate change or global warming. Without the recognition of the Earth's dwindling resources and the unsustainability of the reproduction of global capital as well as the transition away from fossil fuels and toward green growth, renewable energy, and the sustainability of global ecosystems, then the prevailing models of economic sustainability will not be sustainable. In contrast, as the roots of unsustainability are identified in their relationships with the treatment of the ecosystems and climate change, then the 2030 Agenda for Transforming Our World from the United Nations Sustainable Development Summit (see Box 6.2) makes sense for pursing scientific pathways toward democratic capitalism and a healthier, more secure, and sane world.

BOX 6.2 TRANSFORMING OUR WORLD: THE 2030 AGENDA FOR SUSTAINABLE DEVELOPMENT[45]

- Goal 1. End poverty in all its forms everywhere.
- Goal 2. End hunger, achieve food security and improved nutrition, and promote sustainable agriculture.
- Goal 3. Ensure healthy lives and promote well-being for all at all ages.

- Goal 4. Ensure inclusive and equitable quality education, and promote lifelong learning opportunities for all.
- Goal 5. Achieve gender equality and empower all women and girls.
- Goal 6. Ensure availability and sustainable management of water and sanitation for all.
- Goal 7. Ensure access to affordable, reliable, sustainable, and modern energy for all.
- Goal 8. Promote sustained, inclusive, and sustainable economic growth, full and productive employment, and decent work for all.
- Goal 9. Build resilient infrastructure, promote inclusive and sustainable industrialization, and foster innovation.
- Goal 10. Reduce inequality within and among countries.
- Goal 11. Make cities and human settlements inclusive, safe, resilient, and sustainable.
- Goal 12. Ensure sustainable consumption and production patterns.
- Goal 13. Take urgent action to combat climate change and its impacts.
- Goal 14. Conserve and sustainably use the oceans, seas, and marine resources for sustainable development.
- Goal 15. Protect, restore, and promote sustainable use of terrestrial ecosystems, sustainably manage forests, combat desertification, halt and reverse land degradation, and halt biodiversity loss.
- Goal 16. Promote peaceful and inclusive societies for sustainable development, provide access to justice for all and build effective, accountable, and inclusive institutions at all levels.
- Goal 17. Strengthen the means of implementation and revitalize the global partnership for sustainable development.

In the meanwhile and for the foreseeable future, a Global Marshall Plan for the worldwide problem of "joblessness"—expected to surpass more than 200 million unemployed people by the end of 2017—could play a key role while transitioning to sustainability. A strategy of this kind for addressing the structural surplus of global workers, unlike those unemployment forecasting models used by government and industry, takes into account the extraordinary harm or social and economic costs that ensues from these so-called natural rates of unemployment. A worldwide unemployment epidemic, such as the present one, comes equipped with harsh human, environmental, and economic realities. For example, the deep negative impact of joblessness on the physical and mental health of individuals as well as their life satisfaction is well known:

> It's not hyperbole to note … that unemployment kills… Research shows that one in five suicides is related to unemployment, and joblessness causes 32–37 percent excess mortality for men. And while for women the impact is less clear, we know that there are robust and lasting negative effects from

unemployment on social participation and social capital—all prerequisites for a fulfilling and productive life at home and the workplace.[46]

Of course, among criminologists the link between ordinary crime and joblessness is well known, with rates of specific violent and property crimes related to variations in both business cycles and unemployment. In light of the International Labor Organization's findings that "74 million young people are unemployed globally" and with other estimates as high as six or seven times the ILO's, something significant needs to be done to "save these lives" from all of the social dangers, including child/human trafficking and global sexual and labor exploitation, that surround their potential living landscapes. Finally, as for the other 125 million of estimated unemployed adults by the ILO, their joblessness also harms their children and other family members by exacerbating rates of "infant mortality, depression, alcohol consumption, and the spread of infectious disease."[47]

A global Marshall plan for joblessness would be "proactive" rather than "reactive" in its approach. Presently, most governments tackle the issue and related issues of unemployment by trying to counteract their impact after mass layoffs have already occurred. Their monetary and fiscal measures have been designed to produce investment-led growth that is typically too weak and always too late to be either effective or efficient for capital reproduction and consumption. Instead, what is needed are strong fiscal policies that not only move beyond policies that accept unemployment as part of the natural order of things, but that also realize that policies of neoliberalism, privatization, and austerity are the problem and not the solution. Furthermore, a globally coordinated approach to the structurally changing nature of joblessness calls for deliberate and direct actions as well as for mobilizing the planet's most abundant resource—labor—during the transition to economic sustainability. Economist Pavlina Tcherneva describes such a plan:

> No workfare, no bullshit jobs, no compulsory work, no digging holes. A global Marshall plan would offer employment opportunities to the unemployed in every country, while addressing country-specific problems. As the world faces the consequences of climate change, the Marshall Plan can be the big-push policy that puts the unemployed to work in a Global Green New Deal program. Whether it involves green projects, infrastructure projects, community projects, or care projects, there is no shortage of projects that need doing.[48]

One should understand that lasting benefits from "fair" over "free" trade can only be reaped under conditions of full employment, because in the absence of global full employment, trade necessarily produces winners and losers. Similarly, without the substitution of full employment and fair trade agreements, the prevailing "free" trade agreements will continue to lack adequate labor and environmental standards and practices as outlined by various international labor associations and environmental organizations. This global plan could be funded by an international institution, requiring each nation to institute a national safety-net and mandating that government, labor, and business cooperate in devising plans for creating jobs and projects that offset or surpass job losses from trade. These arrangements could possibly be supplanted by a supranational currency—not as money for exchange but rather as a unit of account used to track international flows of assets and liabilities—and a multilateral clearing system or International Clearing Union as first proposed in the 1940s by John M. Keynes and E.F. Schumacher's bancor system and revived more recently by Zhou Xiaochuan, the Governor of the People's Bank of China, in response to the financial crisis of 2007–2010.

Lastly, some "comparative" data reveals how relatively inexpensive such monetary and fiscal policies could be in rendering joblessness obsolete despite the growing worldwide surplus of labor, if all societies were on board. The original price tag for the Marshall Plan that passed the U.S. Congress and was signed into law by President Truman was $5 billion, which represented 2 percent of the GDP and 11 percent of governing spending. Over the next three years the Marshall Plan distributed an additional $8 billion more. "Later, it was replaced by the 1951 Mutual Security Plan and by the time it expired, the US was providing $7 billion annually to Europe until 1961."[49]

More recently, in 2009, the American Recovery and Reinvestment Act (ARRA) authorized $848 billion in economic stimulus. Spread out over four years, this came to a little over 1 percent of GDP per year. Misguidedly, ARRA sought only to save or create some 3–4 million jobs with that money. Had the funds during the Great Recession "been disbursed as they were under the New Deal, namely towards direct employment programs and public investment, the ARRA could have created 20 million living-wage jobs, virtually wiping out all of the unemployment and underemployment in the US."[50]

Notes

1 Leggett, John. C. 1973. *Taking State Power: The Sources and Consequences of Political Challenge*. New York: Harper & Row, p. xi.
2 Ibid.
3 Ibid.
4 Ibid.
5 Ibid.
6 Quoted in de Graaf, John. 2014. "From 'The New Economy' to the Cooperative Commonwealth." *Truthout*. August 8. www.truth-out.org/opinion/item/25401-from-the-new-economy-to-the-cooperative-commonwealth.
7 De Graaf, 2014.
8 Corporate Accountability International. 2016. "About Us." www.stopcorporateabuse.org/about-us.
9 Ibid.
10 Letter mailing from Kelle Louaillier, President of Corporate Accountability International. 2016.
11 Ibid.
12 Chacko, Rinu. 2013. "Top 10 World's Largest Pharmaceutical Companies 2013." *List Dose*. June 29. http://listdose.com/top-10-worlds-largest-pharmaceutical-companies-2013/.
13 Rosenthal, Elisabeth. 2016. "Your Cure: The Side Effects of Ads." *The New York Times*. February 28: Sunday Review, pp. 1 and 4.

14 Ibid.
15 Linebaugh, Peter. 2008. *The Magna Carta Manifesto: Liberties and Commons for All.* Berkeley, CA: University of California Press, p. 6.
16 Ibid.
17 Ibid.
18 Silverman, Jacob. 2016. "All Knowing." *The New York Times Magazine.* June 19: p. 15.
19 Ibid.
20 Ibid.
21 Bishop, Matthew. 2016. "Review of *American Amnesia: How the War on Government Led Us to Forget What Made America Prosper.*" *The New York Times.* April 6. www.nytimes.com/2016/04/10/books/review/american-amnesia-by-jacob-s-hacker-and-paul-pierson.html?_r=0.
22 Ivory, Danielle, Protess, Ben, and Bennett, Kitty. 2016. "When You Dial 911 and Wall Street." *The New York Times.* June 26: front page.
23 Ibid.
24 Ibid.
25 Ibid.
26 Pellegrini, Valeria and Sanelli, Alessandra. 2016. "How Much International Tax Evasion Is There?" *Naked Capitalism.* March 15. www.nakedcapitalism.com/2016/03/how-much-international-tax-evasion-is-there.html.
27 Ibid.
28 Sanders, Bernie. 2016. "Bernie Sanders: Democrats Need to Wake Up." *The New York Times.* June 28. www.nytimes.com/2016/06/29/opinion/campaign-stops/bernie-sanders-democrats-need-to-wake-up.html?emc=edit_th_20160629&nl=todaysheadlines&nlid=34985918&_r=0.
29 Lee, Chisun and Norden, Lawrence. 2016. "The Secret Power Behind Local Elections." *The New York Times.* June 26: Sunday Review, p. 5
30 Ibid.
31 Ibid.
32 Ibid.
33 I would prefer to do away with PACs altogether and substitute public for private funding of elections. To download the Act, go to: http://anticorruptionact.org/whats-in-the-act/. Here is a link to the 2016 State of Washington Government Accountability Act: http://integritywashington.org/wp-content/uploads/2016/04/WAGAA_Summary-2.pdf.
34 Haley, Mark. 2012. "Defining Pollution Down: Forestry, Climate Change and the Dark Figure of Carbon Emissions." In *Criminological and Legal Consequences of Climate Change*, edited by Stephen Farrall, Tawhida Ahmed, and Duncan French. Oxford and Portland, OR: Hart, pp. 169–192 (p. 184).
35 Battistoni, Alyssa. 2016. "Wouldn't a More Democratic World Just Mean a Bigger Environmental Crisis?" In *The ABCs of Socialism* edited by Bhaskar Sunkara. London and Brooklyn: Verso, pp. 94–102 (pp. 98–99).
36 Ibid., p. 100.
37 Ibid., p. 101.
38 Ibid., p. 100.
39 Mazzucato, Mariana. 2015. *The Entrepreneurial State: Debunking Public vs. Private Sector Myths.* New York: Public Affairs, p. 79.
40 Ibid.
41 Porter, Eduardo. 2016. "The Myth of a Return to Manufacturing Greatness." *The New York Times.* April 26. www.nytimes.com/2016/04/27/business/economy/the-mirage-of-a-return-to-manufacturing-greatness.html?_r=0.
42 Quoted in ibid.
43 Ibid.
44 Quoted in *Economic Sustainability*. N.D. www.thwink.org/sustain/glossary/EconomicSustainability.htm.
45 Sustainable Development Knowledge Platform. 2015. "Transforming Our World: The 2030 Agenda for Sustainable Development." From the United Nations Sustainable

Development Summit. September 25. https://sustainabledevelopment.un.org/post2015/transformingourworld.
46 Tcherneva, Pavlina. 2016. "A Global Marshall Plan for Joblessness?" *Naked Capitalism.* May 13. www.nakedcapitalism.com/2016/05/a-global-marshall-plan-for-joblessness.html.
47 Ibid.
48 Ibid.
49 Ibid.
50 Ibid.

CONCLUSION

Democratic capitalism, state-owned multinationals, and sustainable pragmatism

Reflective of a new and emerging paradigm based on a restructuring of sustainable capital markets and of the democratic relations between governments and their electorates, the previous chapter identified alternative pathways for reclaiming the commons, building democratic accountability, and reducing state-routinized crimes in the twenty-first century. Unless there are some basic or structural changes in the need for capital and in some of the ways in which capital is accumulated and reproduced locally and globally and, simultaneously, unless there is also a reordering in the democratic roles and power relationships between governments, markets, and the people, then there is no reason to believe that the typically "non-criminal" treatment of many of the illegalities and harms committed by multinational corporations will discontinue in either the short or long run. On the contrary, staying the neoliberal course of capital accumulation and financialization will exacerbate the inequalities between and within nations, sustain the contradictions of unsustainable economic development, and reinforce the reproduction of multinational harm and criminality.

For example, neoliberal policy stratagems to address the growing poverty, inequality, and low consumption and productivity in the U.S. as well as many other developed economies call for cutting benefits as well as corporate and individual income taxes as the means for stimulating stagnating economies with growth rates like those in the United States of barely 2 percent for 2016. This policy orientation is also for raising the age of retirement, for securing the Trans-Pacific Partnership (TPP), for expanding regressive sales taxes, and for more privatization—pretty much the same counterproductive agenda and policy direction of the past thirty-five years that is at least partially responsible for the current set of contradictory relations of "secular stagnation." Moreover, staying the neoliberal economizing course means that state activities, including the non-enforcement of criminal malfeasance, reinforces the power of those who own capital while it also increases worker subordination to market discipline rather than offering more freedom from its growing demands.

Uncritical criminologists occasionally take some solace in celebrating so-called successes like the 2002 Sarbanes-Oxley Act (SOX), which allegedly has "changed corporate behavior into greater compliance."[1] On the ground, however, nothing could be further from the reality of the non-enforcement of corporate misbehavior. Two years after the law's passage and the re-election of President Bush to a second term of office in 2004, the criminal prosecutions under the law fell to a trickle and shortly thereafter virtually disappeared. Per the 2005 unanimous ruling of the U.S. Supreme Court, which threw out the jury verdict against Arthur Anderson's involvement in cooking the Enron books, future prosecutions under SOX were found to be too risky of a gamble to take so they came unofficially to a halt.[2] Moreover, in the most comprehensive meta-analysis of research studies on the efforts to deter corporate crime published in 2016, the bottom line was that nothing works: not civil law, criminal law, or regulatory law. Nevertheless, the authors are hopeful that more rigorous research will find the right combination of sanctions to deter corporate crime.[3] Good luck with that coming to fruition anytime soon, because 500 years of state-routinized capitalist relations capitulating over and over to the non-enforcement of corporate malfeasance and criminal wrongdoing proves otherwise.[4]

As *Unchecked Corporate Power* has shown throughout its examination, the unfettered crimes of the powerful in general and of multinational corporate crimes in particular are good for these companies' bottom lines so long as there are no real negative consequences or penal sanctions for doing so, which has been and will be the case without any kind of structural transformation of the prevailing relations of the global political economy. The lack of enforcement is especially logical in an age of financialization and the unsustainable expansionism of capital accumulation and reproduction, where at least since the global financial crisis (GFC) of 2007–2008 trade growth has been collapsing everywhere, overall rates of consumption are shrinking, and rising debts have become the driving economic forces behind developed as well as emerging countries alike. Adding to these contradictory forces of a global capital slowdown is the slowdown of the growth in the world's working-age population as well as the rise of insecure impermanent or contingent workers, especially in the DCs.

Presently, after a long hiatus, the 85-year-old billionaire hedge fund founder and socially "left-leaning" philanthropist George Soros has "returned to trading, lured by opportunities to profit from what he sees as coming economic troubles."[5] The last time Mr. Soros was highly involved in his firm's trading was back in 2007, when he had concerns about the housing bubble and began placing bearish wagers over two years that netted more than $1 billion in gains. At the beginning of 2016 Soros began to oversee macro investing at the firm, because over the previous six months his worldview had darkened as economic and political issues in China, Europe and Latin America were becoming more intractable.

A few weeks before the Brexit vote, his concerns revolved primarily around China's capital flight situation that had been depleting foreign currency reserves, which if the situation continued would weaken its economy exerting "deflationary pressure—a damaging spiral of falling wages and prices—on the U.S. and global economies."[6] Soros was also concerned that the European Union might collapse under the weight of the migration crisis, the continuing economic challenges in Greece, and especially if the citizens of the United Kingdom were to vote on June 23, 2016, to exit from the European Union—which they did do, 52 percent to 48 percent. Immediately, the British pound precipitously dropped, as did European, Asian and U.S. stocks, as investments were being transferred into safer government bonds. However, stock markets quickly returned to where they were or better in less than two weeks. The UK departure from the EU, however, represented an ideological blow to both neoliberalism and austerity politics. Politically, the question became, would other member nations of the European Union follow suit, and would this signal the unraveling of the EU? A month after the Brexit vote, Scotland was talking about the likelihood of a pro-EU referendum. As for the other countries that could follow Britain out of the EU, or might be discussing its pros and cons, these include: Sweden, Denmark, Greece, The Netherlands, Hungary, and France.

Even more broadly, and since the recent global financial crisis, DCs have been grappling with the specters of deflation and debt-driven economies. While deflation was

a reflection of the downswing in economic activity in the aftermath of the crisis, such price deflation has proved remarkably impervious to the most expansionary monetary policies and liquidity expansion that the world economy has yet seen. This has had adverse consequences in terms of producers' expectations, which in turn have kept investment low. It has not benefitted working people because wages have stayed low or continued to fall. And it has generated tendencies of the debt deflation-type … whereby the real value of debt and debt servicing keep rising because of falling prices, and make it harder for debtors to deleverage or to increase their spending.[7]

It now appears that at least the two largest ECs—China and India—are both experiencing price deflation. In the case of India, debt default for some time has been placing major strains on bank balance sheets. Similar patterns seem to be emerging in the Global South. For now, at least, and foreseeably into the future, without structural adjustments in both the North and South, continued wage income suppression will extend further ineffective demand/consumption. Coupled with fiscal consolidation and loose monetary policies, these contemporary strategies in place for nearly a decade to stimulate national economies and to reproduce the need for perpetual capital expansionism seem to be sputtering at best.

Meanwhile, the "real-economy investment decisions" continue to be made "by real-economy players, like major corporations who make capital budgeting decisions" as the "overwhelming source of investment funding for companies is retained earnings, not external funding."[8] Moreover, "if capitalists aren't induced to make investments through business subsidies and other incentives, they simply refuse to invest."[9] Similarly, the role of venture capital in start-ups is also minimal. At the same time, the growing concentrations of global wealth only reinforces the "manufacturing of speculation" and the "doubling down" on neoliberal policies of privatization, austerity, and securitization—all of which worsens class stagnation and economic inequality for the deteriorating middle and working classes in the DCs, not to mention the worsening conditions for the vast majority of people living in the ECs and LDCs. These relations of production lower consumptive demands for goods and services that in terms of profitability "versus" sustainability further exacerbate the contradictions of capitalism and global reproduction.

This expanding wealth gap along with the developing, less-secure irregular economies also worsen the asymmetries in social and political power. As these forces of production intensify, the probability is that the crimes of multinational corporations will be even less controllable in the future than they have always been. Critically, a fundamental shift in the power relations of the global political economy and a paradigmatic shift in economic thought and legal intervention away from the prevailing model of capitalism based on a false duality of internal versus external controls of "free" markets is what is required to reign in multinational misbehavior. The alternative pathways for global development based on an understanding of the laws of capital-state development, which have always been inseparable economic institutions tied into the well-being of the other, would pursue the effectiveness of demarginalizing the crimes of the most powerful corporations.

In one examination of corporate criminals and why corporations must be abolished, Steve Tombs and David Whyte demystify the likelihood that corporations can be rational, reasonable "citizens," while revealing that private, profit-making corporations are habitual and routine offenders. They argue that in their present formations, corporations are "permitted, licensed and encouraged to systematically kill, maim and steal for profit" impelling them "to cause harm to people and the environment." Tombs and Whyte contend further "the corporation cannot be easily reformed" and conclude that the "only feasible solution to this 'crime' problem is to abolish the legal and political privileges that enable the corporation to act with impunity."[10] In another work, Tombs argues that there is the need to move beyond regulation. He shows, with respect to "social protections" running up to and after the financial implosion of 2008 in the UK, how the government and state institutions during this period of regulation and re-regulation not only "worked feverishly and relentlessly to further the emergence of norms of regulation" that were "shorn of effective enforcement capacities," but they were also "recast as an overall central and local government *growth function*."[11] As noted back in Chapter 1, I have also underscored that in an age of global capital, change requires moving beyond

> those tinkering efforts in regulation or self-regulation advocated by persons associated with lenient or softer criminal enforcement of corporate crime, such as enhanced self-monitoring, ungraded ethical conduct, or greater social responsibility. For decades now, these and other banal ideas and bankrupt practices have proven themselves inadequate for addressing all forms of corporate misbehavior. In short, these types of sanctions are of little value beyond

their ideological or obfuscating appeal as each misses hitting the proverbial etiological nail with the criminological hammer.[12]

Quite contrarily, I am interested in

long-term revolutionary efforts that, on the one hand, resist those pathways to unsustainable capital expansion and, on the other hand, are supportive of social transformation, involving such changes as breaking up and/or turning those too big to fail (or jail) mega-banks of the global economy into public utilities.[13]

I am also interested "in those other attempts to structurally change the distribution as well as the accumulation of capital as a strategy for addressing both monetary disparities and the asymmetries of political and economic power."[14]

In the contemporary world of capitalization and globalization, most countries find themselves losing their formerly semi-autonomous power relationship with capital, contributing to both regional fragmentation and conflict as well as to social integration and technological cooperation. The capitalist economic system and international economic organizations have certainly spread throughout the globe, as evidenced by the unprecedented role of multinational corporations in generating foreign direct investment, trade, technology, and crime. While some political economists argue that globalization is leading to the development of a "transnational historic block" composed of MNCs, international banks, IEOs, and international business groups from the most powerful capitalist states, other political economists prefer an alternative model of "triadization" where the political, economic, and sociocultural integration of developed countries has been constricted to three regions of the world: Southeast Asia, Western Europe, and North America. Nevertheless, there are the emerging countries such as China, India, South Korea, Russia, Brazil, and South Africa making significant, if uneven, inroads into DCs' dominance, forming their own alliances while at the same time belonging to various trading agreements among the triad nation-states.[15]

As these geopolitical economic relations unfold globally, nation-states are internationally sharing authority with MNCs and international organizations and institutions; domestically, central, or national governments are sharing authority with NGOs and regional and local authorities. During this period of post-industrial financial capital, the effects of these globalizing relations have placed unions and welfare entitlements alike on the defensive, limiting the abilities of countries to regulate or stabilize their national economies because of the massive growth in international capital flows that contribute to destabilizing exchange rate fluctuations. In turn, this increased capital mobility compels most states to adopt capital-friendly policies, because MNCs and international banks can shift their funds to more welcoming locations where there are lower wages, taxes, and environmental standards, not to mention the even laxer or non-enforcement of some multinational corporate crimes. Critics, of course, call on states and international organizations alike to adopt regulations to limit the volatility of capital flows. Critics of global capitalism have also been arguing that political, social, and economic policy-making as well as the "rule of law" and its control or regulation are increasingly being transferred from the once democratically more responsive governments to MNCs, international banks, and allied economic organizations.[16]

Perhaps nothing exemplifies this more than the struggle over the passage of the Trans-Pacific Partnership (TPP) trade agreement and especially Article 9. While Bernie Sanders had always been against "free" trade deals of any kind, Hillary Clinton had always been in favor of them, including the TPP, until the heat of the primary battle for Democratic presidential nomination when she changed her position to align with Sander's, as well as that of Donald Trump, the Republican nominee who railed against the TPP and was elected president in November 2016. President Trump's Democratic predecessor Barack Obama was also opposed to the TPP when he first ran for the highest office in 2004. However, during his two terms of office President Obama was among its biggest cheerleaders, even performing a *slow jam* on NBC's *The Tonight Show Starring Jimmy Fallon*, [June 9, 2016], which included lyrics praising the merits of TPP.

While this treaty should bode well for multinational corporations and their CEOs, as for the member countries and their workers, it appears that would not be the case. Like the previous international trade agreements that have hemorrhaged away millions of jobs in the United States, one governmental study by the International Trade Commission projected that by 2025 "the TPP would augment its member countries' GDP growth by a meager 0.1 percent..." and it estimated by 2032 that "would increase America's economic growth by 0.15 percent ($42.7 billion) and boost incomes by 0.23 percent ($57.3 billion)."[17] The study also found, more tragically, that it would probably cost the U.S. nearly 500,000 jobs.

Article 9 in the popular lingua franca would allow multinational CEOs "to rig the international system through the creation of kangaroo tribunals that [could successfully] destroy effective regulation and the enforcement of rules to protect the public."[18] As Bill Black has been arguing, this agreement crafted in secrecy is less about "free" trade than it is a pretext for an assault on both the rule of law and national sovereignty. As Black underscores:

> Article 9 is the "rule of law" only in the sense that it specifies that the "rule of law" does *not* apply to the kangaroo tribunals that can impose billions of dollars in penalties on a nation for the high crime of trying to discourage smoking.[19]

On the other hand, in the case of Vietnam's membership and ending its practices of slave labor, the TPP agreement only recommends that the country do so, yet there is nothing in place to enforce Vietnam to comply.

More specifically, Article 9 is "designed to bypass one of the most important requisites of national sovereignty—a nation's laws and judicial system."[20] Black refers to Article 9 as an "authoritarian diktat" of, by, and for the CEOs of multinational corporations:

> CEOs share a community of interest to block effective regulation and enforce-
> ment against corporate crimes and abuses. CEOs and their lobbyists were given
> unique access to craft the draft deal while the public was excluded. Everything
> we know from human history tells us that they would use that power and
> secret access to rig the system to benefit their interests and ensure that they
> could use Article 9 to impair the ability of nations to use the "rule of law" to
> prevent corporate abuses and crimes.[21]

Finally, should Article 9 and the TPP become law in its present form not only will the CEOs of those MNCs and those nations that are a part of the agreement benefit at the expense of workers, consumers, and the environment, but Chinese CEOs will also benefit because these Article 9 tribunals "will intensify the 'global race to the bottom' that is eviscerating what remains of the rule of law even in nations that are not parties to the TPP."[22] Should the agreement be ratified, for example, as is, then here are some of the alarming environmental implications:

- The TPP would give corporations in a dozen more countries power over our legal system, with access to the same legal mechanism TransCanada used to sue the United States [to the tune of $15 billion in damages caused to the Cana-dian pipeline developer when President Obama rejected the permit for the XL pipeline to bring tar sands crude across the border into the U.S.]—a legal panel of international lawyers set up under NAFTA, which is not accountable to appeal or review by American courts.
- Corporations could sue to oppose regulations reducing methane emissions from fracking, increasing offshore drilling safety, or stopping oil and gas drilling on public lands.
- The TPP would require the U.S. Department of Energy to automatically approve all exports of natural gas to countries in the deal, thereby removing our government's ability to make decisions about our energy future while expanding dangerous fracking and climate emissions.
- The agreement also lacks strong, enforceable provisions to crack down on environmentally destructive activities like illegal logging and overfishing.[23]

More generally, as historical materialists argue, relations of financialization and global capital have benefitted the most powerful capitalist states and MNCs in the core at the expense of peripheral states and vulnerable societal groups within developed, emerging, and less-developed economies. At the heart of the matter, they argue that energy companies, international markets, and political institutions tend to serve the interests of the global elite of the most dominant states in the world system of capitalism. Similarly, critical environmental theorists and the greens argue that contemporary global capital is linked to the type of economic growth and reproduction that results in environmental pollution and overconsumption of natural resources:

> They cite figures to show that global water consumption, deforestation, and pollutants such as carbon dioxide emissions from automobiles are increasingly exponentially.
>
> Global inequality results in overconsumption by the wealthy and the relegation of the more polluting forms of production to poorer areas and LDCs. Many greens focus specifically on capitalist globalization, which "undermines the quest for an ecologically and socially sustainable future."[24]

A world without multinational corporate harm: making the vision of sustainability a reality

Whether capitalist or socialist, mixed economies of the twenty-first century may be divided up into or organized around both market and non-market forms or relations of production. The market forms retain their use of monetary prices, markets of supply and demand, and even in some instances the profit motive with respect to socially owned enterprises and the allocation of capital goods between them. The non-market forms replace markets of supply and demand as well as money with some kind of calculated, performed-in-kind arrangements or laws other than those based on capitalist development as a means for avoiding the inefficiencies and crises associated with capital accumulation. Mixed economies typically rely on some combination of self-managed or decentralized and state-directed or centralized processes of planning and democratic policy formation. For the globally foreseeable future, whether people are trying to operationalize mixed capitalist or socialist economies, a world without multinational corporate harm would require the abolishment of private and/or for-profit mega multinational corporations. The abolition of the corporation per se is not called for, but abolishing the legal status of corporate personhood is.

As envisioned here, the replacement of for-profit MNCs with state-owned MNCs would accommodate better those economic and social systems—local, national, and international—characterized by the social (rather than the private) and democratic (rather than oligopolistic) control of the means of production. Social ownership can be inclusive of public ownership, cooperative ownership, citizen ownership of equity, or any combination of these. All of these forms of collective ownership are synergistic with the spirit of the greater good and the commonwealth as well as with the practices of reclaiming the commons as well as other social communities.

Some might argue that democratic capitalism is an oxymoron. Why not democratic socialism, especially assuming that global socialism is the desired transformative objective? The answer I would argue is because the present political and economic arrangements of global capitalism are not prepared and ready to go there anytime soon without a great deal of resistance. In preparation or in transition to democratic socialism, winning governmental power by way of organizing and mass popular support and direct participation in the affairs of state will help to shift the balance of influence away from capital and toward labor, at the same time undermining rather than reinforcing market discipline. In the meanwhile, or during what I see as a necessary period of gestation for moving from democratic capitalism to democratic socialism, nation-states will first need to be weaned off the policy teats of financialization and multinational corporate capital, neoliberal economizing, and austerity politics, while they simultaneously ratchet up ecological sustainability and ratchet down material inequality.

Democratic capitalism and state-owned multinational corporations (SOMNC) are political necessities for the transition away from an early twenty-first century global capitalism, which currently revolves around the contradictions of post-industrial, debt-driven financial economies typified again by policies of neoliberalism, privatization, and contraction. These synergistic policies of financialization are represented by and/or are foreshadowing more deterioration of civil societies' basic infrastructures, ecosystems, and biorhythms of everyday life to come. By contrast, democratic capitalism and SOMNCs help to move us toward a twenty-second century of a green and sustainable political economy of global socialism. These Jeffersonian, anti-Hamiltonian, and cooperative ideals and practices of anti-elitist democracy are the means not only for recognizing and addressing the fundamental contradictions of global capitalism while staving off possible human extinction and establishing a genuine commonwealth here on Earth, but also for halting the dangerousness, harm and criminality of MNCs. Ideally, this revolution in the political economy of development and in democratic ownership and control would also resist the rising capitalist security states, privatization, and the shrinking commons especially as these relate to problems of education, immigration, and the spoiling of the environment. Under these altering conditions, government agencies would involve workers and recipients of public schools, immigration and customs enforcement, human service departments, criminal justice systems, community planning departments, and so on to participate in the design and implementation of their socially established products and services.

Once again in terms of realpolitik, however, or in the context of globalization, the commonwealth, and international criminal justice, as underscored by Bassiouni in Chapter 1 and repeated here:

> We are living through a period of decline in the observance of and respect for human rights as they have evolved since the end of World War II. And we may well be witnessing a setback in the evolution of international criminal justice … in a curious, not to say perverse, way—our globalized world is becoming more interdependent and interconnected at the same time that it is becoming less committed to the identification and enforcement of the common good.[25]

Similarly, Amnesty International's 2015/2016 annual report investigating human rights abuses in 160 countries and territories worldwide found that sixty-one countries or more locked up prisoners of conscience (i.e., people who were imprisoned solely for the peaceful expression of their beliefs or identity); 122 countries tortured or otherwise ill-treated people; at least eighty-eight countries conducted unfair trials; thirty or more countries unlawfully forced refugees to return to countries where they would be in danger; and at least 113 countries arbitrarily restricted freedom of expression and the press.[26]

As Bassiouni further emphasizes:

> Globalization has not only enhanced the power and wealth of certain states … it has also given these states a claim of exceptionalism. That claim has also extended to certain multinational corporations and Other non-state actors because of their wealth, worldwide activities, and their economic and political power and influence over national and international institutions. For all practical purposes, many of these multinational entities have grown beyond the reach of the law, whether national or international.[27]

Although it might not make any real difference in practice, international law does not even recognize the "complicit liability" of multinational corporations or any other legal persons in the commission of international crimes such as crimes against humanity, war crimes and genocide. So there is certainly a need for at least a doctrine of corporate liability in international criminal law. Accordingly, Jessie Chella has called for such a doctrine. She has also recommended that the International Criminal Court become the preferred institution to address corporate complicity in these crimes and that the ICC Rome Statute should be revised to develop an appropriate framework.[28]

Historically, at least as far back as ancient Greece and up to the present arrangements of global capitalism, the struggle has always been between the forces of general interests on behalf of equality and democracy, on the one hand, and the forces of private interests on behalf of inequality and monopoly/oligopoly, on the other hand. For more than four decades, both locally and globally, the latter forces have been holding down if not beating up on the former forces and the world has become a less democratic and more unequal playing field of social, political, and economic interaction. A world dominated by fewer and fewer multinational corporations permeating all body politics, cultural institutions, and social policies.

The time is more than past due for tackling monopoly power over our consumption, institutions, and prices. Public-utility-style regulation could be one very significant measure for decreasing monopoly power, as it circumvents tinkering with market incentives or self-regulation. Instead, the state simply

> declares that businesses must adhere to certain principles of access, innovation, and fairness. These principles have been vital since we regulated the railroads and major utilities during the Progressive era, and we need them more than ever in the age of airplanes, Uber, and the Internet.[29]

For example, on June 14, 2016, the Circuit Court of the U.S. District of Columbia in a two-to-one decision ruled to legitimate the doctrine known as net neutrality.[30]

Net neutrality, or treating the Internet as a utility, prohibits broadband companies from blocking or slowing the delivery of Internet content to consumers. This was/ is a public or consumer victory against Internet service providers (ISPs), including such businesses as AT&T, Verizon, and Comcast, dictating the price of accessibility. As law professor Tim Wu comments about net neutrality: "The electric grid does not care if you plug in a toaster, an iron, or a computer. For that reason the electric grid is a model of a neutral, innovation-driving network."[31]

Moreover, net neutrality was a bottom-up campaign that brought millions of citizens together to pressure industry-friendly regulators. It emerged in 2015 when the Federal Communications Commission decided to reclassify "ISPs as tele- communications services, declaring them public utilities like phone companies and allowing net-neutrality rules to go forward."[32] As a public utility service, these for- profit businesses now have to treat all Internet traffic equally instead of charging content creators to reach their audiences. This kind of public-utility regulation means that everyone can rely on those platforms and infrastructures to carry out their activities. Once confined to certain resources and natural monopolies to make them universally accessible to people, in a broader context today they "may be even more important in curtailing monopoly power than just breaking those monopolies up."[33]

By checking monopoly power in this way, for example, and enabling access to a necessary resource, especially for disadvantaged groups, public-utility-style regulation not only creates the obligation or duty to provide services to all comers at a reasonable price, but it also requires acceptable compensation to workers in those fields of endeavor. This was the case with respect to the consumer abuse/protection side of the Dodd–Frank financial reform act, which created public-utility-type regulation over debit card services and limited the fees that credit card companies could charge merchants for business transactions. Such regulations or public-utility restrictions also reduce the power of those who control the networks of credit, information, transportation, and so forth. Thus, these principles of open accessibility are both more democratic and pro-innovation as they resist the tendencies of greater monopolization and increasing inequality.

More generally, what are called for are alternative policies to those under the banner of neoliberalism that contribute to unenlightened self-interest, unregulated financial trading, unfettered harm and victimization, and unsustainable capital reproduction. In the case of U.S. domestic policy, for example, the Earned Income Tax Credit has brought much needed relief to the working poor while it has also served as an indirect subsidy for low-wage employers such as Wal-Mart. Likewise, Medicare Part D offers some subsidies to low-income seniors while it is widely known to be a costly giveaway to the prescription drug industry. Similarly, "Obamacare has increased health insurance coverage, partially through the (con- tested) expansion of Medicaid. But the individual mandate only serves to deepen marketization, adding millions of American to the private, for-profit insurance industry."[34]

The alternative policies identified below reflect a slew of circulating ideas and policies as well as an emerging paradigm based on a restructuring of markets and the relationships between the people and their governments. This alternative economic–legal–social paradigm encourages finance capital to move away from speculative investments that exist primarily to enrich the very few and to expand capital for the near term and toward large-scale public and private investments for the long term, involving commonly shared goods and services, infrastructural development, and greener economies. This emerging paradigm also calls for the reconstituting of multinational corporations as we have known them.

This "new" paradigm is grounded in changing the existing system of ownership, in democratizing wealth and work, and in building community-sustaining economies from the ground up. Such communities are inclusive of co-ops and of both old and new forms of employee stock ownership plans, which currently involves some 10.5 million people in virtually every sector of the U.S. economy. As Gar Alperovitz argues,

> new forms of ownership are important not only on their own, but also in that they begin to offer handholds on a new longer-term vision, a set of ideas about democratization that—if they were to become widespread, embraced, refined, and widely understood—form the basis, potentially, of bringing people together, both to challenge the dominant hegemonic ideology and to build a democratized economic basis for a new vision and new system.[35]

This embryonic paradigm and vision of the possible understands that the material expansion of finance capital for the sole intent of maximizing financial capital rather than for the purposes of expanding sustainable material economies is counterproductive to global well being for numerous reasons. Not the least of these is that maximizing financial capital tends to harm earthly environments as it expands deprivations around the globe. Similarly, an alternate "regulatory regime" would tackle or encourage a prohibition against speculating in hospitable environments, in unsustainable debt, and in economic bubbles, or in what Susan Will has referred to more generally as the Ponzi Cultures of advanced capitalism.[36] Nearly all of the social, political, and economic policy changes advocated here have been implemented in one form or the other somewhere in the world or they have some kind of contemporary backing. Some of these proposed changes may only be relevant to the situation of the United States. However, the vast majority of these are applicable worldwide. Most importantly, this policy agenda should not be mistaken for some kind of a "pie-in-the-sky" laundry list of demands. Rather, these policy-oriented changes should be viewed as consistent with a coherent strategy for addressing the overarching crises (e.g., climate, financial, health) and issues (e.g., labor, war, racial justice) of our time:

- Increase state and federal infrastructure investment.
- Upgrade social programs for the non-working poor.
- Improve family friendly benefits including paid family leave and childcare assistance.

- Tougher labor protection and benefit laws in general.
- Overturn, amend, or repeal *Citizens v. the United States* as well as those rulings of the legal fiction that a corporation is a person.
- Reform if not end private financing of public elections.
- Institute enforceable protections for whistleblowers in the private and public sectors as well as public recognition for their service.
- Limit further or eliminate the use of the filibuster in the U.S. Senate.
- Nationalize or turn all MNCs worth more than $50 billion into state-owned corporations in addition to stronger, transparent, antitrust enforcement measures, the adoption of public interest standards for enforcement actions, and the establishment of placing the burden on merging companies to prove no harm to consumers.
- Break up and/or turn the too big to fail banks into public utilities.
- Ban the speculative use of credit default swaps.
- Exempt securities trading, insurance operations, and real estate transactions from the Federal Deposit Insurance Corporation.
- Reign in or increase regulation of equity traders.
- Standardize derivatives and trade them openly on public exchanges.
- Institute a financial transaction tax to discourage excessive trading and risk.
- Tax earned, unearned, and carried interest income at the same rates.
- Establish independent auditing and rating systems of corporate financial affairs.
- Develop high-tech tagging systems able to monitor and track algorithmic trades.
- Make companies and individuals admit wrongdoing as a condition of settling all civil charges or be forced to fight the charges in court.
- Initiate the empowerment of the Financial Stability Oversight Council under Dodd-Frank to reign in the problem of excessive risk taking by the "shadow banking" industry or by those non-banking financial institutions like AIG.
- Institute tougher restrictions and require more long-term debt, vis-à-vis the Volcker Rule, on speculative trading throughout the banking industry, especially those that include securities and derivatives trading as a part of their "casino banking" activities, to further prevent banks from engaging in proprietary trading or making risky bets with their own money.
- Amend the Volcker Rule adopted on December 10, 2013, which now positively makes it more difficult for banks to buy and sell securities on behalf of clients, to trade with their own cash, and restricts them from investing in risky hedge and private-equity funds, but it also needs to require bank executives not only to guarantee that their firms are in compliance with the Rule, but to hold them liable for such assurances.
- Resurrect a modernized version of Glass-Steagall and/or build stronger firewalls around insured deposits involving commercial banking.
- Integrate financial market incentives with climate change adjustments.
- Support environmental defense organizations like the Business Alliance for Local Living Economies or the American Sustainable Business Council.

- Form state-owned banks and create Benefit or not-for-profit "B" corporations.
- Pass a comprehensive infrastructure-human development fund and Americans job act, appropriating $1 trillion over the next decade.
- Pass a forgive student loan debt and/or payback schedule based on income and/or ability to pay.
- Establish for all working people a livable (minimum) wage and affordable housing combined with an expanded Earned Income Tax Credit—better yet establish a universal basic income (UBI).
- Establish a single-payer healthcare system in which the government rather than private insurers pay for all healthcare costs.
- International criminal law should adopt and formalize a doctrine of corporate liability for corporate complicity with the committing of international crimes.

In the end, any vision of halting the routinization of the crimes of MNCs will remain little more than a pipedream rather than a reality unless we incorporate these and/or similar types of policies and kinds of changes as well as the necessary redistributions of the concentrated pockets of wealth that these social relations of consumption and production will require to establish a new twenty-first century post-industrial commons. At the same time, any visions of a radical transformation of contemporary society capable of moving beyond perpetual global expansionism of unsustainable capital and toward an ecologically sustainable and democratically derived world driven by human needs rather than by private profits will remain a fantasy rather than a reality, as well, without the wholesale abandonment of the philosophies and practices of neoliberal economizing and politicking. Finally, the key to liquidating these counterproductive ideologies of the past four decades and moving toward the realization of a commons agenda lies in the very fact that such an agenda is also capable of bringing together an array of locally and globally based independent social movements.

Notes

1 Paternoster, Ray. 2016. "Deterring Corporate Crime: Evidence and Outlook." *Criminology and Public Policy* 15 (2): 383–386.
2 Barak, Gregg. 2012. *Theft of a Nation: Wall Street Looting and Federal Regulatory Colluding.* Lanham, MD: Roman & Littlefield.
3 Schell-Busey, N., Simpson, S., Rorie, M., and Alper, M. 2016. "What Works? A Systematic Review of Corporate Crime Deterrence." *Criminology and Public Policy* 15 (2): 387–416.
4 Barak, 2012.
5 Zuckerman, Gregory. 2016. "A Bearish George Soros is Trading Again." *The Wall Street Journal.* June 9. www.wsj.com/articles/a-bearish-george-soros-is-trading-again-1465429163.
6 Ibid.
7 Chandrasekhar, C.P. and Ghosh, Jayati. 2016. "And Now, Price Deflation in India and China?" *Naked Capitalism.* June 15. www.nakedcapitalism.com/2016/06/and-now-price-deflation-in-india-and-china.html?utm_source=feedburner&utm_medium=email&utm_campaign=Feed%3A+NakedCapitalism+%28naked+capitalism%29.
8 Smith, Yves. 2016. "Finance Is Just Another Industry." *Naked Capitalism.* June 10. www.nakedcapitalism.com/2016/06/finance-is-just-another-industry.html?utm_source=feed

burner&utm_medium=email&utm_campaign=Feed%3A+NakedCapitalism+%28naked +capitalism%29.

9 Maisano, Chris. 2016. "Isn't America Already Kind of Socialist?" In *The ABCs of Socialism* edited by Bhaskar Sunkara. London and Brooklyn, NY: Verso, pp. 12–21 (p. 18).

10 Tombs, Steve and Whyte, David. 2015. *The Corporate Criminal: Why Corporations Must Be Abolished*. Oxford and New York: Routledge. Quotations are from the back cover.

11 Tombs, Steve. 2016. *Social Protection After the Crisis: Regulation Without Enforcement*. Bristol, UK: Policy Press, p. 182.

12 Barak, Gregg. 2016. "Alternatives to High-Risk Securities Fraud Control: Proposing Structural Transformation in an Age of Financial Expansionism and Unsustainable Global Capital." *Crime, Law and Social Change* 66 (2): 131–145.

13 Ibid.

14 Ibid.

15 Cohn, Theodore. 2016. *Global Political Economy: Theory and Practice*, 7th edition. New York and London: Routledge.

16 Ibid.

17 Sundaram, Jomo Kwame. 2016. "Global Development and Environment Study Finds TPP Will Cost Nearly 500,000 Jobs." *Naked Capitalism*. June 8. www.nakedcapitalism. com/2016/06/global-development-and-environment-study-finds-tpp-will-cost-us-nearly-500000-jobs.html?utm_source=feedburner&utm_medium=email&utm_campaign=Feed% 3A+NakedCapitalism+%28naked+capitalism%29.

18 Black, Bill. 2016. "The Lie That 'China Wins' if the TPP Kangaroo Tribunals are Stopped." *Naked Capitalism*. June 7. www.nakedcapitalism.com/2016/06/bill-black-the-lie-that-china-wins-if-the-tpp-kangaroo-tribunals-are-stopped.html?utm_source=feed burner&utm_medium=email&utm_campaign=Feed%3A+NakedCapitalism+%28naked+ capitalism%29.

19 Ibid.

20 Ibid.

21 Ibid.

22 Ibid.

23 CREDO Action. 2016. Quoted from "The Trans-Pacific Partnership is an environmental disaster," an electronic email communication regarding the Petition to Congress to reject TPP. June 8.

24 Cohn, 2016, pp. 392–393.

25 Bassiouni, M.C. (ed.). 2015. *Globalization and Its Impact on the Future of Human Rights and International Criminal Justice*. Cambridge, UK: Intersentia, Preface.

26 Amnesty Insider. 2016. "The State of the World's Human Rights." Spring. New York: Amnesty International USA, p. 3.

27 Bassiouni, 2015: Preface.

28 Chella, Jessie. 1914. *The Complicity of Multinational Corporations in International Crimes: An Examination of Principles*. Atlanta, GA: Scholars' Press.

29 Konczal, Mike. 2016. "Monopolized." *The Nation*. June 6/13: p. 5.

30 Kang, Celia. 2016. "Court Backs Rules Treating Internet as Utility, Not Luxury." *The New York Times*. June 14. www.nytimes.com/2016/06/15/technology/net-neutrality-fcc-appeals-court.

31 Quoted in Konczal, 2016.

32 Konczal, 2016.

33 Ibid.

34 Maisano, 2016, p. 16.

35 Alperovitz, Gus. 2013. *What Then Must We Do? Straight Talk about the Next American Revolution*. White River Junction, VT: Chelsea Green Publishing, p. 41.

36 Will, Susan. 2013. "America's Ponzi Culture." In *How They Got Away with It: White Collar Criminals and the Financial Meltdown*, edited by Susan Will, Stephen Handelman, and David Brotherton. New York: Columbia University Press, pp. 45–67.

NAME INDEX

SUBJECT INDEX

 **Taylor & Francis eBooks**

Helping you to choose the right eBooks for your Library

Add Routledge titles to your library's digital collection today. Taylor and Francis ebooks contains over 50,000 titles in the Humanities, Social Sciences, Behavioural Sciences, Built Environment and Law.

Choose from a range of subject packages or create your own!

Benefits for you

» Free MARC records
» COUNTER-compliant usage statistics
» Flexible purchase and pricing options
» All titles DRM-free.

Benefits for your user

» Off-site, anytime access via Athens or referring URL
» Print or copy pages or chapters
» Full content search
» Bookmark, highlight and annotate text
» Access to thousands of pages of quality research at the click of a button.

REQUEST YOUR **FREE** INSTITUTIONAL TRIAL TODAY	**Free Trials Available** We offer free trials to qualifying academic, corporate and government customers.

eCollections – Choose from over 30 subject eCollections, including:

Archaeology	Language Learning
Architecture	Law
Asian Studies	Literature
Business & Management	Media & Communication
Classical Studies	Middle East Studies
Construction	Music
Creative & Media Arts	Philosophy
Criminology & Criminal Justice	Planning
Economics	Politics
Education	Psychology & Mental Health
Energy	Religion
Engineering	Security
English Language & Linguistics	Social Work
Environment & Sustainability	Sociology
Geography	Sport
Health Studies	Theatre & Performance
History	Tourism, Hospitality & Events

For more information, pricing enquiries or to order a free trial, please contact your local sales team: www.tandfebooks.com/page/sales

 Routledge Taylor & Francis Group | The home of Routledge books

www.tandfebooks.com